Advanced Operation Research

Advanced Economics: Theory and Practice

Advanced Economics: Theory and Practice

R. Kothekar

2008

CYBER TECH PUBLICATIONS
4264/3, Ansari Road, Daryaganj, New Delhi-110002 (India)
Ph.: 011-23244078. Fax: 011-23280028
E-Mail: cyberpublicationsdelhi@yahoo.com

ADVANCED ECONOMICS: THEORY AND PRACTICE

R. Kothekar

First Edition 2008
Reprint 2024

Published by :

G.S. Rawat for **Cyber Tech Publications**
4264/3, Ansari Road, Daryaganj, New Delhi-110002 (India)
Ph.: 011-23244078. Fax: 011-23280028
E-Mail: cyberpublicationsdelhi@yahoo.com

Printed at : **Amit Enterprises**, Maujpur, Delhi, (9810878184)

Preface

This book examines all essential aspects of economics, viz. demand and supply, inflation, deflation, stagflation, economic development etc. There is, however, no dearth of literature on the subject. Some of the books on the subject deal with particular aspects of the economics, while others are in the form of lecturers delivered by eminent economists from time to time. There are very few books written in the textbook style. But they are mostly accidental in nature. In certain cases their approach and presentation is abstract and difficult. This book like many other books on the subject, has been written under the conviction that is possible to improve upon the textbooks that are already in hand. What the author of this present textbook claims is not the originality but the simplicity and clarity of presentation. I have endeavoured to present the subject in a lucid and intelligible manner as possible as in oriental setting. Clear presentation and further stimulation of interest in this very important field of study has been a motivating force behind the writing of this book.

I like to record my sense of appreciation for all of them who gave me everything I needed, without ever asking for anything in return.

This book, is hoped, will be of great help to those who are studying economics as their subject in their higher studies, and the general readers who are keen to know about their economic machinery. Many of colleagues and friends have read the manuscript and told me that the presentation is clear, logical and systematic. I would now leave the judgement to other readers, and I particularly welcome their comments and constructive criticisms.

Finally, I like to thank the publishers for undertaking to publish this book.

—Author

Contents

1

Economics: An Introduction

Economics is the social science that studies the production, distribution, and consumption of goods and services. The word 'economics' is derived from the Greek word *oikos*: house, and *nomos*: custom or law, hence "rules of the house(hold)."

Although discussions about production and distribution have a long history, economics in its modern sense is conventionally dated from the publication of Adam Smith's The Wealth of Nations in 1776. There Smith defines the subject in practical terms:

Political economy, considered as a branch of the science of a statesman or legislator, proposes two distinct objects: first, to supply a plentiful revenue or product for the people, or, more properly, to enable them to provide such a revenue or subsistence for themselves; and secondly, to supply the state or commonwealth with a revenue sufficient for the public services. It proposes to enrich both the people and the sovereign.

Smith referred to the subject as 'political economy', but that term was gradually replaced by 'economics' with the rise of neoclassical economics after 1870.

A definition that captures much of modern economics is that of Lionel Robbins in a 1932 essay: "the science which studies human behaviour as a relationship between ends and scarce means which have alternative uses." Scarcity means that available resources are insufficient to satisfy all wants and needs. Absent scarcity and alternative uses of available resources, there is no economic problem. The subject thus involves the study of choice, as affected by incentives and resources. Areas of economics may be divided or classified in various ways, including:

- microeconomics and macroeconomics
- positive economics ("what is") and normative economics ("what ought to be")
- fields and broader categories within economics.

Another division is between mainstream economics, used to distinguish economics in general, and heterodox approaches, for example, Austrian economics, Marxian economics, and institutional economics, which proceed from their own perspectives. Thus, in Marx's labour theory of value, value is considered as a measure of labor exploitation, rather than of price.

Methods of economic analysis have been increasingly applied to fields that involve people (officials included) making choices in a social context, such crime, education, the family, politics, health, law, religion, social institutions, and war.

AREAS OF STUDY

One of the uses of economics is to understand how economies work and what the relations are between the main economic players and institutions.

An economy is usually analyzed in either of two ways.

- Microeconomics examines the economic behavior of individual units (including businesses and households) and their interactions through individual markets, given scarcity and government regulation. Within microeconomics, general equilibrium theory aggregates across all markets, including their movements and interactions toward equilibrium.
- Macroeconomics examines an economy as a whole "top down" with a view to understanding interactions between the broadest aggregates such as national income and output, employment and inflation and broad aggregates like total consumption and investment spending and their components.

Macroeconomics since at least the 1960s has been characterized by further micro-based modelling as to rationality of players and efficient use of market information. Today a consensus view is that good macroeconomics has solid microeconomic motivation as to theory and evidence.

A few authors (for example, Kurt Dopfer and Stuart Holland) also argue that 'mesoeconomics', which considers the intermediate level of economic organization such as markets and other institutional arrangements, should be considered an additional branch of economic study. Further, modern developments in consumer psychology suggest an even greater level of disaggregation one might call 'picoeconomics' that reduces the individual consumer's behavior to the psychological components that drive that behavior.

Specialized techniques may be used in the subject, including mathematical economics for representing the theory with simplicity, generality, and precision. A key technique is econometrics, which applies statistical methods to analyze economic data for the purpose of drawing fact-based generalizations and testing theories as to acceptance, rejection, or refinement. Computational economics may use econometric models for forecasting or projecting on the basis of alternative policy assumptions.

Another division of the subject distinguishes positive economics, which seeks to predict and explain economic phenomena, from normative economics, which orders choices and actions by some criterion; such orderings necessarily involve subjective value judgments.

Another trend which is more recent, and closer to microeconomics, is to use social psychology concepts (behavioral economics) and methods (experimental economics) to understand deviations from the predictions of neoclassical economics. Evolutionary economics often deals with the otherwise difficult questions related to the role of 'routines' and 'capabilities' in explaining heterogeneity in firm outcomes. Economic history is the study of economic change, and of economic phenomena in the past. Financial economics has traditionally been considered a part of economics, as its body of results emerges naturally from microeconomics. However, today Finance effectively established itself as a separate, though closely related, discipline.

Economics can also be divided into numerous sub disciplines including: international economics, development economics, labor economics, environmental economics, industrial organization, public finance, economic psychology, economic sociology, institutional economics and economic geography. The JEL classification codes provide a comprehensive, detailed way of classifying and searching for economics articles by subject matter. An alternative classification of often detailed entries by mutually-exclusive categories and subcategories is The New Palgrave: A Dictionary of Economics (1987).

Economic Language and Reasoning

Economics relies on rigorous styles of argument. Economic methodology has several interacting parts:

- Collection of economic data. This data consists of measurable values of price and changes in price, for measurable commodities. For example: the cost to hire a worker for a week, or the cost of a particular commodity, and how much is typically used.
- Formulation of models of economic relationships, for example, the relationship between the general level of prices and the general level of employment. This includes observable forms of economic activity, such as money, consumption, preferences, buying, selling, and prices. Economics typically employs two types of equations:

  (1) Identity equations are used to explain how certain economic values are calculated. An example is the relationship of the quantity theory of money as expressed in Irving Fisher's theory of the price level, which is shown by the equation of exchange. This is often used to find how fast money circulates in the economy and can be considered an accounting measure. Another example is national income. Identity equations are tautological in that the purpose is to define rather than to explain.

(2) Descriptive equations are used to describe how an economic agent behaves. For example, utility and budget equations describe the desires and limitations of consumers. When combined, these yield demand equations which describe the quantities of product consumers will seek to purchase at various prices. Similarly, profit and production equations describe the desires and limitations of firms. When combined, these yield supply equations. Combining demand and supply equations yields equilibrium equations that describe the prices and quantities that will prevail in the markets.

This article will refer to such models as formal models, although they are not formal in the sense of formal logic. Economists often formulate very simple models in order to define the impact of just one variant changing. This is called the ceteris paribus ("other things equal") assumption, meaning that all other things are assumed not to change during the period of observation: for example, "If the price of movie tickets rises, ceteris paribus the demand for popcorn falls." However, it is possible with the use of econometric methods to determine one relationship while removing much of the noise caused by other variables.

- *Production of Economic Statistics:* Taking the data collected, and applying the model being used to produce a representation of economic activity. For example, the "general price level" is a theoretical idea common to macroeconomic models. The specific inflation rate involves taking measurable prices, and a model of how people consume, and calculating what the "general price level" is from the data within the model. For example, suppose that diesel fuel costs 1 euro a litre: to calculate the price level would require a model of how much diesel an average person uses, and what fraction of their income is devoted to this, but it also requires having a model of how people use diesel, and what other goods they might substitute for it.
- *Reasoning within Economic Models:* This process of reasoning sometimes involves advanced mathematics.

For instance, an established (though possibly unexamined) tradition among economists is to reason about economic variables in two-dimensional graphs in which curves representing relations between the axis variables are parameterized by various indices. A good example of this type of reasoning is exhibited by Paul Krugman's online essay, There's something about macro. Paul Samuelson's treatise Foundations of Economic Analysis examines the class of assertions called operationally meaningful theorems in economics, which are those that can be conceivably refuted by empirical data. As usual in science, the conclusions obtained by reasoning have a predictive as well as confirmative (or dismissive) value. An example of the predictive value of economic theory is a prediction as to the effect of current deficits on interest rates 10 years into the future. An example of the confirmative value of economic theory would be confirmation (or dismissal) of theories concerning the relation between marginal tax rates and the deficit.

Formal modeling, which has been adapted to some extent by all branches of economics, is motivated by general principles of consistency and completeness. It is not identical to what is often referred to as mathematical economics; this includes, but is not limited to, an attempt to set microeconomics, in particular general equilibrium, on solid mathematical foundations. Some reject mathematical economics: The Austrian School of economics believes that anything beyond simple logic is often unnecessary and inappropriate for economic analysis. In fact, the entire empirical-deductive framework sketched in this section may be rejected outright by that school. However, the framework sketched here accurately represents the current predominant view of economics.

Many mainstream economists feel that the combination of rigorous theory and empirical data ultimately gives the best understanding of real-world phenomena. Towards this end, economics has undergone a massive formalization of its ideas, concepts and methods. According to critics, sometimes to the detriment of its real-world relevance. This creates a tension in the profession on what economists should do. The traditional Chicago School, with its emphasis on economics being an empirical science aimed at explaining real-world phenomena, has insisted on the power of price theory as the tool of analysis. On the other hand, some economic theorists have formed the view that a consistent economic theory may be useful even if at present no real world economy bears out its prediction.

SCHOOLS OF ECONOMIC THOUGHT

Modern School

Mainstream economics begins with the premise that resources are scarce and that it is necessary to choose between competing alternatives. That is, economics deals with tradeoffs. With scarcity, choosing one alternative implies forgoing another alternative-the opportunity cost. The opportunity cost creates an implicit price relationship between competing alternatives. In addition, in both market oriented and planned economies, scarcity is often explicitly quantified by price relationships.

Economics studies how individuals and societies seek to satisfy needs and wants through incentives, choices, and allocation of scarce resources. Alfred Marshall in the late 19th century informally described economics as "the study of man in the ordinary business of life".

Understanding choices by individuals and groups is central. Economists believe that incentives and desires play an important role in shaping decision making. Concepts from the Utilitarian school of philosophy are used as analytical concepts within economics, though economists appreciate that society may not adopt utilitarian objectives. One example of this is the idea of a utility function, which is assumed to represent how economic agents rank the choices given to them. The utility function ranks available choices from best to worst, and the agent gradually learns to choose the best-ranked choice in the feasible set of his alternatives.

On a microeconomic level, some economists extend economic analysis to all personal decisions. An alternative can be thought of as a vector where the entries are answers not only to questions like "How many eggs should I buy?", but also "How many hours should I spend with my kids?", and "How long should I spend eating a hotdog?".

Modern mainstream economics builds primarily on neoclassical economics, which began to develop in the late 1800s and models choices made in the allocation of scarce resources. Mainstream economics also acknowledges the existence of market failure and some insights from Keynesian economics. It looks to game theory and asymmetric information to solve problems on a microeconomic level. Many important insights on collective behavior (for example, emergence of organizations) have been incorporated from institutional economics via new institutionalism. It is sometimes referred to as the study of choice under conditions of scarcity. Another more simplified way of explaining economics is the study of how people or a society seek to satisfy their needs and wants.

Economics is a broad term given to the social science of how choices are made in face of limited resources. Various definitions include: "the study of people in the ordinary business of life", "the science which studies human behavior as a relationship between given ends and scarce means which have alternative uses", and the "study of how societies use scarce resources to produce valuable commodities and distribute them among different people".

Alternative Approaches

Neoclassical economics is the dominant form of economics used today, and is the main source of theory for mainstream economists. It is often referred to by its critics as Orthodox Economics. The more specific definition this approach implies was captured by Lionel Robbins in 1932: "the science which studies human behavior as a relation between scarce means having alternative uses." Scarcity means that available resources are insufficient to satisfy all wants and needs; if there is no scarcity and no alternative uses of available resources, then there is no economic problem.

There are various forms of heterodox economics, which are less used by mainstream economists. These include institutional economics, Marxist economics, socialism, and green economics. "*Classical economics*: This was the original form of mainstream economics of the Eighteenth and Nineteenth Centuries. Neoclassical economics descended from it.

- *Keynesian Economics:* This school has developed from the work of John Maynard Keynes and focused on macroeconomics in the short-run, particularly the rigidities caused when prices are fixed. It has two successors:
- *Post-Keynesian Economics:* An alternative school-one of the successors to the Keynesian tradition with a focus on macroeconomics. They concentrate on macroeconomic rigidities and adjustment processes, and research micro foundations for their models based on real-life practices rather than simple optimizing models. Generally associated with Cambridge, England and the work of Joan Robinson.
- *New-Keynesian Economics:* The other school associated with developments in the Keynesian fashion. These researchers tend to share with other Neoclassical economists the emphasis on models based on micro foundations and optimizing behavior but focus more narrowly on standard Keynesian themes such as price and wage rigidity. These are usually made to be endogenous features of these models, rather than simply assumed as in older style Keynesian ones.
- *Marxian Economics:* Descended from the work of Karl Marx, this school focuses on the labor theory of value and what Marx considered to be the exploitation of labour by capital.
- *Austrian Economics:* This school focuses on the role of the entrepreneur creating temporary market power and being the drive for economic growth.
- *Other Alternatives:* There are many types of economist, and many of them are considerably outside the mainstream. Socialist economics and green economics are two of the smaller schools.
- *Eclectic Economists:* The term 'eclectic' means selecting and using what seems best from various sources, systems or schools of thought. Eclectic economists tend to

economize to get an optimal result for the problem at hand. The assumption of utility can for example be used, not to imply that people really have such a utility, but as an efficient approximation. Such economists might be 'main stream' or neoclassical in one publication and do political economy in another publication.

- *Complexity Economics:* One of the most recent (dating from the late 1970s early 1980s) school of thoughts in modern economics. Complexity economics theories hold that the economy is a complex adaptive evolving system rather than a closed equilibrium system. Most studies in this new field were done by the Santa Fe Institute in New Mexico, USA.

Famous schools or trends of thought referring to a particular style of economics practiced at and disseminated from well-defined groups of academicians that have become known worldwide, may be generally summarized as follows:

- Austrian School
- Chicago School
- Freiburg School
- Keynesian economics
- Post-Keynesian economics
- School of Lausanne
- Stockholm school

DEFINITIONS OF ECONOMICS

This section extends the discussion of the definitions of Economics:

Wealth Definition

The earliest definitions of political economy were simple, elegant statements defining it as the study of wealth. The first scientific approach to the subject was inaugurated by Aristotle, whose influence is still recognized, inter alia, today by the Austrian School. Adam Smith, author of the seminal work The Wealth of Nations and regarded by some as the "father of neoclassical economics", defines economics simply as "The science of wealth." Smith offered another definition, "The Science relating to the laws of production, distribution and exchange." Wealth was defined as the specialization of labor which allowed a nation to produce more with its supply of labor and resources. This definition divided Smith and Hume from previous definitions which defined wealth as gold. Hume argued that gold without increased activity simply serves to raise prices.

John Stuart Mill defined economics as "The practical science of production and distribution of wealth"; this definition was adopted by the Concise Oxford English Dictionary even though it does not include the vital role of consumption. For Mill, wealth is defined as the stock of useful things.

Definitions in terms of wealth emphasize production and consumption. The accounting measures usually used measure the pay received for work and the price paid for goods, and do not deal with the economic activities of those not significantly involved in buying and selling (for example, retired people, beggars, peasants). For economists of this period, they are considered non-productive, and non-productive activity is considered a kind of cost on society. This interpretation gave economics a narrow focus that was rejected by many as placing wealth in the forefront and man in the background; John Ruskin referred to political economy as a "Bastard science, the science of getting riches."

Welfare Definition

Later definitions evolved to include human activity, advocating a shift toward the modern view of economics as primarily a study of man and of human welfare, not of money. Alfred Marshall in his 1890 book Principles of Economics wrote, "Political Economy or Economics is a study of mankind in the ordinary business of Life; it examines that part of the individual and social action which is most closely connected with the attainment and with the use of material requisites of well-being."

The welfare definition was still criticized as too narrowly materialistic. It ignores, for example, the non-material aspects of the services of a doctor or a dancer. A theory of wages which ignored all those sums paid for immaterial services was incomplete. Welfare could not be quantitatively measured, because the marginal significance of money differs from rich to the poor (that is, $100 is relatively more important to the well-being of a poor person than to that of a wealthy person). Moreover, the activities of production and distribution of goods such as alcohol and tobacco may not be conducive to human welfare, but these scarce goods do satisfy innate human wants and desires.

Marxist economics still focuses on a welfare definition. In addition, several critiques of mainstream economics begin from the argument that current economic practice does not adequately measure welfare, but only monetized activity, which is an inadequate approximation of welfare.

Scarcity Definition

Scarcity suggests all things in the world are in finite supply. People therefore have to make choices.

Scarcity too has its critics. It is most amenable to those who consider economics a pure science, but others object that it reduces economics merely to a valuation theory. It ignores how values are fixed, prices are determined and national income is generated. It also ignores unemployment and other problems arising due to abundance. This definition cannot apply to such Keynesian concerns as cyclical instability, full employment, and economic growth.

The focus on scarcity continues to dominate neoclassical economics, which, in turn, predominates in most academic economics departments. It has been criticized in recent years from a variety of quarters, including institutional economics and evolutionary economics and surplus economics.

Core Concepts

Value

The concept of value is central to economics. An observable measure of it is market price.

Adam Smith defined labor as the underlying source of value, and the "labor theory of value" underlies the work of

Karl Marx, David Ricardo and many other classical economists. This theory argues that a good or service is worth the labor that it takes to produce. For most, this value determines a commodity's price. This labor theory of price and the closely related cost-of-production theory of value dominates the work of most classical economists, but those theories are far from the only accepted basis for "value". For example, Austrian School economists use the marginal theory of value.

Neoclassical economics, as in John R. Hicks's book Value and Capital, distinguishes value (as determined on the demand side) from cost (on the supply side), with price determined by supply and demand. In a competitive market, demand and supply interact to determine price and equate cost and value. Economic analysis considers not only the allocation of output for different uses but the distribution of income to the factors of production, including labour and capital, through factor markets.

SUPPLY AND DEMAND

In microeconomic theory supply and demand attempts to describe, explain, and predict the price and quantity of goods sold in perfectly competitive markets. It is one of the most fundamental economic models, ubiquitously used as a basic building block in a wide range of more detailed economic models and theories.

To define, demand is the quantity of a product that a consumer or buyer would be willing and able to buy at any given price in a given period of time. Demand is often represented as a table or a graph relating price and quantity demanded. Most economic models assume that consumers make rational choices about how much to buy in order to maximize their utility-they spend their income on the products that will give them the most happiness at the least cost. The law of demand states that, in general, price and quantity demanded are inversely related. In other words, the higher the price of a product, the less of it consumers will buy.

Supply is the quantity of goods that a producer or a supplier is willing to bring into the market for the purpose of sale at any given price in a given period of time. Supply is often represented as a table or a graph relating price and quantity supplied. Like consumers, producers are assumed to be utility-maximizing, attempting to produce the amount of goods that will bring them the greatest possible profit. The law of supply states that price and quantity supplied are directly proportional. In other words, the higher the price of a product, the more of it producers will create.

The theory of supply and demand is crucial to explaining the market economy in that it explains the mechanisms by which prices and levels of production are set.

PRICE

In order to measure the ebb and flow of supply and demand, a measurable value is needed. The oldest and most commonly used is price, or the going rate of exchange between buyers and sellers in a market. Price theory, therefore, charts the movement of measurable quantities over time, and the relationship between price and other measurable variables. In Adam Smith's Wealth of Nations, this was the trade-off between price and convenience. A great deal of economic theory is based around prices and the theory of supply and demand. In economic theory, the most efficient form of communication comes about when changes to an economy occur through price, such as when an increase in supply leads to a lower price, or an increase in demand leads to a higher price.

In many practical economic models, some form of "price stickiness" is incorporated to model the fact that prices do not move fluidly in many markets. Economic policy often revolves around arguments about the cause of "economic friction", or price stickiness, and which is, therefore, preventing the supply and demand from reaching equilibrium.

Another area of economic controversy is about whether price measures the value of a good correctly. In mainstream market economics, where there are significant scarcities not factored into price, there is said to be an externalization, which is a cost or benefit to actors other than the buyer and seller; of which many examples exist, including pollution (a cost to others) and education (a benefit to others). Market economics predicts that scarce goods which are under-priced because of externalities are over-consumed, and that scarce goods that are over-priced are under-consumed. This leads into public goods theory. Governments often tax and otherwise restrict the sale of goods that ... e negative externalities and subsidize or otherwise promote the purchase of goods that have positive externalities in an effort to correct the distortion in price caused by these externalities.

SCARCITY

Neoclassical economics is characterized by maximization (leisure time, wealth, health, happiness-all commonly reduced to the concept of utility) subject to constraints. These constraints- or scarcity-inevitably define a trade-off. For example, one can have more money by working harder, but less time (there are only so many hours in a day, so time is scarce). One can have more radishes only at the expense of, for example, fewer carrots (you only have so much land on which to grow food-land is scarce).

All economies in the world face scarcity: Scarcity is defined as: when the price is zero, the quantity demanded exceeds the quantity supplied. Price is a measure of relative scarcity. If all other market variables are held constant. When the price is rising, this indicates the commodity is becoming relatively more scarce. When the price is falling, this indicates the commodity is becoming relatively less scarce.

Adam Smith considered, for example, the trade-off between time, or convenience, and money. He discussed how a person could live near town, and pay more for rent of his home, or live farther away and pay less, "paying the difference out of his convenience".

MARGINALISM

In marginalist economic theory, the price level is determined by the marginal cost and marginal utility. The price of all goods will be the cost of making the last one that people will purchase, and the price of all the employees in a company will be the cost of hiring the last one the business needs. Marginalism looks at decisions based on "the margins", what the cost to produce the next unit is, versus how much it is expected to return in profit. When the marginal return of an action reaches zero, the action stops. Marginal utility is how much more happiness or use a person receives from a purchase in contrast with buying less. Marginal rewards are often subject to diminishing returns: Less reward is obtained from more production or consumption. For example, the 10th bar of chocolate that a person consumes does not taste as good as the first, and so brings less marginal utility.

Marginalism became increasingly important in economic theory in the late 19th century, and is a tool which is used to analyze how economic systems will react. Marginal cost of production divides costs into "fixed" costs which must be paid regardless of how many of a commodity are produced, and "variable costs". The marginal cost is the variable cost of the last unit. Marginalism states that when the profit from the next unit will be zero, that unit will not be produced. This is often termed the marginal revolution in economic thought.

The marginalist theory of price level runs counter to the classical theory of price being determined by the amount of labor congealed in a commodity.

DEVELOPMENT OF ECONOMIC THOUGHT

The term economics was coined around 1870 and popularized by influential "neoclassical" economists such as Alfred Marshall (Welfare definition), as a substitute for the earlier term political economy, which referred to "the economy of polities"-competing states. The term political economy was used through the 18th and 19th centuries, with Adam Smith, David Ricardo and Karl Marx as its main thinkers and which today is frequently referred to as the "classical" economic theory. Both "economy" and "economics" are derived from the Greek oikos-for "house" or "settlement", and nomos for "laws" or "norms".

Actually, etymological sources indicate that the source of "economy" and "economics" is indeed oikos-for "house" or "settlement", but that the second bit is from-nomos meaning "managing," from nemein "manage".

Economic thought may be roughly divided into three phases: Premodern (Greek, Roman, Arab), Early modern (mercantilist, physiocrats) and Modern (since Adam Smith in the late 18th century). Systematic economic theory has been developed mainly since the birth of the modern era. Joseph Schumpeter specifically credits the development of the scientific study of economics to the Late Scholastics, particularly those of 15th and 16th century Spain.

There have been different and competing schools of economic thought pertaining to capitalism from the late 18th century to the present day. Important schools of thought are Mercantilism, Kameralism, Physiocracy, Classical economics, Manchester school, Austrian School, Marxian economics, Chicago School.

Within macroeconomics there is, in general order of their appearance in the literature; Classical economics, Keynesian economics, Neo Classical synthesis, Post-Keynesian economics, Monetarism, New classical economics Supply-side economics and New Keynesian Economics. New alternative developments include The political macroeconomy, Evolutionary economics, Dependency theory, World systems theory and Associative Economics.

CRITICISM AND CONTRARIAN PERSPECTIVES

Is Economics a Science?

One of the marks of a science is the use of a scientific method and the ability to establish hypotheses and make predictions which can then be tested with data and where the results are repeatable by others. Unlike some natural scientists and in a way similar to what happens in other social sciences, it is difficult for economists to conduct formal experiments due to moral and practical issues involved with human subjects. Experimentation, however, has been conducted by social scientists. The sub-fields of experimental economics and consumer behavior focus on conducting experiments using human subjects. The sub-field of econometrics focuses on testing hypotheses when data are not generated via controlled experimentation.

The status of social sciences as an empirical science has been a matter of debate in the 20th century. Unlike the natural sciences, economics yields no natural laws or universal constants due to its reliance on non-physical arguments, so this has led some critics, like Dick Richardson, Ph.D.-Professor of Integrative Biology at the University of Texas at Austin-, to argue economics is not a science. It is also argued by many that difficulty in proving many hypotheses can occur in the natural sciences too, not only in the social sciences. In general, economists reply that while this aspect presents serious difficulties, they do in fact test their hypotheses using statistical methods such as econometrics and data generated in the real world. Some have argued that difficulty in this estimation implies economics is not a soft science, the field simply lacks the controllability of other sciences, and thus has greater difficulty in gathering and establishing evidence. The field of experimental economics has seen efforts to test at least some predictions of economic theories in a simulated laboratory setting-an endeavor which earned Vernon Smith the Bank of Sweden Prize in Economic Sciences in Memory of Alfred Nobel in 2002.

CRITICISMS OF THEORY AND PRACTICE

Economics has been persistently criticized for its heavy reliance on unrealistic, unobservable, or unverifiable assumptions. Some people reply to this criticism by saying that the unrealistic assumptions of economics result from abstraction from unimportant details, and abstraction is necessary for knowledge of a complex real world. So, far from unrealistic assumptions detracting from the epistemic worth of economics, such assumptions are essential for economic knowledge. Denominating this explanation the abstractionist defense, and after clarifying abstraction, unrealistic assumptions and kindred notions, at least one study has shown that this abstractionist defense does not successfully rebut the position of those who criticize economics for its unrealistic assumptions. However, it is important to note that while one school does have a majority in the field, there is far from a consensus on all economic issues and multiple alternative fields claim to have more empirically justified insights.

Economics is a field of study with various schools and currents of thought. As a result, there exists a considerable distribution of opinions, approaches and theories. Some of these reach opposite conclusions or, due to the differences in underlying assumptions, contradict each other. Criticism on several topics in economics can be found elsewhere, in both general and specialized literature (for example, general equilibrium, Pareto efficiency, marginalism, behavioral finance, behavioral economics, feminist economics, Keynesian economics, monetarism, endogenous growth theory, comparative advantage, Kuznets curve, Laffer curve, economic sociology, et al.).

McCloskey Critique

Although the conventional way of connecting an economic model with the world is through econometric analysis, Professor Deirdre McCloskey cites many examples in which professors of econometrics were able to use the same data to both prove and disprove the applicability of a model's conclusions. She argues the vast efforts expended by economists on analytical equations is essentially wasted effort.

Ethics and Economics

The relationship between economics and ethics is complex. Many economists consider normative choices and value judgments, like what needs or wants, or what is good for society, to be political or personal questions outside the scope of economics. Once a person or government has established a set of goals, however, economics can provide insight as to how they might best be achieved.

Others see the influence of economic ideas, such as those underlying modern capitalism, to promote a certain system of values with which they may or may not agree. According to some thinkers such as John Syko, a theory of economics is also, or implies also, a theory of moral reasoning. The premise of ethical consumerism is that one should take into account ethical and environmental concerns, in addition to financial and traditional economic considerations, when making buying decisions.

Effect on Society

Some would say that market forms and other means of distribution of scarce goods suggested by economics affect what people consider to be not just their "desires and wants" but also "needs" and "habits". Much of so-called economic "choice" is involuntary, certainly given the conditioning that people have to expect-a certain quality of life. This leads to one of the most hotly debated areas in economic policy, namely, the effect and efficacy of welfare policies. Libertarians view this as a failure to respect economic reasoning. They argue that redistribution of wealth is morally and economically wrong. And socialists view it as a failure of economics to respect society. They argue that disparities of wealth should not have been allowed in the first place. This led to both 19th century labor economics and 20th century welfare economics before being subsumed into human development theory.

The older term for economics, political economy, is still often used instead of economics, especially by certain economists such as Marxists. Use of this term often signals a basic disagreement with the terminology or paradigm of market economics. Political economy explicitly brings political considerations into economic analysis and is therefore openly normative, although this can be said of many economic recommendations as well, despite claims to being positive. Some mainstream universities (many in the United Kingdom) have a "political economy" department rather than an "economics" department.

Marxist economics generally denies the trade-off of time for money. In the Marxist view, concentrated control over the means of production is the basis for the allocation of resources among classes. Scarcity of any particular physical resource is subsidiary to the central question of power relationships embedded in the means of production.

NEOCLASSICAL ECONOMICS

Neoclassical economics refers to a general approach in economics focusing on the determination of prices, outputs, and income distributions in markets through supply and demand. These are mediated through a hypothesized maximization of income-constrained utility by individuals and of cost-constrained profits of firms employing available information and factors of production. Mainstream economics is largely neoclassical in its assumptions, at least at the microeconomic level. There have been many critiques of neoclassical economics, often incorporated into newer versions of neoclassical theory as circumstances change. Neoclassical economics is often called the marginalist school.

An Overview

Neoclassical economics is the singular element of several schools of thought in economics. There is not complete agreement on what is meant by neoclassical economics, and the result is a wide range of neoclassical approaches to various problem areas and domains--ranging from neoclassical theories of labor to neoclassical theories of demographic changes.

As expressed by E. Roy Weintraub, neoclassical economics rests on three assumptions, although certain branches of neoclassical theory may have different approaches:

1. People have rational preferences among outcomes that can be identified and associated with a value.
2. Individuals maximize utility and firms maximize profits.
3. People act independently on the basis of full and relevant information.

From these three assumptions, neoclassical economists have built a structure to understand the allocation of scarce resources among alternative ends--in fact understanding such allocation is often considered the definition of economics to neoclassical theorists. Here's how William Stanley Jevons presented the basic problem of economics:

Given, a certain population, with certain needs and powers of production, in possession of certain lands and other sources of material: required, the mode of employing their labour which will maximize the utility of their produce.

From the basic assumptions of neoclassical economics comes a wide range of theories about various areas of economic activity. For example, profit maximization lies behind the neoclassical theory of the firm, while the derivation of demand curves leads to an understanding of consumer goods, and the supply curve allows an analysis of the factors of production. Utility maximization is the source for the neoclassical theory of consumption, the derivation of demand curves for consumer goods, and the derivation of factor supply curves and reservation demand. Neoclassical economics emphasizes equilibria, where equilibria are the solutions of individual maximization problems. Regularities in economies are explained by methodological individualism, the doctrine that all economic phenomena can be ultimately explained by aggregating over the behavior of individuals. The emphasis is on microeconomics. Institutions, which might be considered as prior to and conditioning individual behavior, are de-emphasized. Economic subjectivism accompanies these emphases.

Origins of Neoclassical Economics

Classical economics, developed in the 18th and 19th centuries, included a value theory and distribution theory. The value of a product was thought to depend on the costs involved in producing that product. The explanation of costs in Classical economics was simultaneously an explanation of distribution. A landlord received rent, workers received wages, and a capitalist tenant farmer received profits on their investment. This classic approach included the work of Adam Smith and David Ricardo.

However, some economists gradually began emphasizing the perceived value of a good to the consumer. They proposed a theory that the value of a product was to be explained with differences in "utility." Economists began to explore the way that elements such as supply and demand affected price, and neo-classical economics gradually came into being. Neoclassical economics is conventionally dated from William Stanley Jevons's Theory of Political Economy (1871), Carl Menger's Principles of Economics (1871), and Leon Walras's Elements of Pure Economics (1874-1877). These three economists have been said to have promulgated the marginal utility revolution, or Neoclassical Revolution. Historians of economics and economists have debated:

- Whether utility or marginalism was more essential to this revolution (whether the noun or the adjective in the phrase "marginal utility" is more important)

- Whether there was a revolutionary change of thought or merely a gradual development and change of emphasis from their predecessors
- Whether grouping these economists together disguises differences more important than their similarities.

In particular, Walras was more interested in the interaction of markets than in explaining the individual psyche through a hedonistic psychology. Jevons saw his economics as an application and development of Jeremy Bentham's utilitarianism and never had a fully developed general equilibrium theory. Menger emphasized disequilibrium and the discrete. Menger had a philosophical objection to the use of mathematics in economics, while the other two modeled their theories after 19th century mechanics.

Alfred Marshall's textbook, Principles of Economics (1890), was the dominant textbook in England a generation later. Marshall's influence extended elsewhere; Italians would compliment Maffeo Pantaleoni by calling him the "Marshall of Italy". Marshall thought classical economics attempted to explain prices by the cost of production. He asserted that the neoclassicals went too far in correcting this imbalance by overemphasizing utility and demand. Marshall thought the question of whether supply or demand was more important was analogous to the pointless question of which blade of a scissors did the cutting.

Marshall explained prices by the intersection of supply and demand curves. The introduction of different market "periods" was an important innovation of Marshall's:

- *Market Period:* The goods produced for sale on the market are taken as given data, e.g. in a fish market. Prices quickly adjust to clear markets.
- *Short Period:* Industrial capacity is taken as given. The level of output, the level of employment, the inputs of raw materials, and prices fluctuate to equate marginal cost and marginal revenue, where profits are maximized. Economic rents exist in short period equilibrium for fixed factors, and the rate of profit is not equated across sectors.

- *Long Period:* The stock of capital goods, such as factories and machines, is not taken as given. Profit-maximizing equilibria determine both industrial capacity and the level at which it is operated.
- *Very Long Period:* Technology, population trends, habits and customs are not taken as given, but allowed to vary in very long period models.

Marshall took supply and demand as stable functions and extended supply and demand explanations of prices to all runs. He argued supply was easier to vary in longer runs, and thus became a more important determinate of price in the very long run.

Further Developments

An important change in neoclassical economics occurred around 1933. Joan Robinson and Edward H. Chamberlin, with the near simultaneous publication of their respective books, The Economics of Imperfect Competition (1933) and The Theory of Monopolistic Competition (1933), introduced models of imperfect competition. Theories of market forms and industrial organization grew out of this work. They also emphasized certain tools, such as the marginal revenue curve.

Joan Robinson's work on imperfect competition, at least, was a response to certain problems of Marshallian partial equilibrium theory highlighted by Piero Sraffa. Anglo-American economists also responded to these problems by turning towards general equilibrium theory, developed on the European continent by Walras and Vilfredo Pareto. J. R. Hicks's Value and Capital (1939) was influential in introducing his English-speaking colleagues to these traditions. He, in turn, was influenced by the Austrian School economist Friedrich Hayek's move to the London School of Economics, where Hicks then studied.

These developments were accompanied by the introduction of new tools, such as indifference curves and the theory of ordinal utility. The level of mathematical sophistication of neoclassical economics increased. Paul Samuelson's Foundations of Economic Analysis (1947) contributed to this increase in formal rigor. The interwar period in American economics has been argued to have been pluralistic, with neoclassical economics and institutionalism competing for allegiance. Frank Knight, an early Chicago school economist attempted to combine both schools. But this increase in mathematics was accompanied by greater dominance of neoclassical economics in Anglo-American universities after World War II.

Hicks' book had two main parts. The second, which was arguably not immediately influential, presented a model of temporary equilibrium. Hicks was influenced directly by Hayek's notion of intertemporal coordination and paralleled by earlier work by Lindhal. This was part of an abandonment of disaggregated long run models. This trend probably reached its culmination with the Arrow-Debreu model of intertemporal equilibrium. The Arrow-Debreu model has canonical presentations in Gerard Debreu's Theory of Value (1959) and in Arrow and Hahn.

Many of these developments were against the backdrop of improvements in both econometrics, that is the ability to measure prices and changes in goods and services, as well as their aggregate quantities, and in the creation of macroeconomics, or the study of whole economies. The attempt to combine neo-classical microeconomics and Keynesian macroeconomics would lead to the neoclassical synthesis which has been the dominant paradigm of economic reasoning in English-speaking countries since the 1950's. Hicks and Samuelson were for example instrumental in mainstreaming Keynesian economics. Macroeconomics influenced the neoclassical synthesis from the other direction, undermining foundations of classical economic theory such as Say's Law, and assumptions about political economy such as the necessity for a hard money standard. These developments are reflected in neoclassical theory by the search for the occurrence in markets of the equilibrium conditions of Pareto optimality and self-sustainability.

Criticisms of Neoclassical Economics

Neoclassical economics is sometimes criticised for having a normative bias. In this view, it does not focus on explaining actual economies, but instead on describing a "utopia" in which Pareto optimality obtains. Key assumptions of neoclassical economics which are widely criticised as unrealistic include:

- The focus on individuals in the economy may obscure analysis of wider long term issues, such as whether the economic system is desirable and stable on a finite planet of limited natural capital.
- The assumption that individuals act rationally may be viewed as ignoring important aspects of human behavior. Many see the "economic man" as being demonstrably different from a real man on the real earth--they are not human, and are increasingly criticized for not being human. The assumption of rational expectations which has been introduced in some more modern neo-classical models (sometimes also called new classical) may also be strongly criticised on the grounds of realism.
- Large corporations might perhaps come closer to the neoclassical ideal of profit maximisation, but this is not necessarily viewed as desirable if this comes at the expense of neglect of wider social issues. The response to this is that neoclassical economics is descriptive and not normative. It addresses such problems with concepts of private versus social utility.
- Problems with making the neoclassical general equilibrium theory compatible with an economy that develops over time and includes capital goods. This was explored in a major debate in the 1960s-the Cambridge Capital Controversy-about the validity of neoclassical economics, with an emphasis on the economic growth, capital, aggregate theory, and the marginal productivity theory of distribution. There were also internal attempts by neoclassical economists to extend the Arrow-Debreu model to disequilibrium investigations of stability and uniqueness. However a result known as the Sonnenschein-Mantel-Debreu theorem suggests that the assumptions that must be made to insure that the equilibrium is stable and unique are quite restrictive.
- In the opinion of some, these developments have found [illegible] weaknesses in neoclassical economics. Economists,

however, have continued to use highly mathematical models, and many equate neoclassical economics with economics, unqualified. Mathematical models include those in game theory, linear programming, and econometrics, many of which might be considered non-neoclassical. So economists often refer to what has evolved out of neoclassical economics as "mainstream economics". Critics of neoclassical economics are divided in those who think that highly mathematical method is inherently wrong and those who think that mathematical method is potentially good even if contemporary methods have problems.

- The basic theory of a downward sloping aggregate demand curve is critizised for its allegedly strong assumptions.
- In general, allegedly too unrealistic assumptions are one of the most common criticisms towards neoclassical economics. For example, many theories assume perfect knowledge for market actors and the most common theory of finance markets assumes that debts are always paid back and that any actor can raise as much loan as he wants at any given point of time.
- The basic theory of production in neoclassical economics is criticized for incorrect assumptions about the rationales of producers. According to the theory, increasing production costs are the reason for producers not to produce over a certain amount. Some empirical counter arguments claim that most of producers in economies are not making their production decisions in the light of increasing production costs. For example they often may have additional capacity that could be taken into use, if producing more was desirable.
- Often at individual levels, variables such as supply and demand, which are independent, are (allegedly wrongly) assumed to be independent also at aggregate level. This criticism has been applied to many central theories of neoclassical economics.
- The critique of the assumption of rationality is not confined to social theorists and ecologists. Many

> economists, even contemporaries, have criticized this vision of economic man. Thorstein Veblen put it most sardonically: lightning calculator of pleasures and pains, who oscillates like a homogeneous globule of desire of happiness under the impulse of stimuli that shift about the area, but leave him intact.

Herbert Simon's theory of bounded rationality has probably been the most influential of the heterodox approaches. Is economic man a first approximation to a more realistic psychology, an approach only valid in some sphere of human lives, or a general methodological principle for economics? Early neoclassical economists often leaned toward the first two appoaches, but the latter has become prevalent.

- Neoclassical economics is also often seen as relying too heavily on complex mathematical models, such as those used in general equilibrium theory, without enough regard to whether these actually describe the real economy. Many see an attempt to model a system as complex as a modern economy by a mathematical model as unrealistic and doomed to failure. Famous answer to this criticism is Milton Friedman's claim that theories should be judged by their ability to predict events rather than by the realisticity of their assumptions. Naturally, critics claim that neoclassical economics (as well as other branches of economics) has not been very good at predicting events.
- Critics of neoclassical models accuse it of copying of 19th century mechanics and the "clockwork" model of society which seems to justify elite privileges as arising "naturally" from the social order based on economic competititions. This is echoed by modern critics in the anti-globalization movement who often blame the neoclassical theory, as it has been applied by the IMF in particular, for inequities in global debt and trade relations. They assert it ignores the complexity of nature and of human creativity, and seeks mechanical ideas like equilibrium:

And in Poinset's Elements de Statique..., which was a textbook on the theory of mechanics bristling with systems of simultaneous equations to represent, among other things, the mechanical equilibrium of the solar system, Walras found a pattern for representing the catallactic equilibrium of the market system. (William Jaffe)

- The neo-Marxists Michael Hardt and Antonio Negri criticise neoclassical economics and its rejection of Keynesian regulation on philosophical grounds: they assert that neoclassical economics incorrectly posits money as a priori ('monetary Aristotelianism'), even though it is a regulatory instrument.

It is fair to say that many (but not all) of these criticisms can only be directed towards a subset of the neoclassical models. Eg, there are many neoclassical models where unregulated markets fail to achieve pareto-optimality and there has recently been an increased interest in modelling bounded rationality.

2

History of Economics

CHANAKYA

Chanakya (c. 350-283 BC) was adviser and prime minister to the first Maurya Emperor Chandragupta (c. 340-293 BC), and architect of his rise to power.

Kautilya and Vishnugupta, the names by which the political treatise Arthasastra identifies its author, are traditionally identified with Chanakya

Identity

He is generally called Chanakya but, in his capacity as author of the Arthasastra, is generally referred to as Kautilya. The Arthasastra identifies its author by the name Kautilya, except for one verse which refers to him by the name Vishnugupta.

K.C. Ojha puts forward the view that the traditional identification of Vishnugupta with Kautilya was caused by a confusion of editor and originator and suggests that Vishnugupta is in fact a redactor of the original work of Kautilya.

Thomas Burrow goes even further and says that Chanakya and Kautilya are actually two different people.

The Legends

Thomas R. Trautmann lists the following elements as common to different forms of the Chanakya legend:

- Chanakya is born with a complete set of teeth, a sign that he would become king, which is inappropriate for a Brahmin like Chanakya. Chanakya's teeth are therefore broken and it is prophesied that he will rule through another.

- The Nanda King throws Chanakya out of his court, prompting Chanakya to swear revenge.
- Chanakya searches for one worthy for him to rule through. Chanakya encounters a young Candragupta Maurya who is a born leader even as a child.

  "Chanakya's initial attempt to overthrow Nanda fails, whereupon he comes across a mother scolding her child for burning himself by eating from the middle of a bun or bowl of porridge rather than the cooler edge. Chanakya realizes his initial strategic error and, instead of attacking the heart of Nanda territory, slowly chips away at its edges.
- Chanakya betrays his ally the mountain king Parvata.

  "Chanakya enlists the services of a fanatical weaver to rid the kingdom of rebels.
- Chanakya adds poison to the food eaten by Chandragupta, now king, in order to make him immune. Unaware, Chandragupta feeds some of his food to his queen, who is in her ninth month of pregnancy. In order to save the heir to the throne, Chanakya cuts the queen open and extracts the foetus who is named Bindusara because he was touched by a drop (bindu) of blood or of poison.
- Chanakya's political rivalry with Subandhu leads to his death.

Jain Version

According to Jaina accounts Chanakya was born in the village of Chanaka in the Golla district to Chanin and Canesvari, a Jain Brahmin couple.

Death of Chanakya

Chanakya lived to ripe old age and died around 283 BC and was cremated by his grandson/disciple Radhagupta who succeeded Rakshasa Katyayan (great-grand son of Prabuddha Katyayan, who attained Nirvana during the same period as Gautam Budhha) as Prime Minister of the Maurya Empire and was instrumental in backing Ashoka to the throne. There were three non-traditional belief paths in society those days, Jaina, Buddhist and Ajivaka. Ajivaka practising Chankaya brought about the downfall of the Jaina Nandas and their coterie of Jaina ministers. (Chanakya's uncle was Jain, too, and a group of Jains backed Chanakya in his political machinations).

Later on, Chandragupta Maurya took Jainism on abdicating his throne which passed to his Son Bindusara who was an Ajivaka. Even Ashoka was practising Ajivaka who before accession to throne became Buddhist. Bindusara was born before his father ever became Emperor so the below legend is definitely not true. Ashoka's daughter was married in 265 BC and his son Kunala was 18 years of age in 269 BC which means that even the princes married early, Ashoka was born 310 BC and Bindusara around 330 BC. Bindusara means one who encompasses all that is need to be known.

Later on, Ajivikism which was the official religion of the empire since the Kalinga War (261 BC) and for 14 years afterwards, declined and merged into traditional Hinduism. What has been left are a mish mash of contradictory Buddhist and Jaina legends which are even rejected by Sinhalese chronicles.

According to a legend which is a later jaina invention, while Chanakya served as the Prime Minister of Chandragupta Maurya, he started adding small amounts of poison in Chandragupta's food so that he would get used to it. The aim of this was to prevent the Emperor from being poisoned by enemies. One day the queen, Durdha, shared the food with the Emperor while she was pregnant. Since she was not used to eating poisoned food, she died. Chanakya decided that the baby should not die; hence he cut open the belly of the queen and took out the baby. A drop (bindu in Sanskrit) of poison had passed to the baby's head, and hence Chanakya named him Bindusara. Bindusara would go on to become a great king and to father the greatest Mauryan Emperor since Chandragupta-Asoka.

When Bindusara became a youth, Chandragupta gave up the throne and followed the Jain saint Bhadrabahu to present day Karnataka and settled in a place known as Sravana Belagola. He lived as an ascetic for some years and died of voluntary starvation according to Jain tradition.

Chanakya meanwhile stayed as the Prime Minister of Bindusara. Bindusara also had a minister named Subandhu who did not like Chanakya. One day he told Bindusara that Chanakya was responsible for the murder of his mother. Bindusara asked the nurses who confirmed this story and he became very angry with Chanakya.

It is said that Chanakya, on hearing that the Emperor was angry with him, thought that anyway he was at the end of his life. He donated all his wealth to the poor, widows and orphans and sat on a dung heap, prepared to die by total abstinence from food and drink. Bindusara meanwhile heard the full story of his birth from the nurses and rushed to beg forgiveness of Chanakya. But Chanakya would not relent. Bindusara went back and vent his fury on Subandhu, who asked for time to beg for forgiveness from Chanakya.

Subandhu, who still hated Chanakya, wanted to make sure that Chanakya did not return to the city. So he arranged for a ceremony of respect, but unnoticed by anyone, slipped a smoldering charcoal ember inside the dung heap. Aided by the wind, the dung heap swiftly caught fire, and the man behind the Mauryan Empire and the author of Arthashastra was burned to death.

His main philosophy was "A debt should be paid off till the last penny; An enemy should be destroyed without a trace". Ironically, Subandhu followed his main philosophy and destroyed him without a trace.

Other Versions

The 9th century AD Sanskrit play by Vishakhadatta, *Mudra Rakshasa*, is one popular source of Chankaya lore.

A South Indian group of Brahmins in Tamil Nadu called Sholiyar or Chozhiyar, claim that Chanakya was one of them. Though this may sound very improbable considering the vast distance between present day Tamilnadu in the south and Magadha in Bihar, it finds curious echos in Parishista-parvan, where Hemachandra claims that Chankya was a Dramila (Dramila, being a very common variant of Dravida).

Kautilya was educated at Taxila or Takshashila in present day Pakistan. The new states (in present-day Bihar and Uttar Pradesh) by the northern high road of commerce along the base of the Himalayas maintained contact with Takshasilâ and at the eastern end of the northern high road (uttarapatha) was the kingdom of Magadha with its capital city, Pataliputra, now known as Patna. Chanakya's life was connected to these two cities, Pataliputra and Taxila.

In his early years he was tutored extensively in the Vedas-Chanakya memorized them completely at a very early age. He was also taught mathematics, geography and science along with religion. Later he travelled to Taxila, where he became a teacher of politics. Chanakya taught subjects using the best of practical knowledge acquired by the teachers. The age of entering the University was sixteen. The branches of study most sought after around India at that time ranged from law, medicine, warfare and other disciplines. Two of his more famous students were Bhadrabhatt and Purushdutt.

Political turmoil in Western India at that time caused by Greek invasion forced Chanakya to leave the University environment for the city of Pataliputra (presently known as Patna, in the state of Bihar, India), which was ruled by the Nanda king Dhanananda. Although Chanakya initially prospered in his relations with the ruler, being a blunt person he was soon disliked by Dhanananda. This ended with Chanakya being removed from an official position he enjoyed.

According to the Kashmiri version of his legend, Chanakya uproots some grass because it had pricked its foot.

Works

Three books are attributed to Chanakya: Arthashastra, Nitishastra and Chanakya Niti. The Arthashastra discusses monetary and fiscal policies, welfare, international relations, and war strategies in detail. Many of his nitis or policies have been compiled under the book title Chanakya Niti. Nitishastra is a treatise on the ideal way of life, and shows Chanakya's in depth study of the Indian way of life.

CLASSICAL ECONOMICS

Classical economics is widely regarded as the first modern school of economic thought. Its major developers include Adam Smith, David Ricardo, Thomas Malthus and John Stuart Mill. Sometimes the definition of classical economics is expanded to include William Petty, Johann Heinrich von Thünen, and Karl Marx.

The publication of Adam Smith's The Wealth of Nations in 1776 is usually considered to mark the beginning of classical economics. The school was active into the mid 19th century and was followed by neoclassical economics in Britain beginning around 1870.

Classical economists attempted and partially succeeded to explain growth and development. They produced their "magnificent dynamics" during a period in which capitalism was emerging from a past feudal society and in which the industrial revolution was leading to vast changes in society. These changes also raised the question of how a society could be organized around a system in which every individual sought his or her own (monetary) gain. Why would such a society not collapse in chaos?

Classical economists reoriented economics away from an analysis of the ruler's personal interests to a class-based interest. Physiocrat Francois Quesnay and Adam Smith, for example, identified the wealth of a nation with the yearly national income, instead of the king's treasury. Smith saw this income as produced by labor applied to land and capital equipment. Once land and capital equipment are appropriated by individuals, the national income is divided up between laborers, landlords, and capitalists in the form of wages, rent, and interest.

Value Theory

Classical economists developed a theory of value, or price, to investigate economic dynamics. Petty introduced a fundamental distinction between market price and natural price to facilitate the portrayal of regularities in prices. Market prices are jostled by many transient influences that are difficult to theorize about at any abstract level. Natural prices, according to Petty, Smith, and Ricardo, for example, capture systematic and persistent forces operating at a point in time. Market prices always tend toward natural prices in a process that Smith described as somewhat similar to gravitational attraction.

The theory of what determined natural prices varied within the Classical school. Petty tried to develop a par between land and labor and had what might be called a land-and-labor theory of value. Smith confined the labor theory of value to a mythical pre-capitalist past. He stated that natural prices were the sum of natural rates of wages, profits (including interest on capital and wages of superintendence) and rent. Ricardo also had what might be described as a cost of production theory of value. He criticized Smith for describing rent as price-determining, instead of price-determined, and saw the labor theory of value as a good approximation.

Some historians of economic thought, in particular, certain Sraffian economists, see the classical theory of prices as determined from three givens:

1. The level of outputs at the level of Smith's "effectual demand",
2. technology, and
3. wages.

From these givens, one can rigorously derive a theory of value. But neither Ricardo nor Marx, the most rigorous investigators of the theory of value during the Classical period, developed this theory fully. Those who reconstruct the theory of value in this manner see the determinants of natural prices as being explained by the Classical economists from within the theory of economics, albeit at a lower level of abstraction. For example, the theory of wages was closely connected to the theory of population. The Classical economists took the theory of the determinants of the level and growth of population as part of Political Economy. Since then, the theory of population has been seen as part of some other discipline than economics.

In contrast to the Classical theory, the determinants of the neoclassical theory of value:

1. tastes
2. technology, and
3. endowments are seen as exogenous to neoclassical economics.

Classical economics tended to stress the benefits of trade. Its theory of value was largely displaced by marginalist schools of thought (such as the Austrian School) which sees "use value" as deriving from the marginal utility that consumers finds in a good, and "exchange value" (i.e. natural price) as determined by the marginal opportunity-or disutility-cost of the inputs that make up the product. Ironically, considering the attachment of many classical economists to the free market, the largest school of economic thought that still adheres to classical form is the Marxian school.

Monetary Theory

British classical economists in the 19th century had a well-developed controversy between the Banking and the Currency school. This parallels recent debates between proponents of the theory of endogeneous money, such as Nicholas Kaldor, and monetarists, such as one Milton Friedman. Monetarists and members of the currency school argued that banks can and should control the supply of money. According to their theories, inflation is caused by banks issuing an excessive supply of money. According to proponents of the theory of endogeneous money, the supply of money automatically adjusts to the demand, and banks can only control the terms (e.g., the rate of interest) on which loans are made.

Debates Over the Definition of Classical Economics

The theory of value is currently a contested subject. One issue is whether classical economics is a forerunner of neoclassical economics or a school of thought that had a distinct theory of value, distribution, and growth.

Sraffians, who emphasize the discontinuity thesis, see classical economics as extending from Willam Petty's work in the 17th century to the break up of the Ricardian system around 1830.

The period between 1830 and the 1870s would then be dominated by "vulgar political economy", as Karl Marx characterized it. Sraffians argue that the wages fund theory; Senior's abstitence theory of interest, which puts the return to capital on the same level as returns to land and labor; the explanation of equilibrium prices by well-behaved supply and demand functions; and Say's law are not necessary or essential elements of the classical theory of value and distribution.

Perhaps Schumpeter's view that John Stuart Mill put forth a half-way house between classical and neoclassical economics is consistent with this view.

Sraffians generally see Marx as having rediscovered and restated the logic of classical economics, albeit for his own purposes. Others, such as Schumpeter, think of Marx as a follower of Ricardo. Even Samuel Hollander has recently explained that there is a textual basis in the classical economists for Marx's reading, although he does argue that it is an extremely narrow set of texts.

A second position is that neoclassical economics is essentially continuous with classical economics. To scholars promoting this view, there is no hard and fast line between classical and neoclassical economics. There may be shifts of emphasis, such as between the long run and the short run and between supply and demand, but the neoclassical concepts are to be found confused or in embryo in classical economics. To these economists, there is only one theory of value and distribution. Alfred Marshall is a well-known promoter of this view. Samuel Hollander is probably its best current proponent.

A third position sees two threads simultaneously being developed in classical economics. In this view, neoclassical economics is a development of certain exoteric (popular) views in Adam Smith. Ricardo was a sport, developing certain esoteric (known by only the select) views in Adam Smith. This view can be found in W. Stanley Jevons, who referred to Ricardo as something like "that able, but wrong-headed man" who put economics on the "wrong track". One can also find this view in Maurice Dobb's Theories of Value and Distribution Since Adam Smith: Ideology and Economic Theory (1973), as well as in Karl Marx's Theories of Surplus Value.

The above does not exhaust the possibilities. John Maynard Keynes thought of classical economics as starting with Ricardo and being ended by the publication of Keynes' General Theory of Employment Interest and Money. The defining criteria of classical economics, in this view, is Say's law.

One difficulty in these debates is that the participants are frequently arguing about whether there is a non-neoclassical theories that should be reconstructed and applied today to describe capitalist economies. Some, such as Terry Peach, see classical economics as of antiquarian interest.

3

Microeconomics

Microeconomics is a branch of economics that studies how individuals, households, and firms make decisions to allocate limited resources, typically in markets where goods or services are being bought and sold

Microeconomics examines how these decisions and behaviors affect the supply and demand for goods and services, which determines prices, and how prices, in turn, determine the supply and demand of goods and services.

Macroeconomics, on the other hand, involves the "sum total of economic activity, dealing with the issues of growth, inflation, and unemployment and with national economic policies relating to these issues" and the effects of government actions (e.g., changing taxation levels) on them. Particularly in the wake of the Lucas critique, much of modern macroeconomic theory has been built upon 'microfoundations'-*i.e.* based upon basic assumptions about micro-level behaviour.

AN OVERVIEW

One of the goals of microeconomics is to analyze market mechanisms that establish relative prices amongst goods and services and allocation of limited resources amongst many alternative uses. Microeconomics analyzes market failure, where markets fail to produce efficient results, as well as describing the theoretical conditions needed for perfect competition. Significant fields of study in microeconomics include markets under asymmetric information, choice under uncertainty and economic applications of game theory. Also considered is the elasticity of products within the market system.

ASSUMPTIONS AND DEFINITIONS

The theory of supply and demand usually assumes that markets are perfectly competitive. This implies that there are many buyers and sellers in the market and none of them have the capacity to significantly influence prices of goods and services. In many real-life transactions, the assumption fails because some individual buyers or sellers or groups of buyers or sellers do have the ability to influence prices. Quite often a sophisticated analysis is required to understand the demand-supply equation of a good. However, the theory works well in simple situations.

Mainstream economics does not assume a priori that markets are preferable to other forms of social organization. In fact, much analysis is devoted to cases where so-called market failures lead to resource allocation that is suboptimal by some standard (highways are the classic example, profitable to all for use but not directly profitable for anyone to finance). In such cases, economists may attempt to find policies that will avoid waste; directly by government control, indirectly by regulation that induces market participants to act in a manner consistent with optimal welfare, or by creating "missing" markets to enable efficient trading where none had previously existed. This is studied in the field of collective action. It also must be noted that "optimal welfare" usually takes on a Paretian norm which in its mathematical application of Kaldor-Hicks method, does not stay consistent with the Utilitarian norm within the normative side of economics which studies collective action, namely Public Choice. Market failure in positive economics (microeconomics) is limited in implications without mixing the belief of the economist and his or her theory. The demand for various commodities by individuals is generally thought of as the outcome of a utility-maximizing process. The interpretation of this relationship between price and quantity demanded of a given good is that, given all the other goods and constraints, this set of choices is that one which makes the consumer happiest.

MODES OF OPERATION

It is assumed that all firms are following rational decision-making, and will produce at the profit-maximizing output.

Given this assumption, there are four categories in which a firm's profit may be considered.

- A firm is said to be making an economic profit when its average total cost is less than the price of each additional product at the profit-maximizing output. The economic profit is equal to the quantity output multiplied by the difference between the average total cost and the price.
- A firm is said to be making a normal profit when its economic profit equals zero. This occurs where average total cost equals price at the profit-maximizing output.
- If the price is between average total cost and average variable cost at the profit-maximizing output, then the firm is said to be in a loss-minimizing condition. The firm should still continue to produce, however, since its loss would be larger if it were to stop producing. By continuing production, the firm can offset its variable cost and at least part of its fixed cost, but by stopping completely it would lose the entirety of its fixed cost.
- If the price is below average variable cost at the profit-maximizing output, the firm should go into shutdown. Losses are minimized by not producing at all, since any production would not generate returns significant enough to offset any fixed cost and part of the variable cost. By not producing, the firm loses only its fixed cost.

MARKET FAILURE

In microeconomics, the term "market failure" does not mean that a given market has ceased functioning. Instead, a market failure is a situation in which a given market does not efficiently organize production or allocate goods and services to consumers. Economists normally apply the term to situations where the inefficiency is particularly dramatic, or when it is suggested that non-market institutions would provide a more desirable result.

On the other hand, in a political context, stakeholders may use the term market failure to refer to situations where market forces do not serve the "public interest," a subjective assessment that is often made on social or moral grounds.

The four main types or causes of market failure are:

- Monopolies or other cases of abuse of market power where a "single buyer or seller can exert significant influence over prices or output"). Abuse of market power can be reduced by using antitrust regulations.
- Externalities, which occur in cases where the "market does not take into account the impact of an economic activity on outsiders." There are positive externalities and negative externalities. Positive externalities occur in cases such as when a television program on family health improves the public's health. Negative externalities occur in cases such as when a company's processes pollutes air or waterways. Negative externalities can be reduced by using government regulations, taxes, or subsidies, or by using property rights to force companies and individuals to take the impacts of their economic activity into account.
- Public goods such as national defence and public health initiatives such as draining mosquito-breeding marshes. For example, if draining mosquito-breeding marshes was left to the private market, far fewer marshes would probably be drained. To provide a good supply of public goods, nations typically use taxes that compel all residents to pay for these public goods (due to scarce knowledge of the positive externalities to third parties/ social welfare); and
- Cases where there is asymmetric information or uncertainty (information inefficiency). Information asymmetry occurs when one party to a transaction has more or better information than the other party. Typically it is the seller that knows more about the product than the buyer, but this is not always the case. Sellers in some markets have better information than the buyer. For example, used-car salespeople may know how whether a used car has been used as a delivery vehicle or taxi, information that may not be available to buyers. An example of a situation where the buyer may have better information than the seller would be an estate sale of a house, as required by a last will and

testament. A real estate broker purchasing this house may have more information about the house than the family members of the deceased.

This situation was first described by Kenneth J. Arrow in a seminal article on health care in 1963 entitled "Uncertainty and the Welfare Economics of Medical Care," in the American Economic Review. George Akerlof later used the term asymmetric information in his 1970 work The Market for Lemons. Akerlof noticed that, in such a market, the average value of the commodity tends to go down, even for those of perfectly good quality, because the buyer has no way of knowing whether the product they are buying will turn out to be a "lemon" (a defective product).

OPPORTUNITY COST

Although opportunity cost can be hard to quantify, the effect of opportunity cost is universal and very real on the individual level. In fact, this principle applies to all decisions, not just economic ones. Since the work of the Austrian economist Friedrich von Wieser, opportunity cost has been seen as the foundation of the marginal theory of value.

Opportunity cost is one way to measure the cost of something. Rather than merely identifying and adding the costs of a project, one may also identify the next best alternative way to spend the same amount of money. The forgone profit of this next best alternative is the opportunity cost of the original choice. A common example is a farmer that chooses to farm his land rather than rent it to neighbors, wherein the opportunity cost is the forgone profit from renting. In this case, the farmer may expect to generate more profit himself. Similarly, the opportunity cost of attending university is the lost wages a student could have earned in the workforce, rather than the cost of tuition, books, and other requisite items (whose sum makes up the total cost of attendance). The opportunity cost of a vacation in the Bahamas might be the down payment money for a house.

Note that opportunity cost is not the sum of the available alternatives, but rather the benefit of the single, best alternative. Possible opportunity costs of the city's decision to build the hospital on its vacant land are the loss of the land for a sporting center, or the inability to use the land for a parking lot, or the money that could have been made from selling the land, or the loss of any of the various other possible uses--but not all of these in aggregate. The true opportunity cost would be the forgone profit of the most lucrative of those listed.

One question that arises here is how to assess the benefit of dissimilar alternatives. We must determine a dollar value associated with each alternative to facilitate comparison and assess opportunity cost, which may be more or less difficult depending on the things we are trying to compare. For example, many decisions involve environmental impacts whose dollar value is difficult to assess because of scientific uncertainty. Valuing a human life or the economic impact of an Arctic oil spill involves making subjective choices with ethical implications.

APPLIED MICROECONOMICS

Applied microeconomics includes a range of specialized areas of study, many of which draw on methods from other fields. Industrial organization and regulation examines topics such as the entry and exit of firms, innovation, role of trademarks. Law and economics applies microeconomic principles to the selection and enforcement of competing legal regimes and their relative efficiencies.

Labor economics examines wages, employment, and labor market dynamics. Public finance (also called public economics) examines the design of government tax and expenditure policies and economic effects of these policies (e.g., social insurance programs). Political economy examines the role of political institutions in determining policy outcomes. Health economics examines the organization of health care systems, including the role of the health care workforce and health insurance programs. Urban economics, which examines the challenges faced by cities, such as are sprawl, air and water pollution, traffic congestion, and poverty, draws on the fields of urban geography and sociology. The field of financial economics examines topics such as the structure of optimal portfolios, the rate of return to capital, econometric analysis of security returns, and corporate financial behavior. The field of economic history examines the evolution of the economy and economic institutions, using methods and techniques from the fields of economics, history, geography, sociology, psychology, and political science.

SUPPLY AND DEMAND

The supply and demand model describes the interaction in the market for a certain good between producers and consumers, in relation to the price and sales of the good. It is the fundamental model of microeconomics, and is used to explain a variety of microeconomic scenarios, as well as a building block for many other economic models and theories. It was originally described by Alfred Marshall in his influential textbook Principles of Economics.

The model predicts that in a competitive free market, price will function to equalize the quantity demanded by consumers and the quantity supplied by producers, resulting in an economic equilibrium.

Fundamental Theory

The model asserts that in a free market, the amount of a product supplied by the producer and the amount demanded on the consumer are dependent on the market price of the product. The law of supply states that supply is directly proportional to price; the higher the price of the product, the more the producer will supply. The law of demand states that demand is inversely proportional to price; the higher the price of the product, the less the consumer will demand. Thus, supply and demand both vary with price.

The law of supply and demand states that the market price of a good is the intersection of consumer demand and producer supply. If the price for a good is at a low level where consumers demand more of the good than producers are prepared to supply, there will be a shortage of the good, and consumers will be willing to pay more for it. The producers will increase the price until it reaches the level where consumers would not buy any more if the price was increased. Conversely, if the price for a good is at a high level where the suppliers would like to produce more than the consumers will buy, the producers will be willing to lower the price. The price will fall until it reaches the level where consumers would be willing to pay more for the good.

This point to which prices will move towards is the point of economic equilibrium, where the quantity supplied is equal to the quantity demanded-producers are prepared to sell exactly the same quantity of goods as the consumers want to buy.

Supply Schedule

The supply schedule is the relationship between the quantity of goods supplied by the producers of a good and the current market price. It is graphically represented by the supply curve. Since supply is generally directly proportional to price, supply curves are almost always upwards-sloping. Also, the slope of a supply curve is usually increasingly upwards-sloping (i.e., the curve is a convex function) due of the law of diminishing marginal returns.

The supply curve for a given producer is equal to the producer's marginal cost curve because of the equimarginal principle. Thus, the supply curve for the entire market can be expressed as the sum of the marginal cost curves of the individual producers.

Occasionally, supply curves do not slope upwards. A well known example is the backward bending supply curve of labour. Generally, as a worker's wage increases, he is willing to supply a greater amount of labor (working more hours), since the higher wage increases the marginal utility of working (and increases the opportunity cost of not working). But when the wage reaches an extremely high amount, the laborer may experience the law of diminishing marginal utility in relation to his salary. The large amount of money he is making will make further money of little value to him. Thus, he will work less and less as the wage increases, choosing instead to spend his time in leisure.

Another example of a nontraditional supply curve is the supply curve for utility production companies. Because a large portion of their total costs are in the form of fixed costs, the marginal cost (supply curve) for these firms is often depicted as a constant.

Another postulated variant of a supply curve is that for child labor. Supply will increase as wages increase, but at a certain point a child's parents will pull the child from the child labor force due to cultural pressures and a desire to concentrate on education. The supply will not increase as the wage increases, up to a point where the wage is high enough to offset these concerns. For a normal demand curve, this can result in two stable equilibrium points-a high wage and a low wage equilibrium point.

Demand Schedule

Demand is economic want backed up by purchasing power. The demand schedule, depicted graphically as the demand curve, represents the amount of a good that buyers are willing and able to purchase at various prices, assuming all other non-price factors remain the same. The demand curve is almost always downwards-sloping, meaning that as price increases, consumers will buy less of a good.

Just as the supply curves are equal to marginal cost curves, demand curves are equal to marginal utility curves. The main determinants of individual demand are the price of the good, level of income, personal tastes, the price of substitute goods, and the price of complementary goods. The shape of the aggregate demand curve can be convex or concave, possibly depending on income distribution. As described above, the demand curve is generally downward sloping. There may be rare examples of goods that have upward sloping demand curves. A good whose demand curve has an upward slope is known as a Giffen good. The existence of Giffen goods cannot be explained by conspicuous consumption, since an increase in stature associated with buying an expensive product means that more than just price is variable. In fact the actual existence of a Giffen good is debatable. Examples of conspicuous consumption are clearly subjective, but might include the Bugatti Veyron. The social phenomenon often referred to as 'Bling' can also be thought of in this way.

Simple Supply and Demand Curves

Economic theory centers on creating a series of supply and demand relationships, describing them as equations, and then adjusting for factors which produce "stickiness" between supply and demand. Analysis is then done to see what "trade offs" are made in the "market", which is the negotiation between sellers and buyers. Analysis is done as to what point the ability of sellers to sell becomes less useful than other opportunities. This is related to "marginal" costs, or the price to produce the last unit that can be sold profitably, versus the chance of using the same effort to engage in some other activity.

The slope of the demand curve (downward to the right) indicates that a greater quantity will be demanded when the price is lower. On the other hand, the slope of the supply curve (upward to the right) tells us that as the price goes up, producers are willing to produce more goods. The point at which these curves intersect is the equilibrium point. At a price of P* producers will be willing to supply Q* units per period of time and buyers will demand the same quantity. P* in this example, is the equilibrating price that equates supply with demand.

In the figures, straight lines are drawn instead of the more general curves. This is typical in analysis looking at the simplified relationships between supply and demand because the shape of the curve does not change the general relationships and lessons of the supply and demand theory. The shape of the curves far away from the equilibrium point are less likely to be important because they do not affect the market clearing price and will not affect it unless large shifts in the supply or demand occur. So straight lines for supply and demand with the proper slope will convey most of the information the model can offer. In any case, the exact shape of the curve is not easy to determine for a given market. The general shape of the curve, especially its slope near the equilibrium point, does however have an impact on how a market will adjust to changes in demand or supply.

It should be noted that on supply and demand curves both are drawn as a function of price. Neither is represented as a function of the other. Rather the two functions interact in a manner that is representative of market outcomes. The curves also imply a somewhat neutral means of measuring price. In practice any currency or commodity used to measure price is also the subject of supply and demand.

Demand curve Shifts

When more people want something, the quantity demanded at all prices will tend to increase. This can be referred to as an increase in demand. The increase in demand could also come from changing tastes, where the same consumers desire more of the same good than they previously did. Increased demand can be represented on the graph as the curve being shifted right, because at each price point, a greater quantity is demanded. An example of this would be more people suddenly wanting more coffee. This will cause the demand curve to shift from the initial curve D1 to the new curve D2. This raises the equilibrium price from P1 to the higher P2. This raises the equilibrium quantity from Q1 to the higher Q2. In this situation, we say that there has been an increase in demand which has caused an extension in supply.

Conversely, if the demand decreases, the opposite happens. If the demand starts at D2 and then decreases to D1, the price will decrease and the quantity demanded will decrease-a contraction in supply. Notice that this is purely an effect of demand changing. The quantity supplied at each price is the same as before the demand shift (at both Q1 and Q2). The reason that the equilibrium quantity and price are different is the demand is different. At each point a greater amount is demanded (when there is a shift from D1 to D2)

Supply Curve Shifts

When the suppliers' costs change the supply curve will shift. For example, assume that someone invents a better way of growing wheat so that the amount of wheat that can be grown for a given cost will increase. Producers will be willing to supply more wheat at every price and this shifts the supply curve S1 to the right, to S2-an increase in supply. This causes the equilibrium price to decrease from P1 to P2. The equilibrium quantity increases from Q1 to Q2 as the quantity demanded increases at the new lower prices. Notice that in the case of a supply curve shift, the price and the quantity move in opposite directions.

Conversely, if the quantity supplied decreases, the opposite happens. If the supply curve starts at S2 and then shifts to S1, the equilibrium price will increase and the quantity will decrease. Notice that this is purely an effect of supply changing. The quantity demanded at each price is the same as before the supply shift (at both Q1 and Q2). The reason that the equilibrium quantity and price are different is the supply is different. There are only 4 possible movements to a demand/supply curve diagram. The demand curve can move to the left and right, and the supply curve can also move only to the left or right. If they do not move at all then they will stay in the middle where they already are.

Market Clearance

A market clears at the point where the quantity demanded is equal to the quantity supplied. Markets which do not clear will react in some way, either by a change in price, or in the amount produced, or in the amount demanded.

Graphically the situation can be represented by two curves: one showing the price-quantity combinations buyers will pay for, or the demand curve; and one showing the combinations sellers will sell for, or the supply curve. The market clears where the two curves intersect. In a general equilibrium model, all markets in all goods clear simultaneously and the "price" can be described entirely in terms of tradeoffs with other goods. For a century most economists believed in Say's Law, which states that markets, as a whole, would always clear and thus be in balance.

The market clearing price contains no maximization basis. As a result, any disequilibrium (excess demand or excess supply) is just a matter of graphical exercises. Some economists regarded that a demand curve could be represented by a diminishing marginal use value curve (the schedule of a consumer's maximum willing to pay with different quantity endowments). By this framework, people will buy when the market price is low enough, and they will sell when the price is high enough.

In market clearing condition, the market price implies that the marginal use value of all participants are equalized. In other words, mutual gain of exchange is exhausted. Here come the basis of maximization for the concept of market equilibrium.

Elasticity

An important concept in understanding supply and demand theory is elasticity. In this context, it refers to how supply and demand change in response to various stimuli. One way of defining elasticity is the percentage change in one variable divided by the percentage change in another variable (known as arch elasticity because it calculates the elasticity over a range of values, in contrast with point elasticity that uses differential calculus to determine the elasticity at a specific point). Thus it is a measure of relative changes.

Often, it is useful to know how the quantity supplied or demanded will change when the price changes. This is known as the price elasticity of demand and the price elasticity of supply. If a monopolist decides to increase the price of their product, how will this affect their sales revenue? Will the increased unit price offset the likely decrease in sales volume? If a government imposes a tax on a good, thereby increasing the effective price, how will this affect the quantity demanded?

If you do not wish to calculate elasticity, a simpler technique is to look at the slope of the curve. Unfortunately, this has units of measurement of quantity over monetary unit (for example, liters per euro, or battleships per million yen), which is not a convenient measure to use for most purposes. So, for example, if you wanted to compare the effect of a price change of gasoline in Europe versus the United States, there is a complicated conversion between gallons per dollar and liters per euro. This is one of the reasons why economists often use relative changes in percentages, or elasticity. Another reason is that elasticity is more than just the slope of the function: It is the slope of a function in a coordinate space, that is, a line with a constant slope will have different elasticity at various points.

Let's do an example calculation. We have said that one way of calculating elasticity is the percentage change in quantity over the percentage change in price. So, if the price moves from \$1.00 to \$1.05, and the quantity supplied goes from 100 pens to 102 pens, the slope is 2/0.05 or 40 pens per dollar. Since the elasticity depends on the percentages, the quantity of pens increased by 2%, and the price increased by 5%, so the price elasticity of supply is 2/5 or 0.4.

Since the changes are in percentages, changing the unit of measurement or the currency will not affect the elasticity. If the quantity demanded or supplied changes a lot when the price changes a little, it is said to be elastic. If the quantity changes little when the prices changes a lot, it is said to be inelastic. An example of perfectly inelastic supply, or zero elasticity, is represented as a vertical supply curve.

Elasticity in relation to variables other than price can also be considered. One of the most common to consider is income. How would the demand for a good change if income increased or decreased? This is known as the income elasticity of demand. For example, how much would the demand for a luxury car increase if average income increased by 10%? If it is positive, this increase in demand would be represented on a graph by a positive shift in the demand curve, because at all price levels, a greater quantity of luxury cars would be demanded.

Another elasticity that is sometimes considered is the cross elasticity of demand, which measures the responsiveness of the quantity demanded of a good to a change in the price of another good. This is often considered when looking at the relative changes in demand when studying complement and substitute goods. Complement goods are goods that are typically utilized together, where if one is consumed, usually the other is also. Substitute goods are those where one can be substituted for the other, and if the price of one good rises, one may purchase less of it and instead purchase its substitute.

Cross elasticity of demand is measured as the percentage change in demand for the first good that occurs in response to a percentage change in price of the second good. For an example with a complement good, if, in response to a 10% increase in the price of fuel, the quantity of new cars demanded decreased by 20%, the cross elasticity of demand would be-20%/10% or,-2.

Vertical Supply Curve

It is sometimes the case that a supply curve is vertical: that is the quantity supplied is fixed, no matter what the market price. For example, the amount of land in the world can be considered fixed. In this case, no matter how much someone would be willing to pay for a piece of land, the extra cannot be created. Also, even if no one wanted all the land, it still would exist. If land is considered in this way, then it warrants a vertical supply curve, giving it zero elasticity (i.e., no matter how large the change in price, the quantity supplied will not change). On the other hand, the supply of useful land can be increased in response to demand-by irrigation. And land that otherwise would be below sea level can be kept dry by a system of dikes, which might also be regarded as a response to demand. So even in this case, the vertical line is a bit of a simplification.

In the short run near vertical supply curves are more common. For example, if the Super Bowl is next week, increasing the number of seats in the stadium is almost impossible. The supply of tickets for the game can be considered vertical in this case. If the organizers of this event underestimated demand, then it may very well be the case that the price that they set is below the equilibrium price. In this case there will likely be people who paid the lower price who only value the ticket at that price, and people who could not get tickets, even though they would be willing to pay more. If some of the people who value the tickets less sell them to people who are willing to pay more (i.e., scalp the tickets), then the effective price will rise to the equilibrium price.

Supply-side economics argues that the aggregate supply function-the total supply function of the entire economy of a country-is relatively vertical. Thus, supply-siders argue against government stimulation of demand, which would only lead to inflation with a vertical supply curve.

OTHER MARKETS

The model of supply and demand also applies to various specialty markets.

The model applies to wages, which are determined by the market for labor. In this instance, the typical roles of supplier and consumer are reversed. The suppliers are individuals, who attempt to sell their labor for the highest price. Conversely, the consumers of labors are businesses, which attempt to buy the type of labor they need at the lowest price. The equilibrium price for a certain type of labor is the wage.

The model is also held to apply to interest rates, which are determined by the money market. In the short term, the money supply is a vertical supply curve, which the central bank of a country can control through monetary policy. The demand for money intersects with the money supply to determine the interest rate. In a situation in which there are many buyers but a single monopoly supplier that can adjust the supply or price of a good at will, the monopolist will adjust the price so that his profit is maximized given the amount that is demanded at that price. This price will be higher than in a competitive market. A similar analysis using supply and demand can be applied when a good has a single buyer, a monopsony, but many sellers.

Where there are both few buyers or few sellers, the theory of supply and demand cannot be applied because both decisions of the buyers and sellers are interdependent-changes in supply can affect demand and vice versa. Game theory can be used to analyze this kind of situation.

The supply curve does not have to be linear. However, if the supply is from a profit-maximizing firm, it can be proven that supply curves are not downward sloping (i.e., if the price increases, the quantity supplied will not decrease). Supply curves from profit-maximizing firms can be vertical, horizontal or upward sloping. While it is possible for industry supply curves to be downward sloping, supply curves for individual firms are never downward sloping.

Standard microeconomic assumptions cannot be used to prove that the demand curve is downward sloping. However, despite years of searching, no generally agreed upon example of a good that has an upward-sloping demand curve has been found (also known as a giffen good). Non-economists sometimes think that certain goods would have such a curve. For example, some people will buy a luxury car because it is expensive. In this case the good demanded is actually prestige, and not a car, so when the price of the luxury car decreases, it is actually changing the amount of prestige so the demand is not decreasing since it is a different good. Even with downward-sloping demand curves, it is possible that an increase in income may lead to a decrease in demand for a particular good, probably due to the existence of more attractive alternatives which become affordable: a good with this property is known as an inferior good.

History of Supply and Demand

Attempts to determine how supply and demand interact began with Adam Smith's The Wealth of Nations, first published in 1776. In this book, he mostly assumed that the supply price was fixed but that the demand would increase or decrease as the price decreased or increased. David Ricardo in 1817 published the book Principles of Political Economy and Taxation, in which the first idea of an economic model was proposed. In this, he more rigorously laid down the idea of the assumptions that were used to build his ideas of supply and demand.

During the late 19th century the marginalist school of thought emerged. This field mainly was started by Stanley Jevons, Carl Menger, and Léon Walras. The key idea was that the price was set by the most expensive price, that is, the price at the margin. This was a substantial change from Adam Smith's thoughts on determining the supply price.

Finally, most of the basics of the modern school theory of supply and demand were finalized by Alfred Marshall and Léon Walras, when they combined the ideas about supply and the ideas about demand and began looking at the equilibrium point where the two curves crossed. They also began looking at the effect of markets on each other. Since the late 19th century, the theory of supply and demand has mainly been unchanged. Most of the work has been in examining the exceptions to the model (like oligarchy, transaction costs, non-rationality).

Criticism of Marshall's Theory

Marshall's theory of supply and demand runs counter to the ideas of economists from Adam Smith and David Ricardo through the creation of the marginalist school of thought. Although Marshall's theories are dominant in universities today, other economists have disagreed with it. One theory counter to Marshall is that price is already known in a commodity before it reaches the market, negating his idea that some abstract market is conveying price information. The only thing the market communicates is whether an object is exchangeable or not (in which case it would change from an object to a commodity). This would mean that the producer creates the goods without already having customers-blindly producing, hoping that someone will buy them ("buy" meaning exchange money for the commodities). Modern producers often have market studies prepared well in advance of production decisions; however, misallocation of factors of production can still occur.

Keynesian economics also runs counter to the theory of supply and demand. In Keynesian theory, prices can become "sticky" or resistant to change, especially in the case of price decreases. This leads to a market failure. Modern supporters of Keynes, such as Paul Krugman, have noted this in recent history, such as when the Boston housing market dried up in the early 1990s, with neither buyers nor sellers willing to exchange at the price equilibrium.

Gregory Mankiw's work on the irrationality of actors in the markets also undermines Marshall's view of the forces involved in supply and demand.

Empirical Estimation

The demand and supply relations in a market can be statistically estimated from price and quantity data using the simultaneous system estimation ("structural estimation") method in econometrics. An alternative to "structural estimation" is Reduced form estimation. Parameter identification problem is a common issue in "structural estimation." Typically, data on exogenous variables (that is, variables other than price and quantity, both of which are endogenous variables) are needed to perform such an estimation.

Criticism of Supply and Demand

Unlike general equilibrium models, the supply and demand model represents a partial equilibrium which is accurate only in the short term, since it ignores the long-term reinforcing relationship between supply and demand. Objections to free market principles come primarily from Marxists and other Socialists. They would prefer to run an economy so that prices are not permitted to track supply and demand. When shortages occur or demand drops, the price should remain the same, they assert.

Advocates of free markets object to the practices in command economies, particularly in Communist countries. Long-term shortages of basic goods persist, and sporadic supply spikes result in lengthy queues of people waiting to get whatever is available.

CONSUMER SURPLUS

Consumer surplus or Consumer's surplus (or in the plural Consumers' surplus) is the difference between the price consumers are willing to pay (or reservation price) and the actual price. If someone is willing to pay more than the actual price, their benefit in a transaction is how much they saved when they didn't pay that price. For example, a person is willing to pay a tremendous amount for water since he needs it to survive, however since there are competing suppliers of water he is able to purchase it for less than he is willing to pay. The difference between the two prices is the consumer surplus.

The aggregate consumers' surplus is the sum of the consumer's surplus for each individual consumer. This can be represented on a supply and demand figure. If demand is as given as the diagonal line from the price axis to the quantity axis, consumers' surplus in the case of a the initial supply curve (S0) is the triangle above the line formed by price P0 to the demand line (bounded on the left by the price axis and on the top by the demand line). If supply expands (to S1), the consumers' surplus expands, to the triangle above P1 and below the demand line (still bounded by the price axis). The change in consumer's surplus is difference in area between the two triangles, and that is the consumer welfare associated with expansion of supply.

Profit Distribution

The benefits can be thought to accrue to two groups of people.

The first, those who were willing to pay the higher price P0, benefit because of a price reduction. Their benefit is the area in the rectangle formed on the top by P0, on the bottom by P1, on the left by the price axis and on the right by line extending vertically upwards from Q0.

The second set of beneficiaries are new consumers, those who will pay the new lower price (P1) but not the higher price (P0), and are measured as the difference between Q1 and Q0. Their benefit is the triangle formed by on the left by the line extending vertically upwards from Q0, on the right by the demand line, and on the bottom by the line extending horizontally to the right from P1.

Rule of One-half

The rule of one-half estimates the change in consumers' surplus for small changes in supply with a constant demand curve. Following the figure above,

$$\Delta CS = 0.5\ (Q_0 + Q_1)\ (P_0 - P_1)$$

where:

- CS = Consumers' Surplus
- Q_0 and Q_1 are the quantity demanded before and after a change in supply
- P_0 and P_1 are the prices before and after a change in supply

Comparison to Profit

In terms of supply and demand, consumer's surplus is the analog to producer's surplus.

History

The idea of consumer's surplus was due to Jules Dupuit and extended by Alfred Marshall.

ECONOMIC SURPLUS

The term surplus is used in economics for several related quantities. The consumer surplus is the amount that consumers benefit by being able to purchase a product for a price that is less than they would be willing to pay. The producer surplus is the amount that producers benefit by selling at a market price that is higher than they would be willing to sell for. Note that producer surplus flows through to the owners of the factors of production, unlike economic profit which is zero under perfect competition. If the markets for factors are perfectly competitive as well, producer surplus ultimately ends up as economic rent to the owners of scarce inputs such as land.

Details

On a standard supply and demand diagram, consumer surplus shows up as a triangle above the price and below the demand curve, since intramarginal consumers are paying less for the item than the maximum that they would pay. Producer surplus shows up as a triangle below the price and above the supply curve, since that is the minimum that a producer can produce that quantity with. If the government intervenes, using, for example, a tax or a subsidy, then the graph of supply and demand becomes more complicated and will also include an area that represents government surplus. Combined, the consumer surplus, the producer surplus, and the government surplus (if present) make up the social surplus or the total surplus. Total surplus is the primary measure used in Welfare Economics to evaluate the efficiency of a proposed policy.

A basic technique of bargaining for both parties is to pretend that their surplus is less than it really is: sellers may argue that the price they asks hardly leaves them any profit, while customers may play down how eager they are to have the article. In national accounts, operating surplus is roughly equal to distributed and undistributed pre-tax profit income, net of depreciation. In heterodox economics, the economic surplus denotes the total income which the ruling class derives from its ownership of scarce factors of production, which is either reinvested or spent on consumption. In Marxian economics, the term surplus may also refer to surplus value and surplus labour.

Argument

Economics is usually defined as the problem of how best to distribute limited resources, limited because wants are characterised as unlimited. Surplus economics argues that rather than limited resources, there is an abundance of resources and this is the economic problem. The difference is one of perspective. If wants are the focus, then of course resources are limited, but if needs or essentials are used as the foundation, then resources are seen to be abundant. The difference is between a description and an explanation. A focus on wants describes a free market situation, a focus on essentials allows an explanation of the economy to begin. An abundance of resources means that not all need to work productively and that some can use more resources than others. Who shall be the lucky ones and how to keep the unlucky quiet is part of the economic problem. Abundance is also a problem because having more resources than is strictly needed to live presents a danger to the production processes and the command over resources that created an economic surplus in the first place.

SURPLUS ECONOMICS

By economic surplus is meant all production which is not essential for the continuance of existence. That is to say, all production about which there is a choice as to whether or not it is produced. The economic surplus begins when an economy is first able to produce more than it needs to survive, a surplus to its essentials. This definition is no more arbitrary than defining all resources as scarce by definition by declaring all wants infinite. In fact it is much less so since the line between existence and non-existence is a real one.

Alternative definitions are:

1. The difference between the value of a society's annual product and its socially necessary cost of production. (Davis, p.1)
2. The range of economic freedom at its [society's] disposal, extent able to engage in socially discretionary spending that satisfies more than the basic needs of its producers. (Dawson & Foster in Davis, p.45)
3. Income minus essential consumption requirements. (Lippit in Davis p.81)
4. The difference between what a society can produce and what a society must produce to reproduce itself. (Standfield in Davis, p.131)

Argument: Economics is usually defined as the problem of how best to distribute limited resources, limited because wants are characterised as unlimited. Surplus economics argues that rather than limited resources, there is an abundance of resources and this is the economic problem. The difference is one of perspective. If wants are the focus, then of course resources are limited, but if needs or essentials are used as the foundation, then resources are seen to be abundant. The difference is between a description and an explanation. A focus on wants describes a free market situation, a focus on essentials allows an explanation of the economy to begin.

An abundance of resources means that not all need to work productively and that some can use more resources than others. Who shall be the lucky ones and how to keep the unlucky quiet is part of the economic problem. Abundance is also a problem because having more resources than is strictly needed to live presents a danger to the production processes and the command over resources that created an economic surplus in the first place.

Surplus economics seeks to answer such questions as: Why does so much waste exist along side of so much poverty?

The orthodox assumption of scarcity has survived even the staggering levels of surplus of modern economies because this assumption suits the needs of those who command resources and who prefer to ensure that the economy does not become democratised; that unpleasant tasks are done by someone else, that some win and many lose.

4

Welfare and Distribution Economics

Welfare economics is a branch of economics that uses microeconomic techniques to simultaneously determine the allocational efficiency of a macroeconomy and the income distribution associated with it. It attempts to maximize the level of social welfare by examining the economic activities of the individuals that comprise society.

Welfare economics is concerned with the welfare of individuals, as opposed to groups, communities, or societies because it assumes that the individual is the basic unit of measurement. It also assumes that individuals are the best judges of their own welfare, that people prefer greater welfare to less welfare, and that welfare can be adequately measured either in monetary terms or as a relative preference.

Social welfare refers to the overall utilitarian state of society. It is often defined as the summation of the welfare of all the individuals in the society. Welfare can be measured either cardinally in terms of dollars or "utils", or measured ordinally in terms of relative utility. The cardinal method is seldom used today because of aggregation problems that make the accuracy of the method doubtful, as well as strong underlying assumptions.

There are two sides to welfare economics: economic efficiency and income distribution. Economic efficiency is largely positive and deals with the "size of the pie". Income distribution is much more normative and deals with "dividing up the pie".

Two Approaches

There are two approaches that can be taken to welfare economics: the Neoclassical approach and the New welfare economics approach.

The Neoclassical approach was developed by Edgeworth, Sidgwick, Marshall, and Pigou. It assumes that:

- Utility is cardinal, that is, scale-measurable by observation or judgment.
- Additional consumption provides smaller and smaller increases in utility (diminishing marginal utility).
- All individuals have interpersonally comparable utility functions.

With these assumptions, it is possible to construct a social welfare function simply by summing all the individual utility functions.

The New Welfare Economics approach is based on the work of Pareto, Hicks, and Kaldor. It explicitly recognizes the differences between the efficiency part of the discipline and the distribution part and treats them differently. Questions of efficiency are assessed with criteria such as Pareto efficiency and the Kaldor-Hicks compensation tests, while questions of income distribution are covered in social welfare function specification. Further, efficiency dispenses with cardinal measures of utility: ordinal utility, which merely ranks commodity bundles, such as represented by an indifference-curve map is adequate for this analysis.

The Efficiency

Situations are considered to have distributive efficiency when goods are distributed to the people who can gain the most utility from them.

Many economists use Pareto efficiency as their efficiency goal. According to this measure of social welfare, a situation is optimal only if no individuals can be made better off without making someone else worse off. This ideal state of affairs can only come about if four criteria are met:

- The marginal rates of substitution in consumption are identical for all consumers. This occurs when no consumer can be made better off without making others worse off.
- The marginal rate of transformation in production is identical for all products. This occurs when it is impossible to increase the production of any good without reducing the production of other goods.
- The marginal resource cost is equal to the marginal revenue product for all production processes. This takes place when marginal physical product of a factor must be the same for all firms producing a good.
- The marginal rates of substitution in consumption are equal to the marginal rates of transformation in production, such as where production processes must match consumer wants.

There are a number of conditions that, most economists agree, may lead to inefficiency. They include:

- Imperfect market structures, such as a monopoly, monopsony, oligopoly, oligopsony, and monopolistic competition.
- Factor allocation inefficiencies in production theory basics.
- Market failures and externalities; there is also social cost.
- Price discrimination and price skimming.
- Asymmetric information, principle-agent problems.
- Long run declining average costs in a natural monopoly.
- Certain types of taxes and tariffs.

To determine whether an activity is moving the economy towards Pareto efficiency, two compensation tests have been developed. Any change usually makes some people better off while making others worse off, so these tests ask what would happen if the winners were to compensate the losers. Using the Kaldor criterion, an activity will contribute to Pareto optimality if the maximum amount the gainers are prepared to pay is greater than the minimum amount that the losers are prepared to accept. Under the Hicks criterion, an activity will contribute to Pareto optimality if the maximum amount the losers are prepared to offer to the gainers in order to prevent the change is less than the minimum amount the gainers are prepared to accept as a bribe to forgo the change. The Hicks compensation test is from the losers' point of view, while the Kaldor compensation test is from the gainers' point of view. If both conditions are satisfied, both gainers and losers will agree that the proposed activity will move the economy toward Pareto optimality. This is referred to as Kaldor-Hicks efficiency or the Scitovsky criterion.

Income Distribution

There are many combinations of consumer utility, production mixes, and factor input combinations consistent with efficiency. In fact, there are an infinity of consumer and production equilibria that yield Pareto optimal results. There are as many optima as there are points on the aggregate production possibilities frontier. Hence, Pareto efficiency is a necessary, but not a sufficient condition for social welfare. Each Pareto optimum corresponds to a different income distribution in the economy. Some may involve great inequalities of income. So how do we decide which Pareto optimum is most desirable? This decision is made, either tacitly or overtly, when we specify the social welfare function. This function embodies value judgements about interpersonal utility. The social welfare function is a way of mathematically stating the relative importance of the individuals that comprise society.

A utilitarian welfare function (also called a Benthamite welfare function) sums the utility of each individual in order to obtain society's overall welfare. All people are treated the same, regardless of their initial level of utility. One extra unit of utility for a starving person is not seen to be of any greater value than an extra unit of utility for a millionaire. At the other extreme is the Max-Min function. According to the Max-Min criterion, welfare is maximized when the utility of those society members that have the least is the greatest. No economic activity will increase social welfare unless it improves the position of the society member that is the worst off. Most economists specify social welfare functions that are intermediate between these two extremes.

The social welfare function is typically translated into social indifference curves so that they can be used in the same graphic space as the other functions that they interact with. A utilitarian social indifference curve is linear and downward sloping to the right. The Max-Min social indifference curve takes the shape of two straight lines joined so as they form a 90 degree angle. A social indifference curve drawn from an intermediate social welfare function is a curve that slopes downward to the right.

A crude social welfare function can be constructed by measuring the subjective dollar value of goods and services distributed to participants in the economy.

The Seven Equation Model

The basic welfare economics problem is to find the theoretical maximum of a social welfare function, subject to various constraints such as the state of technology in production, available natural resources, national infrastructure, and behavoural constraints such as consumer utility maximization and producer profit maximization. In the simplest possible economy this can be done by simultaneously solving seven equations. This simple economy would have only two consumers (consumer 1 and consumer 2), only two products (product X and product Y), and only two factors of production going into these products (labour (L) and capital (K)). The model can be stated as:

maximize social welfare: $W = f(U^1 U^2)$ subject to the following set of constraints:

$K = K^x + K^y$ (The amount of capital used in the production of goods X and Y)

$L = L^x + L^y$ (The amount of labour used in the production of goods X and Y)

$X = X(K^x L^x)$ (The production function for product X)

$Y = Y(K^y L^y)$ (The production function for product Y)

$U1 = U^1(X^1 Y^1)$ (The preferences of consumer 1)

$U2 = U^2(X^2 Y^2)$ (The preferences of consumer 2)

The solution to this problem yields a Pareto optimum. In a more realistic example of millions of consumers, millions of products, and several factors of production, the math gets more complicated.

Also, finding a solution to an abstract function does not directly yield a policy recommendation! In other words, solving an equation does not solve social problems. However, a model like the one above can be viewed as an argument that solving a social problem (like achieving a Pareto-optimal distribution of wealth) is at least theoretically possible.

Efficiency between Production and Consumption

The relation between production and consumption in a simple seven equation model (2x2x2 model) can be shown graphically. The aggregate production possibility frontier, labeled PQ shows all the points of efficiency in the production of goods X and Y. If the economy produces the mix of good X and Y shown at point A, then the marginal rate of transformation (MRT), X for Y, is equal to 2.

Point A defines the boundaries of an Edgeworth box diagram of consumption. That is, the same mix of products that are produced at point A, can be consumed by the two consumers in this simple economy. The consumers' relative preferences are shown by the indifference curves inside the Edgeworth box. At point B the marginal rate of substitution (MRS) is equal to 2, while at point C the marginal rate of substitution is equal to 3. Only at point B is consumption in balance with production (MRS=MRT). The curve 0BCA (often called the contract curve) inside the Edgeworth box defines the locus of points of efficiency in consumption (MRS1=MRS 2). As we move along the curve, we are changing the mix of goods X and Y that individuals 1 and 2 choose to consume. The utility data associated with each point on this curve can be used to create utility functions.

Social Welfare Maximization

Utility functions can be derived from the points on a contract curve. Numerous utility functions can be derived, one for each point on the production possibility frontier (PQ in the diagram above). A social utility frontier (also called a grand utility frontier) can be obtained from the outer envelope of all these utility functions. Each point on a social utility frontier represents an efficient allocation of an economy's resources; that is, it is a Pareto optimum in factor allocation, in production, in consumption, and in the interaction of production and consumption (supply and demand). The curve MN is a social utility frontier. Point D corresponds with point B from the earlier diagram. Point D is on the social utility frontier because the marginal rate of substitution at point B is equal to the marginal rate of transformation at point A. Point E corresponds with point C in the previous diagram, and lies inside the social utility frontier (indicating inefficiency) because the MRS at point C is not equal to the MRT at point A.

Although all the points on the grand social utility frontier are Pareto efficient, only one point identifies where social welfare is maximized. This is point Z (sometimes called the bliss point) where the social utility frontier MN is tangent to the highest possible social indifference curve labelled SI.

Relation to other Subjects

Welfare economics uses many of the same techniques as microeconomics and can be seen as intermediate or advanced microcconomic theory. Its results are applicable to macroeconomic issues so welfare economics is somewhat of a bridge between the two branches of economics. Cost-benefit analysis is a specific application of welfare economics techniques, but excludes the income distribution aspects.

Political science also looks into the issue of social welfare (political science), but in a less quantitative manner.

Human development theory explores these issues also, and considers them fundamental to the development process itself.

Criticisms

Many doubt whether a cardinal utility function, or cardinal social welfare function, is of any value. The reason given is that it is difficult to aggregate the utilities of various people that have differing marginal utility of money, such as the wealthy and the poor.

Some even question the value of ordinal utility functions. They have proposed other means of measuring well-being as an alternative to price indices, "willingness to pay" functions, and other price oriented measures. These price based measures are seen as promoting consumerism and productivism by many. It should be noted that it is possible to do welfare economics without the use of prices, however this is not always done.

Value assumptions explicit in the social welfare function used and implicit in the efficiency criterion chosen make welfare economics a highly normative and subjective field. This can make it controversial.

DISTRIBUTION

Distribution in economics refers to the way total output and income from it is distributed among individuals and among the factors of production (labor, land, and capital) (Samuelson and Nordhaus, 2001, p. 762). In general theory total output and total income are duals, inseparably bound. So are they bound in their operational counterparts, the national income and product accounts, which represent that each unit of output corresponds to a unit of income, whether expressed in real or nominal terms. One use of national accounts is for classifying factor incomes and measuring them.). But, where focus is on income of persons or households, rather than on returns to different factors of production in their relation to total output, other data sources or adjustments to the national accounts are frequently used. Here, interest is often on the fraction of national (or world) income going to the top (or bottom) say 20 percent of households, to the next 20 percent, and so forth, or on the changes in these fractions over time.

Descriptive, Theoretical, Scientific, and Welfare Uses

Income distribution can describe elements of positive economics. This provides inputs for empirically testable theories explaining the distribution of income, for example human capital theory and the theory of economic discrimination (Becker, 1993, 1971).

In welfare economics, a level of feasible output possibilities may be conveniently distinguished from the distribution of income for those output possibilities. Both can describe elements of positive economics. But in the formal theory of social welfare, rules for selection from feasible distributions of income are a way of representing normative economics at a high level of generality.

Neoclassical Distribution Theory

In neoclassical economics, the supply of and the demand for each factor of production interact in factor markets to determine equilibrium output, income, and the income distribution. Factor demand in turn incorporates the marginal-productivity relationship of that factor in the output market. John R. Hicks's The Theory of Wages (1963) remains a standard neoclassical statement of what determines real wages among labor markets. In a perfectly competitive economy, market equilibrium results in allocative efficiency as to the mix of output produced and distributive efficiency in the least-cost mix of factors of production. In 1908, the efficiency properties of perfect competition were shown by Enrico Barone to be required as well for efficient resource use in collectivist planning.

The neoclassical growth model provides an account of how distribution of income between capital and labor are determined in competitive markets at the macroeconomic level over time with technological change and changes in the size of the capital stock and labor force. More recent developments of the distinction between human capital and physical capital and between social capital and personal capital have deepened analysis of distribution.

5

Economics and Accounting

A good or commodity in economics is any object or service that increases utility, directly or indirectly, not be confused with good in a moral or ethical sense. A good that cannot be used by consumers directly, such as an office building or capital equipment, can also be referred to as a good as an indirect source of utility through resale value or as a source of income. A 'good' in economic usage does not imply moral acceptance or even legality.

If an object or service is sold for a positive price, then it is a good since the purchaser considers the utility of the object or service more valuable than the money. Some things are useful but not scarce such as air and are referred to as free goods.

In macroeconomics and accounting, a good is contrasted with a service. A good here is defined as a physical (tangible) product capable of being delivered to a purchaser and involves the transfer of ownership from seller to customer, as opposed to an (intangible) service. A more general term that preserves the distinction between goods and services is 'commodities'. In microeconomics s 'good' is often used in this more inclusive sense of a commodity.

UTILITY CHARACTERISTICS OF GOODS

A good is an object whose consumption increases the utility of the consumer, for which the quantity demanded exceeds the quantity supplied at zero price. Goods are usually modeled as having decreasing marginal utility. The first car an individual purchases is very valuable; the fourth is much less useful.

Thus, in these and similar goods, the marginal utility of additional units approaches zero as the quantity consumed increases. Assuming that one cannot re-sell it, there is a point at which a consumer would decline to purchase an additional car, even at a price very near zero. This is the consumer's satiation point.

In some cases, such as the above example of a car, the lower limit of utility as quantity increases is zero. In other goods, the utility of a good can cross zero, changing from positive to negative through time. This means that what initially is a good can become a bad if too much of it is consumed. For example, shots of vodka can have positive utility, but beyond some point, additional units make the consumer less happy, that is, they would not be chosen. In economics a bad is the opposite of a good. Ultimately, whether an object is a good or a bad depends on each individual consumer, and therefore, it is important to realize that not all goods are good all the time, and not all goods are goods to all people.

ACCOUNTANCY

Accountancy (profession) or accounting (methodology) is the measurement, disclosure or provision of assurance about financial information primarily used by managers, investors, tax authorities and other decision makers to make resource allocation decisions. The names come from the use of financial accounts. Financial accounting is one branch of accounting and historically has involved processes by which financial information about a business is recorded, classified, summarized, interpreted, and communicated. Accounting is also widely referred to as the "language of business".

Auditing, a related but separate discipline, has two sub-disciplines: Internal and External auditing. External auditing is the process whereby an independent auditor examines an organization's financial statements and accounting records in order to express an opinion-that conveys reasonable but not absolute assurance-as to the truth and fairness of the statements and the accountant's adherence to Generally Accepted Accounting Principles (GAAP), or International Financial Reporting Standards (IFRS), in all material respects.

Internal auditing is an examination in which management, and not the external public, is the main beneficiary. It is carried out usually by auditors employed by the company, but sometimes by external service providers. The internal auditor's role is broader, and basically depends on what kind of assurance management wants. It usually certifies the efficiency and effectiveness of processes, departments, projects or internal controls. The Institute of Internal Auditors is generally accepted as the custodian of Internal Auditing best practice.

At the heart of accounting is the measurement of financial transactions which are transfers of legal property rights made under contractual relationships. Non-financial transactions are specifically excluded due to conservatism and materiality principles.

Practitioners of accountancy are known as accountants. There are many professional bodies for accountants throughout the world. Many allow their members to use titles indicating their membership. Examples are Chartered Certified Accountant (ACCA or FCCA), Chartered Accountant (FCA, CA or ACA), Management Accountant (ACMA, FCMA or AICWA) and Certified Public Accountant (CPA).

Accountancy attempts to create accurate financial reports that are useful to managers, regulators, and other stakeholders such as shareholders, creditors, or owners. The day-to-day record-keeping involved in this process is known as bookkeeping.

At the heart of modern financial accounting is the double-entry bookkeeping system. This system involves making at least two entries for every transaction: a debit in one account, and a corresponding credit in another account. The sum of all debits should always equal the sum of all credits. This provides an easy way to check for errors. This system was first used in medieval Europe, although claims have been made that the system dates back to Ancient Greece.

According to critics of standard accounting practices, it has changed little since. Accounting reform measures of some kind have been taken in each generation to attempt to keep bookkeeping relevant to capital assets or production capacity. However, these have not changed the basic principles, which are supposed to be independent of economics as such. In recent times, the divergence of accounting from economic principles has resulted in controversial reforms to make financial reports more indicative of economic reality.

HISTORY

Accountancy's infancy dates back to the earliest days of human agriculture and civilization (the Sumerians in Mesopotamia), when the need to maintain accurate records of the quantities and relative values of agricultural products first arose. Simple accounting is mentioned in the Christian Bible in the book of Matthew, in the Parable of the Talents (Matt. 25:19). The Quran also mentions simple accounting for trade and credit arrangements (Quran 2: 282).

Twelfth century writer Ibn Taymiyyah mentioned in his book Hisba (verification, calculation), detailed accounting systems used by the Muslims as early as in the mid-seventh century. The accounting practices were influenced by the Roman and the Persian civilizations that Muslims interacted with. The most detailed example of a complex governmental accounting system is the Divan of Umar, the second Caliph of Islam in which all revenues and disbursements were recorded. The Divan of Umar has been described in detail by various Islamic historians and was used by Muslim rulers with modifications and enhancements until the fall of the Ottoman Empire.

BIRTH OF MODERN ACCOUNTANCY

The first book on accounting was written by a Croatian merchant Benedetto Cotrugli, who is also known as Benedikt Kotruljevic, from the city of Dubrovnik. During his life in Italy he met many merchants and decided to write, Della Mercatvra et del Mercante Perfetto (On Trade and the Perfect Merchant) in which he elaborated on the principles of modern, double-entry book-keeping. He finished his lifework in 1458. However, his work was not published until 1573, as a result of which his contributions to the field have been overlooked by the general public..

For this reason, Luca Pacioli (1445-1517), also known as Friar Luca dal Borgo, is credited for the "birth" of accounting.

His Summa de arithmetica, geometrica, proportioni et proportionalita (Venice 1494), a synthesis of the mathematical knowledge of his time, includes the first published description of the method of keeping accounts that Venetian merchants used at that time, known as the double-entry accounting system. Although Pacioli codified rather than invented this system, he is widely regarded as the "Father of Accounting". The system he published included most of the accounting cycle as we know it today. He described the use of journals and ledgers, and warned that a person should not go to sleep at night until the debits equalled the credits! His ledger had accounts for assets (including receivables and inventories), liabilities, capital, income, and expenses-the account categories that are reported on an organization's balance sheet and income statement, respectively. He demonstrated year-end closing entries and proposed that a trial balance be used to prove a balanced ledger. His treatise also touches on a wide range of related topics from accounting ethics to cost accounting.

The first known book in the English language on accounting was published in London by John Gouge (or Gough) in 1543. It is described as A Profitable Treatyce called the Instrument or Boke to learn to knowe the good order of the kepyng of the famouse reconynge, called in Latin, Dare and Habere, and, in English, Debitor and Creditor.

A short book of instructions was also published in 1588 by John Mellis of Southwark, in which he says, "I am but the renuer and reviver of an ancient old copie printed here in London the 14 of August 1543: collected, published, made, and set forth by one Hugh Oldcastle, Scholemaster, who, as appeareth by his treatise, then taught Arithmetics, and this booke in Saint Ollaves parish in Marko Lane." John Mellis refers to the fact that the principle of accounts he explains (which is a simple system of double entry) is "after the forme of Venice".

A book described as The Merchants Mirrour, or directions for the perfect ordering and keeping of his accounts formed by way of Debitor and Creditor, after the (so termed) Italian manner, by Richard Dafforne, accountant, published in 1635, contains many references to early books on the science of accountancy. In a chapter in this book, headed "Opinion of Book-keeping's Antiquity," the author states, on the authority of another writer, that the form of book-keeping referred to had then been in use in Italy about two hundred years, "but that the same, or one in many parts very like this, was used in the time of Julius Caesar, and in Rome long before." He gives quotations of Latin book-keeping terms in use in ancient times, and refers to "ex Oratione Ciceronis pro Roscio Comaedo"; and he adds:

"That the one side of their booke was used for Debitor, the other for Creditor, is manifest in a certain place, Naturalis Historiae Plinii, lib. 2, cap. 7, where hee, speaking of Fortune, saith thus:

Huic Omnia Expensa.

Huic Omnia Feruntur accepta et in tota Ratione mortalium sola.

Utramque Paginam facit."

An early Dutch writer appears to have suggested that double-entry book-keeping was even in existence among the Greeks, pointing to scientific accountancy having been invented in remote times.

There were several editions of Richard Dafforne's book-the second edition in 1636, the third in 1656, and another in 1684. The book is a very complete treatise on scientific accountancy, beautifully prepared and containing elaborate explanations. The numerous editions tend to prove that the science was highly appreciated in the 17th century. From this time on, there has been a continuous supply of literature on the subject, many of the authors styling themselves accountants and teachers of the art, and thus proving that the professional accountant was then known and employed.

QUALIFICATIONS AND REGULATION

The requirements for entry in the profession of accounting vary from country to country.

Accountants may be licensed by a variety of organisations, such as the British qualified accountancy bodies including

Association of Chartered Certified Accountants (ACCA) and Institute of Chartered Accountants, and are recognized by titles such as Chartered Certified Accountant (ACCA or FCCA) and Chartered Accountant (UK, Australia, New Zealand, Canada, India, Pakistan, South Africa), Certified Public Accountant (Ireland, Japan, US, Singapore, Hong Kong, the Philippines), Certified Management Accountant (Canada, U.S.), Certified General Accountant (Canada), or Certified Practising Accountant (Australia). Some Commonwealth countries (Australia and Canada) often recognise both the certified and chartered accounting bodies. The majority of "public" accountants in New Zealand and Canada are Chartered Accountants; however, Certified General Accountants are also authorized by legislation to practise public accounting and auditing in all Canadian provinces, except Ontario and Quebec, as of 2005. There is, however, no legal requirement for an accountant to be a paid-up member of one of the many Institutes and other bodies which are effectively a form of professional trade union. Unlike the Law Society, which can legally stop a solicitor from practising, accountancy institutes do not have such authority. However, auditors are regulated.

THE "BIG FOUR" ACCOUNTANCY FIRMS

The "Big Four auditors" are the largest multinational accountancy firms.

- Pricewater house Coopers
- Deloitte Touche Tohmatsu
- Ernst & Young
- KPMG

These firms are associations of the partnerships in each country rather than having the classical structure of holding company and subsidiaries, but each has an international 'umbrella' organization for coordination.

Before the Enron and other accounting scandals, there were five large firms and were called the Big Five. Since Arthur Andersen's assurance practice split (after the firm was implicated in the Enron scandal, however it was found not guilty), with a plurality joining KPMG in the US and

Deloitte & Touche outside of the US, Arthur Andersen left from the group. Previous to this there were also groupings referred to as the "Big Six" (Arthur Andersen, plus Coopers & Lybrand before its merger with Price Waterhouse) and the "Big Eight" (Ernst and Young prior to their merger were Ernst& Whinney and Arthur Young and Deloitte & Touche was formed by the merger of Deloitte, Haskins and Sells with the firm Touche Ross).

Enron turned out to be only the first of a series of accounting scandals that enveloped the accounting industry in 2002.

This is likely to have far-reaching consequences for the U.S. accounting industry. Application of International Accounting Standards originating in International Accounting Standards Board headquartered in London and bearing more resemblance to UK than current US practices is often advocated by those who note the relative stability of the UK accounting system (which reformed itself after scandals in the late 1980s and early 1990s). Accounting reform of a far more comprehensive sort is advocated by those who see issues with capitalism or economics, and seek ecological or social accountability.

MARKET SIZE OF UK

According to Accountancy Age's 2005 league table, fee income amongst the Top 50 accounting firms in the UK rose from £6.3bn to £7.0bn. This followed two successive years in which fee income had declined, largely a result of the sale by some of the larger firms of their consultancy arms. As detailed in the next section, fee income in most business areas-audit, tax, corporate finance and consultancy-rose in the 2005 survey, with insolvency and wealth management being the only segments where revenue fell.

Price water house Coopers remains the largest firm with fee income totalling £1,780m followed by Deloitte (£1,350m), KPMG (£1,066m) and Ernst & Young (£945m). The combined revenue of the Big Four accounted for £5.0bn, 72% of the fee income of the Top 50, down from 78-79% in the years up to the 2002 survey and the third year in succession a decline in their share has occurred. Ernst & Young's fee income is the smallest of the largest four firms, but still over three times that of the next largest firm, Grant Thornton. The amount of fee income tapers off amongst the mid-tier firms so that in total there were only 25 firms that each generated more than £15m of revenue in the 2005 survey.

ACCOUNTING REFORM

Accounting reform is an expansion to accounting rules that goes beyond the realm of financial measures for both individual economic entities and national economies. It is advocated by those who consider the focus of the present standards and practices wholly inadequate to the task of measuring and reporting the activity, success, and failure of modern enterprise, including government. The basic bookkeeping concepts underlying contemporary accounting date back about 500 years to Renaissance Italian practices. Obviously, the vast majority of articulations by modern standard setters have little in common with the accounting practices then used. Real debate concerns concepts such as whether to report transactions, such as asset acquisitions, at their cost or to report them at their current market values. The former, traditional approach, appeals for its reliability but can quickly lose its relevance due to inflation and other factors; the latter, increasingly common approach, appeals for its relevance but may be less reliable due to its resort to appraisals or other subjective measures. This trade off is essentially impossible to overcome. The relative virtue of either approach depends on the subject matter in question.

BUSINESS

Limited reforms within professional management circles have led in the past to activity-based costing, economic value added, regret and risk measures. Not only do most businesses raise capital based on numbers derived from current standards, there are extensive lobbying efforts by the accounting industry to keep those standards roughly as they are: complex, loopholed, and unable to be applied or audited easily by laymen.

Heads of the U.S. Securities and Exchange Commission since the 1980s have consistently complained that this lobbying makes it impossible for them to apply meaningful reform, even in the wake of accounting scandals, e.g. that which felled Arthur Andersen in 2002.

NATIONAL ECONOMIES

Any comprehensive scheme of accounting reform is a major professional and academic enterprise; Typically it requires examination of the role of each of the fundamental factors of production, an analysis of capital indicating how many types there are and how each supports each factor of a production process.

A comprehensive scheme that would affect, for instance, the United Nations standards for national accounts, the rules of the Bank for International Settlements, or listing requirements on the major stock exchanges, would have to defend any change against critics that advocated lesser reforms-making it extraordinarily difficult to achieve simultaneous consent.

Marilyn Waring, who deeply criticized the UN account system for systematically under-valuing the social and economic contributions of women, stated also that she had to read literally an entire room full of books in order even to understand the standards applied today. It seems unlikely that most advocates of reform have the stamina to do so, nor the background required to debate each issue with economists or accountants that build their careers on the detailed extension and improvement of standards that already exist. Most critics considered reform prospects bleak.

The critique from ecological economics was even more fundamental, claiming that most means of measuring well-being indicated that the developed nations were in a state of "uneconomic growth" through the 1980s and 1990s, due mostly to failures of measurement, most or all of which could be tracked back to the practice of using the Gross National Product as a means of making money supply decisions. This is perhaps the most obvious and widely-held critique of current national accounting and economic growth reporting systems-the creators of the GNP and GDP measures themselves advise against its use as a single measure of economic growth-but politicians and press typically do so without caveat nor apology.

Robert Costanza, Paul Hawken, Amory Lovins and others who advocate a consistent global system for valuing natural capital, note that failures in this area are particularly grim: promoting extinction, loss of biodiversity, climate change and destructive weather for the sake of such "growth". John McMurtry characterized this as "the cancer stage of capitalism".

What makes "economic sense" under current standards, they argue, is in fact leading to ecological catastrophe, social conflict, and economic chaos.

GOVERNMENTS

One barrier to accounting reform are governments themselves. They have the authority to determine what are accepted accounting principles, while using questionable accounting practices themselves. Governments, for example, pay off operating costs with longer-term debt and thus overstate budgetary surpluses or conceal operating deficits. This is not unlike the allegedly fraudulent practices of some corporations.

ACTUARY

Actuaries are those with a deep understanding of financial security systems, their reasons for being, their complexity, their mathematics, and the way they work. (Trowbridge 1989, p. 7). They evaluate the likelihood of events and quantify the contingent outcomes in order to minimize losses, both emotional and financial, associated with uncertain undesirable events. Since many events, such as death, cannot be totally avoided, it is helpful to take measures to minimize their financial impact when they occur. These risks can impact both sides of the balance sheet, and require asset management, liability management, and valuation skills. Analytical skills, business knowledge and understanding of human behavior and the vagaries of information systems are required to design and manage programs that control risk (Be An Actuary 2005).

Actuaries' insurance disciplines may be classified as life; health; pensions, annuities, and asset management; social welfare programs; property; casualty; liability; general insurance; and reinsurance. Life, health, and pension actuaries deal with mortality risk, morbidity, and consumer choice regarding the ongoing utilization of drugs and medical services risk, and investment risk. Products prominent in their work include life insurance, annuities, pensions, mortgage and credit insurance, short and long term disability, and medical, dental, health savings accounts and long term care insurance. In addition to these risks, social insurance programs are greatly influenced by public opinion, politics, budget constraints, changing demographics and other factors such as medical technology, inflation and cost of living considerations (Bureau of Labor Statistics 2006).

Casualty actuaries, also known as non-life or general insurance actuaries, deal with catastrophic, unnatural risks that can occur to people or property. Products prominent in their work include auto insurance, homeowners insurance, commercial property insurance, workers' compensation, title insurance, malpractice insurance, products liability insurance, directors and officers liability insurance, environmental and marine insurance, terrorism insurance and other types of liability insurance. Reinsurance products have to accommodate all of the previously mentioned products, and in addition have to properly reflect the increasing long term risks associated with climate change, cultural litigiousness, acts of war, terrorism and politics (Bureau of Labor Statistics 2006).

In 2002, a Wall Street Journal survey on the best jobs in the United States listed actuary as the second best job, while in previous editions of the list, actuaries had been the top rated job (Lee 2002). The survey used six key criteria to rank jobs: environment, income, employment outlook, physical demands, security and stress.

History

Need for Insurance

The basic requirements of communal interests gave rise to risk sharing since the dawn of civilization. For example, people who lived their entire lives in a camp had the risk of fire, which would leave their band or family without shelter. After basic exchange came into existence, more complex forms developed beyond a basic barter economy, and new forms of risk manifested.

Merchants embarking on trade journeys bore the risk of losing goods entrusted to them, their own possessions, or even their lives. Intermediaries developed to warehouse and trade goods, and they often suffered from financial risk. The primary providers in any extended families or household always ran the risk of premature death, disability or infirmity, leaving their dependents to starve. Credit procurement was difficult if the lender worried about repayment in the event of the borrower's death or infirmity. Alternatively, people sometimes lived too long, exhausting their savings, if any, or becoming a burden on others in the extended family or society (Faculty and Institute of Actuaries 2004).

Early Attempts

In the ancient world there was no room for the sick, suffering, disabled, aged, or the poor-these were largely not part of the cultural consciousness of societies (Perkins 1995). Early methods of protection involved charity; religious organizations or neighbors would collect for the destitute and needy. By the middle of the third century, 1,500 suffering people were being supported by charitable operations in Rome (Perkins 1995). Charitable protection is still an active form of support to this very day (Tong 2006). However, receiving charity is uncertain and is often accompanied by social stigma. Elementary mutual aid agreements and pensions did arise in antiquity (Thucydides c. 431BCE). Early in the Roman empire, associations were formed to meet the expenses of burial, cremation, and monuments-precursors to burial insurance and friendly societies. A small sum was paid into a communal fund on a weekly basis, and upon the death of a member, the fund would cover the expenses of rites and burial. These societies sometimes sold shares in the building of columbaria, or burial vaults, owned by the fund-the precursor to mutual insurance companies (Johnston 1903, §475-§476). Other early examples of mutual surety and assurance pacts can be traced back to various forms of fellowship within the Saxon clans of England and their Germanic forbears, and to Celtic society (Loan 1992). However, many of these earlier forms of surety and aid would fail due to lack of understanding and knowledge (Faculty and Institute of Actuaries 2004).

DEVELOPMENT OF THEORY

The 17th century was a period of extraordinary advances in mathematics in Germany, France, and England. At the same time there was a rapidly growing desire and need to place the valuation of personal risk on a more scientific basis. Independently from each other, compound interest was studied and probability theory emerged as a well understood mathematical discipline. Another important advance came in 1662 from a London draper named John Graunt, who showed that there were predictable patterns of longevity and death in a defined group, or cohort, of people, despite the uncertainty about the future longevity or mortality of any one individual person. This study became the basis for the original life table. It was now possible to set up an insurance scheme to provide life insurance or pensions for a group of people, and to calculate with some degree of accuracy how much each person in the group should contribute to a common fund assumed to earn a fixed rate of interest. The first person to demonstrate publicly how this could be done was Edmond Halley. In addition to constructing his own life table, Halley demonstrated a method of using his life table to calculate the premium someone of a given age should pay to purchase a life-annuity (Halley 1693).

Early Actuaries

James Dodson's pioneering work on the level premium system led to the formation of the Society for Equitable Assurances on Lives and Survivorship (now commonly known as Equitable Life) in London in 1762. This was the first life insurance company to use premium rates which were calculated scientifically for long-term life policies, using Dodson's work. The company still exists, though it has run into difficulties recently. After Dodson's death in 1757, Edward Rowe Mores took over the leadership of the group that eventually became the Society for Equitable Assurances in 1762. It was he who specified that the chief official should be called an 'actuary' (Ogborn, 1956). Previously, the use of the term had been restricted to an official who recorded the decisions, or 'acts', of ecclesiastical courts, in ancient times originally the secretary of the Roman senate, responsible for compiling the Acta Senatus (Faculty and Institute of Actuaries 2004). Other companies which did not originally use such mathematical and scientific methods most often failed or were forced to adopt the methods pioneered by Equitable (Bühlmann 1997 p. 166).

Development of the Modern Profession

In the eighteenth and nineteenth centuries, computational complexity was limited to manual calculations. The actual calculations required to compute fair insurance premiums are rather complex. The actuaries of that time developed methods to construct easily-used tables, using sophisticated approximations called commutation functions, to facilitate timely, accurate, manual calculations of premiums (Slud 2006). Over time, actuarial organizations were founded to support and further both actuaries and actuarial science, and to protect the public interest by ensuring competency and ethical standards (Hickman 2004 p. 4). However, calculations remained cumbersome, and actuarial shortcuts were commonplace. Non-life actuaries followed in the footsteps of their life compatriots in the early twentieth century. The 1920 revision to workers compensation rates took over two months of around-the-clock work by day and night teams of actuaries (Michelbacher 1920 p. 224, 230). In the 1930s and 1940s, however, rigorous mathematical foundations for stochastic processes were developed (Bühlmann 1997 p. 168). Actuaries could now begin to forecast losses using models of random events instead of deterministic methods. Computers further revolutionized the actuarial profession. From pencil-and-paper to punchcards to microcomputers, the modeling and forecasting ability of the actuary has grown exponentially (MacGinnitie 1980 p.50-51).

Another modern development is the convergence of modern financial theory with actuarial science (Bühlmann 1997 p. 169-171). In the early twentieth century, actuaries were developing many techniques that can be found in modern financial theory, but for various historical reasons, these developments did not achieve much recognition (Whelan 2002). However, in the late 1980s and early 1990s, there was a distinct effort for actuaries to combine financial theory and stochastic methods into their established models (D'arcy 1989). Today, the profession, both in practice and in the educational syllabi of many actuarial organizations, combines tables, loss models, stochastic methods, and financial theory (Feldblum 2001 p. 8-9), but is still not completely aligned with modern financial economics (Bader & Gold 2003 p. 1-39).

Responsibilities

Actuaries use skills in mathematics, economics, finance, probability and statistics, and business to help businesses assess the risk of certain events occurring, and to formulate policies that minimize the cost of that risk. For this reason, actuaries are essential to the insurance and reinsurance industry, either as staff employees or as consultants, as well as to government agencies such as the Government Actuary's Department in the UK or the Social Security Administration in the US. Actuaries assemble and analyze data to estimate the probability and likely cost of the occurrence of an event such as death, sickness, injury, disability, or loss of property. Actuaries also address financial questions, including those involving the level of pension contributions required to produce a certain retirement income and the way in which a company should invest resources to maximize its return on investments in light of potential risk. Using their broad knowledge, actuaries help design and price insurance policies, pension plans, and other financial strategies in a manner which will help ensure that the plans are maintained on a sound financial basis (Bureau of Labor Statistics 2006).

Traditional Employment

On both the life and casualty sides, the classical function of actuaries is to calculate premiums and reserves for insurance policies covering various risks. Premiums are the amount of money the insurer needs to collect from the policyholder in order to cover the expected losses, expenses, and a provision for profit. Reserves are provisions for future liabilities and indicate how much money should be set aside now to reasonably provide for future payouts. If you inspect the balance sheet of an insurance company, you will find that the liability side consists mainly of reserves.

On the casualty side, this analysis often involves quantifying the probability of a loss event, called the frequency, and the size of that loss event, called the severity. Further, the amount of time that occurs before the loss event is also important, as the insurer will not have to pay anything until after the event has occurred. On the life side, the analysis often involves quantifying how much a potential sum of money or a financial liability will be worth at different points in the future. Since neither of these kinds of analysis are purely deterministic processes, stochastic models are often used to determine frequency and severity distributions and the parameters of these distributions. Forecasting interest yields and currency movements also plays a role in determining future costs, especially on the life side.

Actuaries do not always attempt to predict aggregate future events. Often, their work may relate to determining the cost of financial liabilities that have already occurred, called retrospective reinsurance, or the development or re-pricing of new products.

Actuaries also design and maintain products and systems. They are involved in financial reporting of companies' assets and liabilities. They must communicate complex concepts to clients who may not share their language or depth of knowledge. Actuaries work under a strict code of ethics that covers their communications and work products, but their clients may not adhere to those same standards when interpreting the data or using it within different kinds of businesses.

Non-traditional Employment

Many actuaries are general business managers or financial officers. They analyze prospective business prospects with their financial skills in valuing or discounting risky future cash flows, and many apply their pricing expertise from insurance to other lines of business. Some actuaries act as expert witnesses by applying their analysis in court trials to estimate the economic value of losses such as lost profits or lost wages.

There has been a recent widening of the scope of the actuarial field to include investment advice and asset management. Further, there has been a convergence from the financial fields of risk management and quantitative analysis with actuarial science. Now, actuaries also work as risk managers, quantitative analysts, or investment specialists. Even actuaries in traditional roles are now studying and using the tools and data previously in the domain of finance (Feldblum 2001 p. 8). One of the latest developments in the industry, insurance securitization, requires both the actuarial and finance skills (Krutov 2006). (Tong 2006).

Credentialing and Exams

Becoming a fully credentialed actuary requires passing a rigorous series of exams, usually taking several years. In some countries, such as France, most study takes place in a university setting. In others, such as the U.S. and the UK, most study takes place during employment.

UK and Republic of Ireland

Qualification in the United Kingdom and the Republic of Ireland consists of a combination of exams and courses provided by the professional bodies, the Institute of Actuaries based in London, England, and the Faculty of Actuaries based in Edinburgh, Scotland-separate but coinciding bodies. No geographic limitations exist for these bodies. Students and actuaries in any part of the UK or the Republic of Ireland may be a member of either or both bodies. The exams may only be taken upon having officially joined the body, unlike many other countries where exams may be taken earlier. However, a candidate may offer proof of having previously covered topics, usually while at university, in order to be exempt from taking certain subjects. The exams themselves are now split into four sections: Core Technical (CT), Core Applications (CA), Specialist Technical (ST), and Specialist Applications (SA). For students that joined the Profession after June 2004, a further requirement that the student carry out a "Work-based skills" exercise has been brought into effect. This involves the student submitting a series of essays to the Profession detailing the work that he or she has been involved in. In addition to exams, essays and courses, it is required that the candidate have at least three years' experience of actuarial work under supervision of a recognized actuary for him or her to qualify as a "Fellow of the (Institute/Faculty) of Actuaries" (FIA/FFA) (Faculty and Institute of Actuaries 2006).

Budding actuaries can also gain partial credit towards Fellowship of either the Faculty or Institute of Actuaries by following an actuarial science degree at an accredited university. In the UK these include the University of Southampton, Heriot Watt University, the Cass Business School, and the University of Kent.

UNITED STATES

In the U.S., for life and health actuaries, exams are given by the Society of Actuaries, while for property and casualty actuaries the exams are administered by the Casualty Actuarial Society. The Society of Actuaries' membership requirements include passing six examinations for Associateship, and an additional two exams, together with the completion of a professional paper, for Fellowship (SOA 2006). The Casualty Actuary Society requires the successful completion of seven examinations for Associateship and two additional exams for Fellowship. In addition to these requirements, casualty actuarial candidates must also complete professionalism education and be recommended for membership by existing members (CAS 2006). Continuing education is required after certification for all actuaries.

In order to sign statements of actuarial opinion, however, American actuaries must be members of the American Academy of Actuaries. Academy membership requirements include membership in one of the recognized actuarial societies, at least three years of full-time equivalent experience in responsible actuarial work, and either residency in the United States for at least three years or a non-resident or new resident who meets certain requirements (AAA 2006). In the pension area, American actuaries must past three examinations to become an Enrolled Actuary. Some pension-related filings to the Internal Revenue Service and the Pension Benefit Guaranty Corporation require the signature of an Enrolled Actuary. Many Enrolled Actuaries belong to the Conference of Consulting Actuaries or the American Society of Pension Professionals and Actuaries.

CANADA

The Canadian Institute of Actuaries (the CIA) recognizes 'lows of both the Society of Actuaries and the Casualty Actuary

Society, provided that they have specialized study in Canadian actuarial practice. For fellows of the SOA, this is fulfilled by taking the CIA's Practice Education Course (PEC). For fellows of the Casualty Actuarial Society, this is fulfilled by taking exam 7C (Canada) instead of exam 7US. Unlike their American counterparts, the CIA only has one class of actuary-Fellow. Further, the CIA requires three years of actuarial practice within the previous decade, and 18 months of Canadian actuarial practice within the last three years, to become a fellow (CIA 2004).

SWEDEN

Actuarial training in Sweden takes place at Stockholm University. The four year master's program covers the subjects mathematics, mathematical statistics, insurance mathematics, financial mathematics, insurance law and insurance economics. The program operates under the Division of Mathematical Statistics (Stockholm University 2006).

Denmark

In Denmark it normally takes five years of study at the University of Copenhagen to become an actuary with no professional experience requirement. There is a focus on statistics and probability theory, and a requirement for a master's thesis (Norberg 1990). By Danish law, responsibility for the practise of any life insurance business must be taken by a formally acknowledged and approved actuary. In order to be approved as a formally responsible actuary, three to five years of professional experience is required (Haastrup and Nielsen).

OTHER COUNTRIES

Many other countries pattern their requirements after the larger societies of the US or UK. In general, the websites of these organizations are often the easiest source for finding out about membership requirements.

Exam Support

As these qualifying exams are rigorous, support is usually available to people progressing through the exams. Often, employers provide paid on-the-job study time and paid attendance at seminars designed for the exams (Be An Actuary 2005). Also, many companies which employ actuaries have automatic pay raises or promotions when exams are passed. As a result, actuarial students have strong incentives for devoting adequate study time during off-work hours. A common rule of thumb for exam students is that roughly 400 hours of study time are necessary for each full exam (Sieger 1998). Thus, thousands of hours of study time should be anticipated over several years, assuming no failures (Feldblum 2001 p. 6). In practice, as the historical passing percentages remain below 50% for these exams, the "travel time" to credentialing is extended and more study time is needed. This process resembles formal schooling, so that actuaries who are sitting for exams are still called "students" or "candidates" despite holding important positions with substantial responsibilities.

6

Balance of Payments

The balance of payments (or BOP) measures the payments that flow between any individual country and all other countries. It is used to summarize all international economic transactions for that country during a specific time period, usually a year. The BOP is determined by the country's exports and imports of goods, services, and financial capital, as well as financial transfers. It reflects all payments and liabilities to foreigners (debits) and all payments and obligations received from foreigners (credits).

MAIN COMPONENTS

The Balance of Payments for a country is the sum of the Current account, the Capital account, the Financial account, and the change in Official Reserves.

Current Account

The current account is the sum of net sales from trade in goods and services, net factor income (such as interest payments from abroad), and net unilateral transfers from abroad. Positive net sales from abroad corresponds to a current account surplus; negative net sales from abroad corresponds to a current account deficit. Because exports generate positive net sales, and because the trade balance is typically the largest component of the current account, a current account surplus is usually associated with positive net exports. The Income Account or Net Factor Income, a subaccount of the Current Account, is usually presented under the headings "Income Payments", as outflows, and "Income Receipts", as inflows. If the Income Account is negative, the country is paying more than it is taking in interest, dividends, etc. For example, the United States' net income has been declining exponentially since it allowed the Dollar's price relative to other currencies be determined by the market to a point where income payments and receipts are roughly equal. The various subcategories in the Income Account are linked to specific respective subcategories in the Financial account. From here, economists and central banks determine implied rates of return on the different types of capital exchanged in the Financial Account. The United States, for example, gleans a substantially larger rate of return from foreign capital than foreigners from domestic capital.

When analyzing the current account theoretically, it is often written as a function X of the real exchange rate, p, domestic GDP, Y, and foreign GDP, Y*. Thus the current account can be written as X(p, Y, Y*). According to theory, the current account X should increase if (1) the domestic currency depreciates (p increases), (2) domestic GDP decreases, or (3) foreign GDP increases. A domestic currency depreciation makes domestic goods relatively cheaper, boosting exports relative to imports. A decrease in domestic GDP reduces domestic demand for foreign goods, lowering imports without affecting exports. An increase in foreign GDP increases foreign demand for domestic goods, increasing exports without affecting imports.

Current account =

- Trade Balance
    - o Net Exports (Exports-Imports) of Merchandise (tangible goods)
    - o Net Exports (Exports-Imports) Services (such as legal and consulting services)
- + Net Factor Income From Abroad (such as interest and dividends)
- + Net Unilateral Transfers From Abroad (such as foreign aid, grants, gifts, etc.)

Capital Account

The capital account used to entitle the section now familiarly known as the financial account. This section usually includes special debt transactions between nations and migrants' goods as they cross a country's borders.

Official Reserves

The official reserve account records the government's current stock of reserves. Reserves include official gold reserves, foreign exchange reserves, and IMF Special Drawing Rights (SDRs). Reserve accounts typically are dominated by monetary authority intervention in the official currency's exchange rate.

Countries who try to control the price of their currency will have large net changes in their Official Reserve Accounts. Some of the most extreme examples include China and Japan. Japan in particular recently had a change in its reserves approximately one half of the entire net reported Balance of Payments. In 2003 and 2004, Japan had an outflow of reserves, yen, by more than equivalently one third of one trillion US Dollars.

In general, net increases in the Official Reserve Account will indicate that a country is buying its currency to try to keep the price dear from the perspective of whatever resource is being sold to acquire the currency. Countries with net decreases in the Official Reserve Account are usually attempting to keep the price of their currency cheap relative to whatever resource they are purchasing in exchange for the currency.

Some countries are much more difficult to detect in this regard. The United Kingdom is a good example. Its net changes in the Official Reserve Account are small, but this is because the monetary authorities of the UK borrow from one source, principally the IMF and its' SDR reserve, to buy back pounds in the form of bonds and money market accounts. This interesting example can be found in Section 7.9 in the Pink Book.

Financial Account

The financial account is the net change in foreign ownership of domestic assets. If foreign ownership of domestic assets has increased more quickly than domestic ownership of foreign assets in a given year, then the domestic country has a financial account surplus. On the other hand, if domestic ownership of foreign assets has increased more quickly than foreign ownership of domestic assets, then the domestic country has a financial account deficit

The accounting entries in the financial account record the purchase and sale of domestic and foreign assets. These assets are divided into categories such as Foreign Direct Investment (FDI), Portfolio Investment (which includes trade in stocks and bonds), and Other Investment (which includes transactions in currency and bank deposits).

Financial account =

- Increase in foreign ownership of domestic assets
- Increase of domestic ownership of foreign assets

BALANCE OF PAYMENTS IDENTITY

The Balance of Payments is the sum of the Current Account and the Capital Account. The Balance of Payments Identity states that:

Current Account + Capital Account = Change in Official Reserve Account

Typically, in the United States, the change in official reserves in a given year is small relative to the Current Account and the Capital Account. Therefore it is sometimes approximated as zero. For example, if a government runs a current account deficit and has no change in official reserves, then the current account deficit must be balanced by a capital account surplus. The basic principle behind the identity is that a country can only consume more than it produces (a current account deficit) if it borrows from abroad (a capital account surplus). The United States has been carrying a negative current account balance for many years, and this debt has been primarily financed by issuing securities. This interpretation of the data, however, is disputed by Milton Friedman (Balance of Trade) claiming that cheaper, riskier, foreign capital is exchanged for "riskless", expensive, US capital and that the difference is made up with extra goods and services. Nevertheless, Friedman's interpretation is incomplete with respect to countries that interfere with the market prices of their currencies through the changes in their reserves.

A country will have a negative balance of payments (a net decrease in official reserves) if the net of the current account and the capital account is a deficit. Similarly, there will be a positive balance of payments (a net increase in official reserves) if the net of the current and the capital account results in a surplus.

History

Historically these flows simply were not carefully measured, and the flow proceeded in many commodities and currencies without restriction, clearing being a matter of judgement by individual banks and the governments that licensed them to operate. Mercantilism was a theory that took special notice of the balance in payments and sought simply to monopolize gold, in part to keep it out of the hands of potential military opponents (a large "war chest" being a prerequisite to start a war, whereupon much trade would be embargoed).

As mercantilism gave way to classical economics, these crude systems were later regulated in the 19th century by the gold standard which linked central banks by a convention to redeem "hard currency" in gold. After World War II this system was replaced by the Bretton Woods institutions (the International Monetary Fund and Bank for International Settlements) which pegged currency of participating nations to the US dollar, which was redeemable nominally in gold. In the 1970s this redemption ceased, leaving the system without a formal base. Some consider the system today to be based on oil, a universally desirable commodity due to the dependence of so much infrastructural capital on oil supply. Since OPEC prices oil in US dollars, the US dollar remains a reserve currency, but is increasingly challenged by the euro, and to a small degree the Japanese yen.

CURRENT ACCOUNT

The current account of the balance of payments is the sum of the balance of trade (exports less imports of goods and services), net factor income (such as interest and dividends) and net transfer payments (such as foreign aid). A current account surplus increases a country's net foreign assets by the corresponding amount, and a current account deficit does the reverse. Both government and private payments are included in the calculation. The balance of trade is typically the most important part of the current account. This means that changes in the patterns of trade are key drivers of the current account. However, for the few countries with substantial overseas assets or liabilities, net factor payments may be significant.

The current account, capital account, financial account and change in official reserves together sum to zero as a result of accounting definitions. This sum is known as the balance of payments. Typically, the change in official reserves is very small. Action to reduce a substantial current account deficit usually involves increasing exports or decreasing imports. This may be accomplished directly through import restrictions, quotas, or duties (though these may indirectly limit exports as well), or subsidizing exports. Influencing the exchange rate to make exports cheaper for foreign buyers will indirectly affect the balance of payments. This can be accomplished by increasing domestic inflation (e.g. by cutting interest rates), loosening monetary policy (making more money available), or adjusting government spending tc favor domestic suppliers.

Less obvious but more effective methods to reduce a current account deficit include measures that increase domestic savings (or reduced domestic borrowing), including a reduction in borrowing by the national government.

It should be noted that a current account deficit is not always a problem. The "Pitchford Thesis" states that a current account deficit does not matter if it is driven by the private sector. Some feel that this theory has held true for the Australian economy, which has had a persistent current account deficit, yet has experienced economic growth for the past 14 years (1991-2005). Others argue that Australia is accumulating a substantial foreign debt that could become problematic, especially if interest rates increase.

The Interrelationships

Absent changes in official reserves, the current account is the mirror image of the sum of the capital and financial accounts. One might then ask: Is the current account driven by the capital and financial accounts or is it vice versa? The traditional response is that the current account is the main causal factor, with capital and financial accounts simply reflecting financing of a deficit or investment of funds arising as a result of a surplus. However, more recently some observers have suggested that the opposite causal relationship may be important in some cases. In particular, it has controversially been suggested that the United States current account deficit is driven by the desire of international investors to acquire U.S. assets. However, the main viewpoint undoubtedly remains that the driving factor is the current account and that the positive financial account mainly reflects the need to finance the U.S. current account deficit.

CAPITAL ACCOUNT

The capital account is one of two primary components of the balance of payments, the other being the current account. The capital account records all transactions between a domestic and foreign resident that involves a change of ownership of an asset. It is the net result of public and private international investment flowing in and out of a country. This includes foreign direct investment, plus changes in holdings of stocks, bonds, loans, bank accounts, and currencies. By convention, resident acquiring a domestic asset (a capital inflow). A capital account debit is recorded if a transaction leads to a domestic resident acquiring a foreign asset (a capital outflow). This convention ensures that the sum of the current and capital account balances is always zero. Along with transactions pertaining to non-financial and non-produced assets, the capital account may also include debt forgiveness, the transfer of goods and financial assets by migrants leaving or entering a country,. the transfer of ownership on fixed assets, the transfer of funds received to the sale or acquisition of fixed assets, gift and inheritance taxes, death levies, patents, copyrights, royalties, and uninsured damage to fixed assets.

BALANCE OF TRADE

The balance of trade (or net exports, NX) is the difference between the monetary value of exports and imports in an economy over a certain period of time. A positive balance of trade is known as a trade surplus and consists of exporting more than your imports; a negative balance of trade is known as a trade deficit or, informally, a trade gap. The balance of trade is sometimes divided into a goods and a services balance; especially in the United Kingdom the terms visible and invisible balance are used.

Definition

The balance of trade forms part of the current account, which also includes other transactions such as income from the international investment position as well as international aid. If the current account is in surplus, the country's net international asset position increases correspondingly. Equally, a deficit decreases the net international asset position.

The trade balance is identical to the difference between a country's output and domestic demand (the difference between what goods a country produces and how many goods it buys from abroad, this does not include money respent on foreign stocks, nor does it factor the concept of importing goods to produce for the domestic market).

Measuring the balance of payments can be problematic because of problems with recording and collecting data. As an illustration of this problem, when official data for all the world's countries are added up, exports exceed imports by a few percent; it appears the world is running a positive balance of trade with itself. This cannot be true, because all transactions involve an equal credit or debit in the account of each nation. The discrepancy is widely believed to be explained by transactions intended to launder money or evade taxes, and other visibility problems. However, especially for developed countries, accuracy is likely to be good. Factors that can affect the balance of trade figures include:

- Prices of goods manufactured at home (influenced by the responsiveness of supply)
- Exchange rates
- Trade agreements or barriers
- Other tax, tariff and trade measures
- Business cycle at home or abroad.

The balance of trade is likely to differ across the business cycle. In export led growth (such as oil and early industrial goods), the balance of trade will improve during an economic expansion. However, with domestic demand led growth (as in the United States and Australia) the trade balance will worsen at the same stage in the business cycle.

Economic Impact

Since the falling from favor of mercantilism, most economists do not believe that trade deficits are inherently good or bad, but must be judged based on the circumstances in which they arose. Large imbalances may sometimes be a sign of underlying economic problems or rigidities. An example includes a situation where exchange rates have been fixed or pegged for political reasons at levels impeding a correction of a trade imbalance.

In order to maintain a negative balance of trade, it must be financed either by income or transfers, or by running down the country's net international assets. This may be done for example by selling assets, through foreign direct investment or by international borrowing. An increase in net foreign liabilities tends to lead to an increase in the net outflow of income on international investments. Such payments to foreigners have intergenerational effects: by shifting consumption over time, some generations may gain at the expense of others . However, a trade deficit may lead to higher consumption in the future if, for example, it is used to finance profitable domestic investment, which generates returns in excess of that paid on the net foreign liabilities (a situation that might arise if a country experiences an unexpected gain in productivity). Similarly, a surplus on the current account implies an increase in the net international investment position and the shifting of consumption to future rather than current generations.

However, trade imbalances are not always indicative of the smooth operation of the market given differences in international productivity and intertemporal consumption preferences. Trade deficits have often been associated with a loss of international competitiveness, or unsustainable 'booms' in domestic demand. Similarly, trade surpluses have been associated with policies that inefficiently bias a country's economic activity towards external demand, resulting in lower living standards. An example of an economy in which a positive balance of payments was regarded as a bad thing by some was Japan in the 1990s. The positive balance was partly the result of protectionist measures that also caused the price of goods in Japan to be much higher than they would have been, had imports been freely allowed. The foreign currency Japanese companies earned overseas remained largely unconverted into yen in order to suppress the yen's value, further preventing Japanese consumers from benefiting from the trade surplus. In addition, the potential benefit from the trade surpluses were partly squandered by spending it on prestige real estate purchases in the United States that often proved unprofitable.

Milton Friedman's View

Milton Friedman, the Nobel Prize-winning economist and father of Monetarism, argued that many of the fears of trade deficits are unfair criticisms in an attempt to push macroeconomic policies favorable to exporting industries. He stated that these deficits are not harmful to the country as the currency always comes back to the country of origin in some form or another (country A sells to country B, country B sells to country C who buys from country A, but the trade deficit only includes A and B). In fact, in his view, the "worst case scenario" of the currency never returning to the country of origin was actually the best possible outcome: the country actually purchased its goods by exchanging for pieces of cheaply-made paper. As Friedman put it, this would be the same result as if the exporting country burned the dollars it earned, never returning it to market circulation.

From a mainstream perspective, Friedman's argument is believed to be correct but incomplete. In particular, it is seen by many as ignoring the intergenerational consequences of deficits. If country A has a trade deficit because of large imports of consumer goods, other countries accumulate cash from country A. That money can be used to purchase existing investment assets and government bonds within country A. As a result, the return from those assets will accrue not to citizens of country

A but to foreigners. The consumption standard of future generations in country A may therefore potentially decline as a result of the deficit. In particular, Americans are increasingly paying taxes to finance the interest on federal bonds held by foreigners. However, a criticism of this argument notes that all transactions are win-win. In the case of foreign investment in American assets, it helps fuel American economic growth and keeps US interest rates low.

Friedman also believed that deficits would be corrected by free markets as floating currency rates rise or fall with time to encourage or discourage imports in favor of the exports, reversing again in favor of imports as the currency gains strength. A potential difficulty however is that currency markets in the real world are far from completely free, with government and central banks being major players, and this is unlikely to change within the foreseeable future.

Friedman and other economists have also pointed out that a large trade deficit (importation of goods) signals that the country's currency is strong and desirable. To Friedman, a trade deficit simply meant that consumers had opportunity to purchase and enjoy more goods at lower prices; conversely, a trade surplus implied that a country was exporting goods its own citizens did not get to consume or enjoy, while paying high prices for the goods they actually received.

Perhaps most significantly, Friedman contended strongly that the current structure of the balance of payments is misleading. In an interview with Charlie Rose, he stated that "on the books" the US is a net borrower of funds, using those funds to pay for goods and services. He pointed to the income receipts and payments showing that the US pays almost the same amount as it receives: thus, U.S. citizens are paying lower prices than foreigners for capital assets to exchange roughly the same amount of income. The reasons why the U.S. (and UK) appear to earn a higher rate of return on their foreign assets than they pay on their foreign liabilities are not clearly understood.

Friedman presented his analysis of the balance of trade in Free to Choose, widely considered his most significant popular work.

United States Trade Deficit

The United States has posted a trade deficit since the 1970s, and it has been rapidly increasing since 1997. The US trade deficit hit a record high of 763.6 billion dollars in 2006, up from 716.7 billion dollars in 2005.

Physical Trade Balance

Monetary trade balance is different from physical trade balance (which is expressed in amount of raw materials). Developed countries usually import a lot of primary raw materials from developing countries at low prices. Often, these materials are then converted into finished products, and a significant amount of value is added. Although for instance the EU (as well as many other developed countries) has a balanced monetary trade balance, its physical trade balance (especially with developing countries) is negative, meaning that in terms of materials a lot more is imported than exported. That means the ecological footprint of developed countries is larger than that of developing countries.

COMPARATIVE ADVANTAGE

In economics, the theory of comparative advantage (sometimes known as "Ricardo's Law") explains why it can be beneficial for two parties (countries, regions, individuals and so on) to trade without barriers if one is more efficient at producing goods or services needed by the other. What matters is not the absolute cost of production, but rather the ratio between how easily the two countries can produce different goods. The concept is highly important in modern international trade theory.

Under "absolute advantage", each state in an unregulated international economy would find a productive niche based on absolute advantage, i.e. it would benefit by specializing in those goods it produced most efficiently and by trading with other states. With comparative advantage, even if one country has no "absolute advantage" when it manufactures a product, it should specialize in and export those products with which it has a relative advantage (i.e. the least cost advantage).

Origins of the Theory

Comparative advantage was first described by Robert Torrens in 1815 in an essay on the corn trade. He concluded that it was to England's advantage to trade various goods with Poland in return for corn, even though it might be possible to produce that corn more cheaply in England than Poland.

However, the theory is usually attributed to David Ricardo who created a systematic explanation in his 1817 book The Principles of Political Economy and Taxation using an example involving England and Portugal. In Portugal it is possible to produce both wine and cloth with less work than it takes in England. However, the relative costs of producing those two goods are different in the two countries. In England it is very hard to produce wine, and only moderately difficult to produce cloth. In Portugal both are easy to produce. Therefore, while it is cheaper to produce cloth in Portugal than England, it is cheaper still for Portugal to produce excess wine, and trade that for English cloth. Conversely, England benefits from this trade because its cost for producing cloth has not changed but it can now get the cheaper Portuguese wine.

Stanislaw Ulam once challenged Nobel laureate Paul Samuelson to name one theory in all of the social sciences which is both true and nontrivial. Several years later, Samuelson responded with David Ricardo's theory of comparative advantage: "That it is logically true need not be argued before a mathematician; that it is not trivial is attested by the thousands of important and intelligent men who have never been able to grasp the doctrine for themselves or to believe it after it was explained to them."-Paul Samuelson

Critical analysis of Ricardo's Theory

Ricardo's principle relies on a variety of implicit assumptions that are debatable, such as that there is no (or a low) cost for transportation, and that the advantages of increased production outweigh externalities such as environmental contamination or social inequities.

Opponents of free trade often point out that globalized communications and transportation unavailable in Ricardo's time invalidate the assumption of capital immobility and cause capital to gravitate toward absolute advantage. It has also been argued that comparative advantage may reduce economic diversity to risky levels.

Free trade advocates would disagree, however, and say that modernization has decreased transportation and logistics costs through inventions such as the airplane or the internet which were unavailable in Ricardo's time, making his theory ever increasingly sound. Furthermore, despite the increased movement of capital, differences in capacities of production are still wide. In fact, free trade creates a wider gap of production in many areas despite the larger increases it makes in absolute wealth. In theory, as long as a country has one more worker, one more machine, or one extra source of natural resources, comparative advantage will still apply.

As to perfect competition, supporters of free trade claim that perfect competition is the result of universal free trade, not its precondition. For free trade advocates, comparative advantage is what a capitalist country must embrace to gain an advantage in an existing mercantilist world. On a final note, Gottfried Haberler showed in the 1930s that Ricardo's thinking on comparative advantage could also be expressed in neoclassical terms of opportunity cost.

Few Examples

The following worked examples explain the reasoning behind the theory. In Example 3 all assumptions are italicized for easy reference, and some are explained at the end of the example.

Example 1

Two men land alone in an isolated island. To survive they must undertake a few basic economic activities like water carrying, fishing, cooking and shelter construction and maintenance. The first man is young, strong, and educated and is faster, better, more productive at everything. He has an absolute advantage in all activities. The second man is old, weak, and uneducated. He has an absolute disadvantage in all economic activities. In some activities the difference between the two is great; in others it is small.

Is it in the interest of either of them to work in isolation? No, specialization and exchange (trade) can benefit both of them. How should they divide the work? According to comparative, not absolute advantage: the young man must spend more time on the tasks in which he is much better and the old man must concentrate on the tasks in which he is only a little worse. Such an arrangement will increase total production and/or reduce total labor. It will make both of them richer. Specialization and exchange will not be possible if there is an absolute resource constraint. If, for example, the amount of fresh water available on the island is enough for only one man, then there will be war.

Example 2

A Needs 100 P1 and 100 P2

B Needs 100 P1 and 100 P2

A: No trade

Product	Cost	Produced	Cost
P1	10	100	1000
P2	20	100	2000
Net	-	200	3000

B: No trade

Product	Cost	Produced	Cost
P1	15	100	1500
P2	25	100	2500
Net	-	200	4000

A with trade: 100P1 for 56 P2

Product	Cost	Produced	Cost
P1	10	200	2000
P2	20	44	880
Net	-	244	2880

B With trade: 56 P2 for 100 P1

Product	Cost	Produced	Cost
P1	15	0	0
P2	25	156	3900
Net	-	156	3900

So A saved 120 cost units or 4% and B saved 100 cost units or 2.5%. Clearly A gained more from the trade, but both parties experienced growth. Now if B adds some taxes to protect the producers of P1 he can try to get a larger percentage of the trade but his savings goes down as do the overall savings.

Example 3

Suppose for example we have two countries of equal size, Northland and Southland, that both produce and consume two goods, Food and Clothes. The productive capacities and efficiencies of the countries are such that if both countries devoted all their resources to Food production, output would be as follows:

- Northland: 100 tonnes
- Southland: 200 tonnes

Conversely if all of the resources of the countries were allocated to the production of Clothes, output would be:

- Northland: 100 tonnes
- Southland: 100 tonnes

We need to assume that each of the countries has constant opportunity costs of production between the two products, and that both economies have full employment at all times. Also all factors of production are perfectly mobile within the countries between clothing and food industries, but are immobile between the countries. Finally the price mechanism must be working to provide perfect competition.

So Southland has an absolute advantage over Northland in the production of Food, and both countries are equally efficient in the production of Clothes. Intuitively it would seem that there is no mutual benefit in trade between the economies. But an examination of the opportunity costs shows something different. For Northland the opportunity cost of producing one tonne of Food is one tonne of Clothes and vice versa. But for Southland the opportunity cost of one tonne of Food is 0.5 tonne of Clothes; and the opportunity cost of one tonne of Clothes is 2 tonnes of Food. Looked at this way, Southland has a comparative advantage in Food production because of its lower opportunity cost of production with respect to Northland. And Northland also has a comparative advantage over Southland in the production of Clothes, the opportunity cost of which is lower in Southland with respect to Food than in Northland.

To show that these different opportunity costs can lead to mutual benefit if the countries specialise production and trade, consider the following starting position. Both countries produce and consume only domestically. The volumes are:

Production and consumption before trade

	Food	**Clothes**
Northland	50	50
Southland	100	50
World total	150	100

We now examine the consequences of trade between the two countries. This example includes no formulation of the preferences of consumers in the two economies which would allow the determination of the international exchange rate of Clothes and Food. But given the production capabilities of each country, in order for trade to be worthwhile Northland requires a price of at least one tonne of Food in exchange for one tonne of Clothes; and Southland requires at least one tonne of Clothes for two tonnes of Food. It follows that the actual exchange price will be somewhere between the two. The remainder of the example works with an international trading price of one tonne of Food for 2/3 tonne of Clothes.

If both countries specialise completely in the goods in which they have comparative advantage, their outputs will be:

Production after trade

	Food	Clothes
Northland	0	100
Southland	200	0
World total	200	100

Note that world production of Food had increased and Clothing production has remained the same. Using the exchange rate of one tonne of Food for 2/3 tonne of Clothes, Northland and Southland are able to trade to yield the following level of consumption:

Consumption after trade

	Food	Clothes
Northland	75	50
Southland	125	50
World total	200	100

Northland has traded 50 tonnes of Clothing for 75 tonnes of Food. Both countries have benefited. In fact, both countries are now consuming at points outside their production possibility frontiers.

Assumptions in Example 3

- Two countries, two goods-the theory is no different for larger numbers of countries and goods, but the principles are clearer and the argument easier to follow in this simpler case.
- Equal size economies-again, this is a simplification to produce a clearer example.
- Full employment-if one or other of the economies has less than full employment of factors of production, then this excess capacity must usually be used up before the comparative advantage reasoning can be applied.
- Constant opportunity costs-a more realistic treatment of opportunity costs the reasoning is broadly the same,

but specialization of production can only be taken to the point at which the opportunity costs in the two countries become equal. This does not invalidate the principles of comparative advantage, but it does limit the magnitude of the benefit.

- Perfect mobility of factors of production within countries-this is necessary to allow production to be switched without cost. In real economies this cost will be incurred: capital will be tied up in plant (sewing machines are not sowing machines) and labour will need to be retrained and relocated. This is why it is sometimes argued that 'nascent industries' should be protected from fully liberalised international trade during the period in which a high cost of entry into the market (capital equipment, training) is being paid for.
- Immobility of factors of production between countries-why are there different rates of productivity? Capital includes production technology and know-how. If it can be moved between countries then the production capabilities of the countries will change. Similarly the movement of labour will change that factor cost and productivity. Perfect transnational mobility of factors of production would invalidate comparative advantage. Imperfect transnational mobility reduces the mutual benefit of trade.
- Perfect competition-this is a standard assumption that allows perfectly efficient allocation of productive resources in an idealized free market.

IMPORT SUBSTITUTION

Import substitution industrialization (also called ISI) is a trade and economic policy based on the premise that a developing country should attempt to substitute products which it imports, mostly finished goods, with locally produced substitutes. The theory is similar to that of mercantilism in that it promotes high exports and minimal imports to increase national wealth.

The policy has three major tenets: an active industrial policy to subsidize and orchestrate production of strategic substitutes, protective barriers to trade (namely, tariffs), and a monetary policy that keeps the domestic currency undervalued. Hence import substitution policies are not favored by advocates of absolute free trade.

A major (theoretical) advantage touted by proponents, which grew out of the Great Depression was this. If most of an ISI-practicing country's industries were native-food, consumer goods like clothing, automobiles, electronics, and even industrial goods-that nation would only be affected slightly, if at all, in the case of another massive worldwide economic shock like that of 1929, being insulated by its self-contained ISI policies.

Latin America

Import substitution policies were adopted by most nations in Latin America in the 1930s and 1940s because of the Great Depression of the 1930s. In the 1950s the Argentine economist and UNECLAC head Raúl Prebisch was a visible proponent of the idea. Prebisch believed that developing countries needed to create forward linkages domestically, and could only succeed by creating the industries that used the primary products already being produced by these countries. The tariffs were designed to allow domestic infant industries to prosper.

ISI did not succeed only in creating, in some countries, moderate growth, at best, often resulting in inferior, or mediocre substitutes for higher quality products that were cheaper in the world market. For example, Brasilian small arms production is a result of ISI, though these goods could very easily, and at much lower cost, have be attained from any number of other manufacturing nations. As a result, Brasil now has a native weapons industry, even exporting such to countries as Venezuela, yet these weapons are of inferior quality to, as an example, German manufactured small arms. ISI was most successful in countries with large populations or high living standards, having already a more solid economic basis upon which to function. Latin American countries such as Argentina, Brazil, Mexico, and, to a lesser extent, Chile and Uruguay had the most success with ISI (Blouet and Blouet, 2002). Smaller and poorer countries such as Ecuador, Honduras, and Dominican Republic were not very successful in implementing ISI policies.

In Latin American countries where ISI was most successful, it was accompanied by structural changes to the government. Old neocolonial governments came crashing down to be replaced by more or less democratic governments. Banks and utilities and certain foreign-owned companies were nationalized.

Many economists contend that ISI failed in Latin America, being one of many factors leading to the so-called Lost Decade of Latin American economics. Other economists contend that ISI led to the "Mexican Miracle," the period that lasted from 1940 to 1970 in which economic growth of 6 percent or more. A lack of comparative advantage in many industries led to gross inefficiencies, not to mention that their domestic markets were not large nor strong enough. Government subsidies to support domestic production led to a lack of incentive for innovation and improving efficiency.

East Asia

ISI was rejected by most nations in East Asia in the 1960s, and many economists attribute the superior performance of East Asia in the 1970s and 1980s to this difference in policies. Typically, import substitution policies resulted in inefficient industries.

In addition, the focus of import substitution in promoting industrialization typically resulted in policies which benefited industrial workers at the expense of farmers which made up most of the population of the nations involved. For example to reduce the cost of industrialization, the cost of food was often fixed at an artificially low level. In addition the licensing schemes required for an import substitution strategy led also to rent seeking behaviors which decreased economic efficiency.

In order to build up their manufacturing bases, many countries imposed high tariffs on manufactured goods, so that multinational companies would instead produce or assemble them locally. One example of this was in the motor industry, in which manufacturers exported vehicles in 'completely knocked down' (CKD) kit form, for local assembly. This often resulted in products that were of poorer quality and more expensive than those imported 'completely built up'. It also became increasingly inefficient for manufacturers to have identical products assembled locally in several countries in the same region, which only served to duplicate resources and reduce economies of scale.

South Korea

One strategy that Korea adopted to boost its competitiveness in the 1970s were export oriented and import substitution industrialization strategy. Investments were made into heavy and chemical industries, such as shipbuilding, steel and petrochemicals.

Perceived Failure

The policy began to fail in the early 1980s, as a result of overspending by the governments involved, mostly from spending foreign exchange reserves trying to keep the currency stable. As the Latin American governments failed, they began to default on their debts and were forced to turn to the International Monetary Fund for help. The failure of ISI led to the rise of the Washington Consensus.

However, some economists have pointed out that the failure of import substitution should not necessarily be taken as an endorsement of globalization. They note that most East Asian countries while rejecting import substitution also maintained high tariff barriers. The strategy followed by those countries was to focus subsidies and investment on industries which would make goods for export. The focus on export markets allowed them to create competitive industries. Although these policies later created inefficiencies and other problems, as seen during the Asian financial crisis.

By the end of the 1990's, the Washington consensus was being questioned. Nevertheless, there has not been a return to import substitution as a developmental strategy.

7

WTO, IMF and World Bank

The World Trade Organization (WTO) (OMC-French: Organisation Mondiale du Commerce, Spanish: Organización Mundial del Comercio) is an international organization that establishes rules for international trade through consensus among its member states. It also resolves disputes between the members, which are all signatories to its set of trade agreements.

The organization's headquarters are located in Geneva, Switzerland. There are 150 member states in the organization, the latest to join being Vietnam on January 11, 2007. Pascal Lamy is the current Director-General of the World Trade Organization. Since its inception in 1995, the WTO has been a major focus for protests by civil society groups in many countries.

HISTORY OF THE WTO

The Bretton Woods Conference of 1944 proposed the creation of an International Trade Organization (ITO) to establish rules and regulations for trade between countries. Members of the UN Conference on Trade and Employment in Havana agreed to the ITO charter in March 1948, but ratification was blocked by the U.S. Senate (WTO, 2004b). Some historians have argued that the failure may have resulted from fears within the American business community that the International Trade Organization could be used to regulate big business (Lisa Wilkins, 1997; Helen Milner 1993).

Only one element of the ITO survived: the General Agreement on Tariffs and Trade (GATT). Seven rounds of negotiations occurred under the GATT before the eighth round-known as the Uruguay Round-which began in 1986 and concluded in 1995 with the establishment of the WTO. The GATT principles and agreements were adopted by the WTO, which was charged with administering and extending them and approximately 30 other agreements and resolving trade disputes between member countries. Unlike the GATT, the WTO has a substantial institutional structure.

The Marrakesh Agreement, signed in Marrakech, Morocco, on April 15, 1994, established the World Trade Organization, which came into being upon its entry into force on January 1, 1995. The Marrakesh Agreement developed out of the General Agreement on Tariffs and Trade, which it includes; but it supplemented it with several other agreements, on such issues as trade in services, sanitary and plant health measures, trade-related aspects of intellectual property, and technical barriers to trade. It also established a new, more efficient and legally binding means of dispute resolution. The various agreements which make up the Marrakesh Agreement combine as an indivisible whole; no entity can be party to any one agreement without being party to them all. It was the culmination of the Uruguay Round of trade negotiations originally launched in 1986.

OBJECTIVES AND PRINCIPLES

The WTO states that its aims are to increase international trade by promoting lower trade barriers and providing a platform for the negotiation of trade and to their business. The WTO discussions should follow these fundamental principles of trading.

1. A trading system should be free of discrimination in the sense that one country cannot privilege a particular trading partner above others within the system, nor can it discriminate against foreign products and services.
2. A trading system should tend toward more freedom, that is, toward fewer trade barriers (tariffs and non-tariff barriers).
3. A trading system should be predictable, with foreign companies and governments reassured that trade

barriers will not be raised arbitrarily and that markets will remain open.

4. A trading system should tend toward greater competition.
5. A trading system should be more accommodating for less developed countries, giving them more time to adjust, greater flexibility, and more privileges.

FORMAL STRUCTURE

According to WTO rules, all WTO members may participate in all councils, committees, etc., except Appellate Body, Dispute Settlement panels, and plurilateral committees. In practice, most of the WTO's decisions are made in informal meetings, often called "Green Room" meetings, to which most members are not invited. The topmost decision-making body of the WTO is the Ministerial Conference, which has to meet at least every two years. It brings together all members of the WTO, all of which are countries or separate customs territories. The Ministerial Conference can make decisions on all matters under any of the multilateral trade agreements.

The daily work of the ministerial conference is handled by three groups: the General Council, the Dispute Settlement Body, and the Trade Policy Review Body. All three consist of the same membership-representatives of all WTO members-but each meets under different rules.

1. The General Council is the WTO's highest-level decision-making body in Geneva, meeting regularly to carry out the functions of the WTO. It has representatives (usually ambassadors or equivalent) from all member governments and has the authority to act on behalf of the ministerial conference which only meets about every two years. The council acts on behalf on the Ministerial Council on all of the WTO affairs. The current chairman is Amb. Eirik Glenne (Norway).
2. *The Dispute Settlement Body:* Made up of all member governments, usually represented by ambassadors or equivalent. The current chairperson is H.E. Mr. Muhamad Noor Yacob (Malaysia).

3. *The Trade Policy Review Body (TPRB):* The WTO General Council meets as the Trade Policy Review Body to undertake trade policy reviews of Members under the TRPM. The TPRB is thus open to all WTO Members. The current chairperson is H.E. Ms. Claudia Uribe (Colombia).

The Councils for Trade work under the General Council. There are three councils-Council for Trade in Goods, Council for Trade-Related Aspects of Intellectual Property Rights, and Council for Trade in Services-each council works in different fields. Apart from these three councils, six other bodies report to the General Council reporting on issues such as trade and development, the environment, regional trading arrangements and administrative issues.

1. *Council for Trade in Goods:* The workings of the General Agreement on Tariffs and Trade (GATT) which covers international trade in goods, are the responsibility of the Council for Trade in Goods. It is made up of representatives from all WTO member countries. The current chairperson is Amb. Yonov Frederick Agah (Nigeria).
2. *Council for Trade:* Related Aspects of Intellectual Property Rights-Information on intellectual property in the WTO, news and official records of the activities of the TRIPS Council, and details of the WTO's work with other international organizations in the field.
3. *Council for Trade in Services:* The Council for Trade in Services operates under the guidance of the General Council and is responsible for overseeing the functioning of the General Agreement on Trade in Services (GATS). It's open to all WTO members, and can create subsidiary bodies as required.

There are subsidiary bodies under each of the three councils.

1. The Goods Council-subsidiary under the Council for Trade in Goods. It has 11 committees consisting of all member countries, dealing with specific subjects such as agriculture, market access, subsidies, anti-dumping measures and so on. Committees include the following:

- Information Technology Agreement (ITA) Committee
- State Trading Enterprises
- Textiles Monitoring Body-Consists of a chairman and 10 members acting under it.
- Groups dealing with notifications-process by which governments inform the WTO about new policies and measures in their countries.

2. The Services Council-subsidiary under the Council for Trade in Services which deals with financial services, domestic regulations and other specific commitments.
3. Dispute Settlement panels and Appellate Body-subsidiary under the Dispute Settlement Body to resolve disputes and the Appellate Body to deal with appeals.

Other Committees:

- Committees on
  - o Trade and Environment
  - o Trade and Development (Subcommittee on Least-Developed Countries)
  - o Regional Trade Agreements
  - o Balance of Payments Restrictions
  - o Budget, Finance and Administration
- Working parties on
  - o Accession
- Working groups on
  - o Trade, debt and finance
  - o Trade and technology transfer

TRADE NEGOTIATIONS

While most international organizations operate on a one country, one vote or even a weighted voting basis, many WTO decisions, such as adopting agreements (and revisions to them) are officially determined by consensus of all members. The advantage of consensus decision-making is that it encourages efforts to find the most widely acceptable decision. Main disadvantages include large time requirements and many rounds of negotiation to develop a consensus decision, and the tendency for-final agreements to use ambiguous language on contentious points that makes future interpretation of treaties difficult.

In reality, WTO negotiations proceed not by consensus of all members, but by a process of informal negotiations between small groups of countries. Such negotiations are often called "Green Room" negotiations (after the colour of the WTO Director-General's Office in Geneva), or "Mini-Ministerials", when they occur in other countries. These processes have been regularly criticized by many of the WTO's developing country members which are often totally excluded from the negotiations.

Richard Steinberg (2002) argues that although the WTO's consensus governance model provides law-based initial bargaining, trading rounds close through power-based bargaining favouring Europe and the United States, and may not lead to Pareto improvement.

Doha Round

The WTO began the current round of negotiations, the Doha round, at the Fourth Ministerial Conference in Doha, Qatar in November 2001. The talks have been highly contentious and agreement has not been reached, despite continuing talks at Fifth Ministerial Conference in Cancún in 2003 and at the Sixth Ministerial Conference in Hong Kong on December 13-December 18, 2005 and Seventh Ministerial Conference in Geneva-July 2006.

Dispute Resolution

Apart from hosting negotiations on trade rules, one of the principal functions of the WTO is to act as an arbiter of disputes between member countries. Countries can bring disputes to the WTO's Dispute Settlement Body (DSB) if they believe another member has breached WTO rules. The DSB is the WTO General Council acting in a specialized role under a separate chair. It administers the Understanding on Rules and Procedures Governing Settlement of Disputes (DSU), which regulates dispute settlement under all covered WTO agreements.

Disputes are heard by a Dispute Settlement Panel, usually made up of three trade officials. The panels meet in secret and are not required to alert national parliaments that their laws have been challenged by another country.

Either side can appeal a panel's ruling. Appeals have to be based on points of law such as legal interpretation-they cannot reexamine existing evidence or examine new issues. Each appeal is heard by three members of a permanent seven-member Appellate Body set up by the Dispute Settlement Boay and broadly representing the range of WTO membership. Members of the Appelate Body have four-year terms. They have to be individuals with recognized standing in the field of law and international trade, not affiliated with any government. The appeal can uphold, modify or reverse the panel's legal findings and conclusions. Normally appeals should not last more than 60 days, with an absolute maximum of 90 days. The Dispute Settlement Body has to accept or reject the appeals report within 30 days-and rejection is only possible by consensus.

Unlike most other international organizations, the WTO has significant power to enforce its decisions through the authorization of trade sanctions against members which fail to comply with its decisions.

The WTO dispute settlement system has been quite active since the founding of the organization. Proceedings have produced a huge corpus of what is sometimes called WTO law.

If decisions of the Dispute Settlement Body are not complied with, it may authorize "retaliatory measures"-trade sanctions-in favour of the member(s) which brought the dispute. While such measures are a strong mechanism when applied by economically powerful countries like the United States or the European Union, when applied by economically weak countries against stronger ones, they can often be ignored. This has been the case, for example, with the March 2005 Appellate Body ruling in case DS 267, which declared US cotton subsidies illegal.

In order to assist developing countries overcome their limited expertise in WTO law and assist them in the management of complex trade disputes, an Advisory Centre on WTO Law was established in 2001. The aim is to level the playing field for these countries and customs territories in the WTO system by enabling them to have a full understanding of their rights and obligations under the WTO Agreement.

MEMBERSHIP

The WTO has 150 members (almost all of the 123 nations participating in the Uruguay Round signed on at its foundation, and the rest had to get membership). The 27 states of the European Union are represented also as the European Communities. Some non-sovereign autonomous entities of member states are included as separate members.

The Kingdom of Tonga was admitted on 15 December 2005 during the ministerial conference. However, Tonga has yet to finalize ratification of this admittance, and is not expected to do so until July 2007. A current list of members can be found here.

The shortest accession negotiation was that of the Kyrgyz Republic, lasting 2 years and 10 months. The longest was that of the People's Republic of China, lasting 15 years and 5 months. Russia, having first applied to join GATT in 1993, is still in negotiations for membership. Recently, it has made much bigger strides by securing a bilateral trade agreement with the US. It is expected to form trade agreements with Moldova and Georgia, the remaining two nations that Russia must make agreements with, very soon despite minor trade issues. Russia is expected to join the WTO in mid 2007.

A number of non-members have been observers (31) at the WTO and are currently negotiating their membership: Algeria, Andorra, Azerbaijan, Bahamas (process frozen in 2001), Belarus, Bhutan, Bosnia and Herzegovina, Cape Verde, Equatorial Guinea (expected to start membership negotiations until 4 April 2007), Ethiopia, Holy See (Vatican; special exception from the rules allows it to remain observer without starting negotiations), Iran 1, Iraq, Kazakhstan, Lao People's Democratic Republic, Lebanon, Libya, Montenegro, Russian Federation, Samoa, Sao Tome and Principe, Serbia, Seychelles (negotiations frozen since 1998), Sudan, Tajikistan, Ukraine, Uzbekistan,

Vanuatu (accession agreed in 2001, but not ratified by Vanuatu itself), and Yemen. Iran first applied to join the WTO in 1996, but the United States, accusing Tehran of supporting international terrorism, veto its application 22 times. The U.S. said in March it would drop its veto on a start to Iran's accession negotiations. The U.S. has chosen not to veto Iran's latest application for membership as part of a nuclear related compromise.

Syria first applied to join the WTO in October 2001, then again in January 2004 and September 2005. Its application for membership is currently still pending, waiting for WTO General Council approval to start negotiations.

The following states (15) and territories (2) so far have no official interaction with the WTO: the states of Eritrea, Somalia, Liberia, Turkmenistan, North Korea, Monaco, San Marino, East Timor, Comoros, Nauru, Tuvalu, Palau, Kiribati, Micronesia, Marshall Islands and the territories of Western Sahara, Palestine.

AGREEMENTS

The WTO oversees about 60 different agreements which have the status of international legal texts. Member countries must sign and ratify all WTO agreements on accession. A list of WTO agreements can be found here A discussion of some of the most important agreements follows.

Agreement on Agriculture (AoA)

The AoA came into effect with the establishment of the WTO at the beginning of 1995. The AoA has three central concepts, or "pillars": domestic support, market access and export subsidies.

Domestic Support

The first pillar of the AoA is "domestic support". The AoA structures domestic support (subsidies) into three categories or "boxes": a Green Box, an Amber Box and a Blue Box. The Green Box contains fixed payments to producers for environmental programmes, so long as the payments are "decoupled" from current production levels. The Amber Box contains domestic subsidies that governments have agreed to reduce but not eliminate. The Blue Box contains subsidies which can be increased without limit, so long as payments are linked to production-limiting programmes.

The AoA's domestic support system currently allows Europe and the USA to spend $380 billion annually on agricultural subsidies alone. "It is often still argued that subsidies are needed to protect small farmers but, according to the World Bank, more than half of EU support goes to 1% of producers while in the US 70% of subsidies go to 10% of producers, mainly agri-businesses.". The effect of these subsidies is to flood global markets with below-cost commodities, depressing prices and undercutting producers in poor countries-a practice known as dumping.

Market Access

"Market access" is the second pillar of the AoA, and refers to the reduction of tariff (or non-tariff) barriers to trade by WTO members. The 1995 AoA required tariff reductions of:

- 36% average reduction by developed countries, with a minimum per tariff line reduction of 15% over five years.
- 24% average reduction by developing countries with a minimum per tariff line reduction of 10% over nine years.

Least Developed Countries (LDCs) were exempted from tariff reductions, but either had to convert non-tariff barriers to tariffs-a process called tariffication-or "bind" their tariffs, creating a "ceiling" which could not be increased in future.

Export Subsidies

"Export subsidies" is the third pillar of the AoA. The 1995 AoA required developed countries to reduce export subsidies by at least 35% (by value) or by at least 21% (by volume) over the five years to 2000.

Criticism

The AoA is criticized for reducing tariff protections for small farmers-a key source of income for developing countries-while allowing rich countries to continue to pay their farmers massive subsidies which developing countries cannot afford.

The Agreement on the Application of Sanitary and Phytosanitary Measures-also known as the SPS Agreement was negotiated during the Uruguay Round of the General Agreement on Tariffs and Trade, and entered into force with the establishment of the WTO at the beginning of 1995.

Under the SPS agreement, the WTO sets constraints on members' policies relating to food safety (bacterial contaminants, pesticides, inspection and labelling) as well as animal and plant health (imported pests and diseases).

SPS and Genetically Modified Organisms (GMOs)

In 2003, the United States challenged a number of EU laws restricting the importation of Genetically Modified Organisms (GMOs), arguing they are "unjustifiable" and illegal under SPS agreement. In May 2006, the WTO's dispute resolution panel issued a complex ruling which took issue with some aspects of the EU's regulation of GMOs, but dismissed many of the claims made by the U.S.

Criticism

Quarantine policies plays an important role in ensuring the protection of human, animal and plant health. Yet under the SPS agreement, quarantine barriers can be a 'technical trade barrier' used to keep out foreign competitors. The SPS agreement gives the WTO the power to override a country's use of the precautionary principle-a principle which allows them to act on the side of caution if there is no scientific certainty about potential threats to human health and the environment. Under SPS rules, the burden of proof is on countries to demonstrate scientifically that something is dangerous before it can be regulated, even though scientists agree that it is impossible to predict all forms of damage posed by insects or pest plants.

Agreement on Technical Barriers to Trade (TBT)

The Agreement on Technical Barriers to Trade-also known as the TBT Agreement is an international treaty of the World Trade Organization. It was negotiated during the Uruguay

Round of the General Agreement on Tariffs and Trade, and entered into force with the establishment of the WTO at the end of 1994.

The object of the TBT Agreement is to "to ensure that technical negotiations and standards, as well as testing and certification procedures, do not create unnecessary obstacles to trade"

CHRONOLOGY

- 1986-1994-Uruguay Round of GATT negotiations culminating in the Marrakech Agreement that established the WTO.
- January 1, 1995-The WTO came into existence.
- May 1, 1995-Renato Ruggiero became director-general for a 4-year term.
- December 9-December 13, 1996-The inaugural ministerial conference in Singapore. Disagreements between largely developed and developing economies emerged during this conference over four issues initiated by this conference, which led to them being collectively referred to as the "Singapore issues".
- May 18-May 20, 1998-2nd ministerial conference in Geneva, Switzerland.
- September 1, 1999-Mike Moore became director-general. The post had been fiercely contested; eventually a compromise was reached with Mike Moore and Supachai Panitchpakdi taking half each of a six-year term.
- November 30-December 3, 1999-3rd ministerial conference in Seattle, Washington, USA. The conference itself ended in failure, with massive demonstrations and riots drawing worldwide attention.
- November 9-November 13, 2001-4th ministerial conference in Doha, Qatar begins the Doha round. Issuance of the Doha Declaration.
- December 11, 2001-The People's Republic of China joined the WTO after 15 years of negotiations (the longest in GATT history).

- January 1, 2002-Taiwan joined under the name "Separate Customs Territory of Taiwan, Penghu, Kinmen and Matsu".
- September 1, 2002-Supachai Panitchpakdi became director-general.
- September 10-September 14, 2003-5th ministerial conference in Cancún, Mexico aims at forging agreement on the Doha round. An alliance of 22 southern states, the G20 (led by India, People's Republic of China and Brazil), resisted demands from the North for agreements on the so-called "Singapore issues" and called for an end to agricultural subsidies within the EU and the US. The talks broke down without progress, although trade facilitation, one of the Singapore issues, re-emerged with the support from both developed and developing countries in later Doha trade round discussion.
- August 2004-Geneva talks achieve a framework agreement on the Doha round. Developed countries will lower agricultural subsidies, and in exchange the developing countries will lower tariff barriers to manufactured goods.
- May 2005-Paris talks aimed at finalizing issues for agreement before the December 2005 ministerial conference in Hong Kong are hung over technical issues. The group of five (U.S., Australia, the EU, Brazil and India) fail to agree over chicken, beef and rice. France continues to protest restrictions on subsidies to farmers. Oxfam accuses the EU of delaying tactics which threaten to scupper the Doha round.
- November 11-WTO General Council successfully adopts Saudi Arabia's terms of Accession
- December 13-December 18, 2005-6th ministerial conference in Hong Kong.
- July 24, 2006-The Doha Development Agenda negotiations were suspended, because gaps between key players remained too wide.

CRITICISM

The stated aim of the WTO is to promote free trade and stimulate economic growth. Many people argue that free trade does not make ordinary people's lives more prosperous but only results in the rich (both people and countries) becoming richer. WTO treaties have also been accused of a partial and unfair bias toward multinational corporations and wealthy nations.

Critics contend that small countries in the WTO wield little influence, and despite the WTO aim of helping the developing countries, the influential nations in the WTO focus on their own commercial interests. They also claim that the issues of health, safety and environment are steadfastly ignored.

Martin Khor argues that the WTO does not manage the global economy impartially, but in its operation has a systematic bias toward rich countries and multinational corporations, harming smaller countries which have less negotiation power. Some examples of this bias are:

- Rich countries are able to maintain high import duties and quotas in certain products, blocking imports from developing countries (e.g. clothing);
- The increase in non-tariff barriers such as anti-dumping measures allowed against developing countries;
- The maintenance of high protection of agriculture in developed countries while developing ones are pressed to open their markets;
- Many developing countries do not have the capacity to follow the negotiations and participate actively in the Uruguay Round; and
- The TRIPs agreement which limits developing countries from utilizing some technology that originates from abroad in their local systems (including medicines and agricultural products).

Jagdish Bhagwati, although pro-free trade and pro-globalization, has strongly criticized the introduction of TRIPs (forum shifting) into the WTO/GATT framework. His fear is that other non-trade agendas might overwhelm the organization's function.

Many non-governmental organizations, such as the World Federalist Movement, are calling for the creation of a WTO parliamentary assembly to allow for more democratic participation in WTO decision making. Dr Caroline Lucas recommended that such an assembly "have a more prominent role to play in the form of parliamentary scrutiny, and also in the wider efforts to reform the WTO processes, and its rules". However, Dr. Raoul Marc Jennar argues that a consultative parliamentary assembly would be ineffective for the following reasons:

- It does not resolve the problem of "informal meetings" whereby industrialized countries negotiate the most important decisions;
- It does not reduce the de facto inequality which exists between countries with regards to an effective and efficient participation to all activities within all WTO bodies;
- It does not rectify the multiple violations of the general principles of law which affect the dispute settlement mechanism.

INTERNATIONAL MONETARY FUND

The International Monetary Fund (IMF) is an international organization that oversees the global financial system by observing exchange rates and balance of payments, as well as offering financial and technical assistance when requested. Its headquarters are located in Washington, D.C. and offices around the world.

Organization and Purpose

IMF describes itself as "an organization of 185 countries, Montenegro being the 185th as of January 18th, 2007, working to foster global monetary cooperation, secure financial stability, facilitate international trade, promote high employment and sustainable economic growth, and reduce poverty". With the exception of North Korea, Cuba, Andorra, Monaco, Liechtenstein, Tuvalu and Nauru, all UN member states participate directly in the IMF. Some are represented by other member states. The Vatican City, the Republic of China (Taiwan), the Palestinian Authority and the Sahrawi Arab Democratic Republic (Western Sahara) are the other entities not participating in the IMF.

History

In the Great Depression of the 1930s, as economic activity in the major industrial countries diminished, countries began to adopt mercantilist practices, as an attempt to defend their economies by increasing restrictions on imports. To conserve diminishing reserves of gold and foreign currency, some countries restricted foreign imports, some devalued their currencies, and some began policies of complicated restrictions on foreign exchange accounts held by their citizens. These measures were arguably detrimental to the countries themselves as the theory of Ricardian comparative advantage states that all countries gain from trade without restrictions. It is noteworthy to mention that, although the "size of the pie" is enhanced according to this theory of free trade, improving all industries, when distributional concerns are taken into account, there are always industries that lose out even as others benefit in any given country. World trade declined sharply, as did employment and living standards in many countries.

As World War II came to a close, the leading allied countries considered various plans to restore order to international monetary relations, and at the Bretton Woods conference the IMF emerged. The founding members drafted a charter (or Articles of Agreement) of an international institution to oversee the international monetary system and to promote both the elimination of exchange restrictions relating to trade in goods and services, and the stability of exchange rates.

The IMF came into existence in December 1945, when the first 29 countries signed its Articles of Agreement. The statutory purposes of the IMF today are the same as when they were formulated in 1944.

Presnt Scenario

From the end of World War II until the late-1970s, the capitalist world experienced unprecedented growth in real incomes. (Since then, the People's Republic of China's integration into the capitalist system has added substantially to the growth of the system.) Within the capitalist system, the benefits of growth have not flowed equally to all (either within or among nations) but overall there has been an increase in prosperity that contrasts starkly with the conditions within capitalist countries during the interwar period.

The lack of a recurring global depression is likely due to improvements in the conduct of international economic policies that have encouraged the growth of international trade and helped smooth the economic cycle of boom and bust.

In the decades since World War II, apart from rising prosperity, the world economy and monetary system have undergone other major changes that have increased the importance and relevance of the purposes served by the IMF, but that has also required the IMF to adapt and reform. Rapid advances in technology and communications have contributed to the increasing international integration of markets and to closer linkages among national economies. As a result, financial crises, when they erupt, now tend to spread more rapidly among countries.

The IMF's influence in the global economy steadily increased as it accumulated more members. The number of IMF member countries has more than quadrupled from the 44 states involved in its establishment, reflecting in particular the attainment of political independence by many developing countries and more recently the collapse of the Soviet bloc. The expansion of the IMF's membership, together with the changes in the world economy, have required the IMF to adapt in a variety of ways to continue serving its purposes effectively.

Data Dissemination Systems

The IMF established standards to guide members in the dissemination to the public of their economic and financial data. Currently there are two such systems: General Data Dissemination System (GDDS) and its superset Special Data Dissemination System (SDDS) for those member countries having or seeking access to international capital markets.

Some countries initialy used the GDDS, but lately upgraded to SDDS. Some entities that are not IMF members also contribute statistical data to the systems:

- Palestinian Authority-GDDS
- Hong Kong-SDDS
- European Union institutions:
  - o the European Central Bank for the Eurozone-SDDS
  - o Eurostat for the whole EU.-SDDS, thus providing data from Cyprus (not using any DDSystem on its own) and Malta (using only GDDS on its own)

Membership Qualifications

Any country may apply for membership of the IMF. The application will be considered first by the IMF's Executive Board. After its consideration, the Executive Board will submit a report to the Board of Governors of the IMF with recommendations in the form of a "Membership Resolution." These recommendations cover the amount of quota in the IMF, the form of payment of the subscription, and other customary terms and conditions of membership. After the Board of Governors has adopted the "Membership Resolution," the applicant state needs to take the legal steps required under its own law to enable it to sign the IMF's Articles of Agreement and to fulfill the obligations of IMF membership.

A member's quota in the IMF determines the amount of its subscription, its voting weight, its access to IMF financing, and its allocation of SDRs. A member state cannot unilaterally increase its quota-increases must be approved of by the Executive Board. For example, in 2001, China was prevented from increasing its quota as high as it wished, ensuring it remained at the level of the smallest G7 economy (Canada). Since then, its contribution has been allowed to be increased slightly further. As of 2006, participating nations were discussing changes to the voting formula, to increase equity.

Assistance and Reforms

The primary mission of the IMF is to provide financial assistance to countries that experience serious financial difficulties. Member states with balance of payments problems may request loans and/or organizational management of their national economies. In return, the countries are usually required to launch certain reforms, which have often been derisively dubbed the "Washington Consensus" by critics. These reforms are generally required because countries with fixed exchange rate policies can engage in fiscal, monetary, and political practices which may lead to the crisis itself. For example, nations with severe budget deficits, rampant inflation, strict price controls, or significantly over-valued or under-valued currencies run the risk of facing balance of payment crises in their future. Thus, the structural adjustment programs are at least ostensibly intended to ensure that the IMF is actually helping to prevent financial crises rather than merely funding financial recklessness.

However, this approach is not without its critics, as described below. Many proponents of the IMF contend that some criticisms are the result of the fact that many people are not familiar with the operations and objectives of the IMF, and blame a lack of transparency within the IMF for this, as well as the dense nature of international finance in general. Suggestions for improving these understandings have included greater community outreach efforts, tighter accounting standards, possible regulatory oversight, and changes in the organizational structure of the IMF to include fewer economists, whom many fear are attempting to use developing countries as nothing more than lab rats. Some fear, however, that some of these reforms to the IMF itself introduce political considerations rather than economic considerations, many of which may have resulted in the financial crises in the first place. According to Ulrich Beck, the International Monetary Fund is an international risk community combating the threat of a global financial crisis.

Criticism

The role of the two Bretton Woods institutions has been controversial to some since the late Cold War period. Critics claim that IMF policy makers deliberately supported capitalistic military dictatorships friendly to American and European corporations. Critics also claim that the IMF is generally apathetic or hostile to their views of democracy, human rights, and labor rights. The controversy has helped spark the anti-globalization movement. Others claim the IMF has little power to democratize sovereign states, although that is not its stated objective, which is to advise and promote financial stability. Arguments in favor of the IMF say that economic stability is a precursor to democracy.

Two criticisms from economists have been that financial aid is always bound to so-called "Conditionalities", including Structural Adjustment Programs. Conditionalities, it is claimed, retard social stability and hence inhibit the stated goals of the IMF, while Structural Adjustment Programs lead to an increase in poverty in recipient countries.

Typically the IMF and its supporters advocate a Keynesian approach. As such, adherents of supply-side economics generally find themselves in open disagreement with the IMF. The IMF frequently advocates currency devaluation, criticized by proponents of supply-side economics as inflationary. Secondly they link higher taxes under "austerity programmes" with economic contraction.

Currency devaluation is recommended by the IMF to the governments of poor nations with struggling economies. Supply-side economists claim these Keynesian IMF policies are destructive to economic prosperity.

That said, the IMF sometimes advocates "austerity programmes," increasing taxes even when the economy is weak, in order to generate government revenue and balance budget deficits, which is the opposite of Keynesian policy. These policies were criticised by Joseph E. Stiglitz, former chief economist and Senior Vice President at the World Bank, in his book Globalization and Its Discontents. He argued that by converting to a more Monetarist approach, the fund no longer had a valid purpose, as it was designed to provide funds for countries to carry out Keynesian reflations.

Complaints are also directed toward International Monetary Fund gold reserve being undervalued. At its inception in 1945, the IMF pegged gold at 35 dollars per Troy ounce of gold. In 1973 the Nixon administration lifted the fixed asset value of gold in favour of a world market price. Hence the fixed exchange rates of currencies tied to gold were switched to a floating rate, also based on market price and exchange. This largely came about because Petrodollars outside the United States were more than could be backed by the gold at Fort Knox under the fixed exchange rate system. The fixed rate system only served to limit the amount of assistance the organization could use to help debt-ridden countries. Current IMF rules prohibit members from linking their currencies to gold.

Most altermondialists, like ATTAC, believe that IMF interventions aggravate the poverty and debt of Third World and developing countries. According to the analysis by Yves Engler, the IMF is considered to be responsible for worsening or actually creating famine in Malawi (2002), Ethiopia (2003) and Niger (2005).

Opposition to the IMF is often fragmented. For instance, advocates of supply-side economics would generally regard the policies advocated by ATTAC to be little different in form to the ideas peddled by the IMF. In other words, they would see ATTAC tax-and-spend policies and the IMF's austerity policies as being fundamentally similar.

Argentina, which had been considered by the IMF to be a model country in its compliance to policy proposals by the Bretton Woods institutions, experienced a catastrophic economic crisis in 2001, generally believed to have been caused by IMF-induced budget restrictions-which undercut the government's ability to sustain national infrastructure even in crucial areas such as health, education, and security-and privatization of strategically vital national resources. The crisis added to widespread hatred of this institution in Argentina and other South American countries, with many blaming the IMF for the region's economic problems. The current-as of early 2006-trend towards moderate left-wing governments in the region and a growing concern with the development of a regional economic policy largely independent of big business pressures has been ascribed to this crisis.

Another example of where IMF Structural Adjustment Programmes aggravated the problem was in Kenya. Before IMF got involved in the country, the Kenya central bank oversaw all currency movement in and out of the country. IMF mandated that Kenya central bank had to allow easier currency movement. However, the adjustment resulted in very little foreign investment, but allowed Kamlesh Manusuklal Damji Pattni, with the help of corrupt government officials, to siphon out billions of Kenya shillings in what came to be known as the Goldenberg scandal, leaving the country in a state worse than that which it was in before the IMF reforms were implemented.

That the IMF intervenes only in countries that experience years of dire economic conditions has certainly hurt its reputation. The financial collapses it intervenes in are products of uneven capitalist development sometimes exacerbated by government mismanagement, but mismanagement is often cited by rich nations as the source of the financial crises. These collapses tend to lead to years of economic difficulty that can be addressed in various ways, but IMF Structural Adjustment Policies consistently serve to open up or "liberalize" economies to foreign capital rather than provide for economic recovery through statist policies such as government financed projects to achieve full employment. Thus, IMF policies further the notion that economic development in underdeveloped countries is dependent on attracting foreign investment rather than through a state-managed approach centered on full employment and progressive taxation. It is also true that politicians have used the IMF as an easy target for blame when they themselves have erred, using nationalism to gain easy political points.

Overall the IMF success record is limited. While it was created to help stabilize the global economy, since 1980 over 100 countries have experienced a banking collapse that reduced GDP by four percent or more, far more than at any previous time in history. The considerable delay in IMF response to a crisis, and the fact that it tends to only respond to rather than prevent them, has led many economists to argue for reform.

Whatever the feelings people in the Western world have for the IMF, research by the Pew Research Center shows that more than 60 percent of Asians and 70 percent of Africans feel that the IMF and the World Bank have a positive effect on their country. This may largely be due to the fact that the media and textbooks in developing countries' schools describe the IMF as having a positive role in their countries, despite the increase in poverty, increase in the debt-burden, and reduction of economic growth that IMF opponents argue its policies have resulted in.

The documentary Life and Debt deals with the IMF's policies' influence on Jamaica and its economy, from a critical point of view.

The IMF has long been criticized for what has been considered an incredibly unfair advantage to the world powers in concern for the IMF funds distribution especially among third world countries.

WORLD BANK GROUP

The World Bank Group is a group of five international organizations responsible for providing finance and advice to countries for the purposes of economic development and eliminating poverty. The Bank came into formal existence on 27 December 1945 following international ratification of the Bretton Woods agreements, where the United Nations Monetary and Financial Conference that led to their establishment took place (1 July-22 July 1944). Commencing operations on 25 June 1946, it approved its first loan on 9 May 1947 ($250m to France for postwar reconstruction, in real terms the largest loan issued by the Bank to date). Its five agencies are:

- International Bank for Reconstruction and Development (IBRD)
- International Finance Corporation (IFC)
- International Development Association (IDA)
- Multilateral Investment Guarantee Agency (MIGA)
- International Centre for Settlement of Investment Disputes (ICSID)

The World Bank's activities are focused on developing countries, in fields such as human development (e.g. education, health), agriculture and rural development (e.g. irrigation, rural services), environmental protection (e.g. pollution reduction, establishing and enforcing regulations), infrastructure (e.g. roads, urban regeneration, electricity), and governance (e.g.

anti-corruption, legal institutions development). The IBRD and IDA provide loans at preferential rates to member countries, as well as grants to the poorest countries. Loans or grants for specific projects are often linked to wider policy changes in the sector or the economy. For example, a loan to improve coastal environmental management may be linked to development of new environmental institutions at national and local levels and to implementation of new regulations to limit pollution. The activities of the IFC and MIGA include investment in the private sector and providing insurance respectively.

Organizational Structure

Together with four affiliated agencies created between 1956 and 1988, the IBRD is part of the World Bank Group. The Group's headquarters are in Washington, D.C. It is an international organization owned by member governments; although it makes profits, these profits are used to support continued efforts in poverty reduction. Technically the World Bank is part of the United Nations system, but its governance structure is different: each institution in the World Bank Group is owned by its member governments, which subscribe to its basic share capital, with votes proportional to shareholding. Membership gives certain voting rights that are the same for all countries but there are also additional votes which depend on financial contributions to the organization.

As a result, the World Bank is controlled primarily by developed countries, while clients have almost exclusively been developing countries. Some critics argue that a different governance structure would take greater account of developing countries' needs. As of November 1, 2006 the United States held 16.4% of total votes, Japan 7.9%, Germany 4.5%, and the United Kingdom and France each held 4.3%. As major decisions require an 85% super-majority, the US can block any such major change.

World Bank Group Agencies

The World Bank Group consists of:

- the International Bank for Reconstruction and Development (IBRD), established in 1945, which provides debt financing on the basis of sovereign guarantees;

- the International Finance Corporation (IFC), established in 1956, which provides various forms of financing without sovereign guarantees, primarily to the private sector;
- the International Development Association (IDA), established in 1960, which provides concessional financing (interest-free loans or grants), usually with sovereign guarantees;
- the Multilateral Investment Guarantee Agency (MIGA), established in 1988, which provides insurance against certain types of risk, including political risk, primarily to the private sector; and,
- the International Centre for Settlement of Investment Disputes (ICSID), established in 1966, which works with governments to reduce investment risk.

The term "World Bank" generally refers to the IBRD and IDA, whereas the World Bank Group is used to refer to the institutions collectively.

Governments can choose which of these agencies they sign up to individually. The IBRD has 185 member governments, and the other institutions have between 140 and 176 members. The institutions of the World Bank Group are all run by a Board of Governors meeting once a year. Each member country appoints a governor, generally its Minister of Finance. On a daily basis the World Bank Group is run by a Board of 24 Executive Directors to whom the governors have delegated certain powers. Each Director represents either one country (for the largest countries), or a group of countries. Executive Directors are appointed by their respective governments or the constituencies.

The agencies of the World Bank are each governed by their Articles of Agreement that serve as the legal and institutional foundation for all of their work.

The Bank also serves as one of several Implementing Agencies for the UN Global Environment Facility (GEF).

Presidency

The World Bank Group is headed by Paul Wolfowitz, appointed on June 1, 2005. Wolfowitz, a former United States Deputy Secretary of Defense and well-known neo-conservative, was nominated by George W. Bush to replace James D. Wolfensohn. By convention, the Bank President has always been a US citizen, while the Managing Director of the IMF has been a European. Although nominated by the US Government, the World Bank President is subject to confirmation by the Board of Directors. The President serves a term of five years, which may be renewed.

List of Presidents

By tradition, the bank president is a national of and is nominated by the largest shareholder in the bank, the United States. The President is elected by the Board of Governors for a five-year, renewable term. By the same tradition, the IMF's managing director is nominated by its European governors.

- Eugene Meyer (June 1946-December 1946)
- John J. McCloy (March 1947-June 1949)
- Eugene R. Black (1949-1963)
- George D. Woods (January 1963-March 1968)
- Robert S. McNamara (April 1968-June 1981)
- Alden W. Clausen (July 1981-June 1986)
- Barber B. Conable (July 1986-August 1991)
- Lewis T. Preston (September 1991-May 1995)
- James Wolfensohn (May 1995-June 2005)
- Paul Wolfowitz (June 2005-Present)

List of Chief Economists

- Anne Krueger-1982-1986
- Stanley Fischer-1988-1990
- Lawrence Summers-1991-1993
- Joseph E. Stiglitz-1997-2000

- Nicholas Stern-2000-2003
- François Bourguignon-2003-current

Criticism

The World Bank has long been criticized by a range of non-governmental organizations and academics. In addition the Bank's internal evaluations can produce negative conclusions. It has been accused of being a US or Western tool for imposing economic policies that support Western interests. Critics argue that the free market reform policies-which the Bank advocates in many cases-in practice are often harmful to economic development if implemented badly, too quickly ("shock therapy"), in the wrong sequence, or in very weak, uncompetitive economies. In Russia, for example, shock therapy has raised poverty from 2 million to 60 million, a 3000% increase. UNICEF noted that this resulted in 500,000 'extra' deaths per year.

The World Bank has been criticized because of a perceived conflict between their stated goals, and their actual goals. Critics argue that the adverse effects created by the World Bank are apparent when observing the numerous countries on the African continent which are in essence "owned" by the World Bank. National debt is common in many African countries, especially those being "helped" by the World Bank. This is due in part to the economic ideals used to work in this extremely impoverished region. Water and sanitation are needed, yet the companies that bring that to the poorest people in the world are large westernized companies out to make profit. Because the World Bank supports these enterprises, critics cite that the organization makes the poor poorer and the rich richer. Following decolonization, many African countries were ruled by dictators. These corrupt dictators took the financial support lent by the World Bank, and began to build an enormous national debt in their countries. Despite harsh criticisms, the World Bank is one of the most highly-regarded financial institutions in the world, especially in the field of development economics and related research. In addition, World Bank standards and methods have been adopted in many areas such as transparent procedures for competitive procurement and environmental standards for project evaluation. World Bank also engages in funding the education of a few promising young people from developing countries through its graduate scholarship programs.

AIDS Controversy

In debates about the World Bank's role, the arguments are complex and often rely as much upon political judgment as economic proof. For example, in the 2005 Massey Lecture, entitled "Race Against Time", Stephen Lewis argued that the structural adjustment policies of the World Bank and the International Monetary Fund have aggravated and aided the spread of the AIDS pandemic by limiting the funding allowed to health and education sectors. However, it should also be noted that, although finances hardly help stop the spread of the AIDS pandemic, the World Bank is a major source of funding for combating AIDS in poor countries, and in the past six years it has committed about US$ 2 billion through grants, loans and credits for programs to fight HIV/AIDS).

Opposition

Although relied upon by poor countries as a contributor of development finance, the World Bank is often criticized, primarily by opponents of corporate "neo-colonial" globalization. These advocates of alter-globalization fault the bank for undermining the national sovereignty of recipient countries through various structural adjustment programs that pursue economic liberalization and de-emphasize the role of the state.

A related critique is that the Bank operates under essentially "neo-liberal" principles. In this perspective, reforms born of "neo-liberal" inspiration are not always suitable for nations experiencing conflicts (ethnic wars, border conflicts, etc.), or that are long-oppressed (dictatorship or colonialism) and do not have stable, democratic political systems.

One general critique is that the Bank is under the marked political influence of certain countries (notably, the United States) that would profit from advancing their interests. In this point of view, the World Bank would favor the installation of foreign enterprises, to the detriment of the development of the local economy and the people living in that country.

Furthermore, it is frequently suggested that the Bank intervenes in order to salvage irresponsible loans from private institutions to governments in developing countries, and thus shifts the risk from the original risk-takers to the public of the rich countries, who ultimately back the Bank. This may be referred to as a problem of moral hazard, if private lenders believe that public lenders will not allow the borrower to fail.

In her book Masters of Illusion: The World Bank and the Poverty of Nations (1996), author Catherine Caufield makes a sharp criticism of the assumptions and structure of the World Bank operation, arguing that at the end it harms southern nations rather than promoting them. In terms of assumption, Caufield first criticizes the highly homogenized and Western recipes of "development" held by the Bank. To the WB, different nations and regions are indistinguishable, and ready to receive the "uniform remedy of development". The danger of this assumption is that to attain even small portions of success, western approaches to life are adopted and traditional economic structures and values are abandoned. A second assumption is that poor countries cannot modernize without money and advice from abroad. This generates a cycle of indebtedness that with the payment of interest means currently a net transfer from the poor to the rich nations of $1.7 billion yearly.

In terms of the structure of the bank, Caufield criticizes two elements. First, the structure of repayment; the Bank is a lender of foreign currency and demands to be repaid in the same currency. The borrower countries, in order to obtain the currencies to repay the loans, must sell to the rich countries more than they buy from them. However, the rich countries want to be net exporters, not importers. This generates "the transfer problem", often the only way of repaying loans is to engage in other loans, resulting in an accumulation of debts. Second, she criticizes the high influence of the bank over national sovereignty. As a condition of the credit, the Bank offers advice on how countries should manage their finances, make their laws, provide services, and conduct themselves in the international market. The Bank has great power of persuasion, because if it decides to ostracize a borrower, other major international powers will follow the lead. On top of this, by excessive lending, the Bank has added to its own power and depleted that of its borrowers, generating a blatant inconsistency with its stated mission.

John Perkins in Confessions of an Economic Hit Man sees the World Bank as an instrument of American imperial policy, providing loans to developing countries for projects that enormously benefit a ruling elite as well as American companies and making such countries subject to American influence and pressure.

Defenders of the World Bank contend that no country is forced to borrow its money. The Bank provides both loans and grants. Even the loans are concessional since they are given to countries that have no access to international capital markets. Furthermore, the loans, both to poor and middle-income countries, are at below market-value interest rates. The World Bank argues that it can help development more through loans than grants, because money repaid on the loans can then be lent for other projects. Finally, it has made a major effort in recent years to address criticism, particularly regarding the environment and corruption, as well as to the legitimacy of its enormous influence and power.

EVALUATION AT THE WORLD BANK

Social and Environmental Concerns

Throughout the period from 1972 to 1989, the Bank did not conduct its own environmental assessments and did not require assessments for every project that was proposed. Assessments were required only for a varying, small percentage of projects, with the environmental staff, in the early 1970s, sending check-off forms to the borrowers and, in the latter part of the period, sending more detailed documentation and suggestions for analysis.

During this same period, the Bank's failure to adequately consider social environmental factors was most evident in the 1974 Indonesian Transmigration program (Transmigration V). This project was funded after the establishment of the Bank's OESA (environmental) office in 1971. According to the Bank critic Le Prestre, Transmigration V was the "largest resettlement program ever attempted... designed ultimately to transfer, over a period of twenty years, 65 million of the nation's 165 million inhabitants from the overcrowded islands of Java, Bali, Madura, and Lombok..." (175). The objectives were: relief of the economic and social problems of the inner islands, reduction of unemployment on Java, relocation of manpower to the outer islands, the "strengthening of national unity through ethnic integration, and improvement of the living standard of the poor" (ibid, 175).

Putting aside the possibly Machiavellian politics of such a project, it otherwise failed as the new settlements went out of control; local populations fought with the migrators and the tropical forest was devastated (destroying the lives of indigenous peoples). Also, "some settlements were established in inhospitable sites, and failures were common;" these concerns were noted by the Bank's environmental unit whose recommendations (to Bank management) and analyses were ignored (Le Prestre, 176). Funding continued through 1987, despite the problems noted and despite the Bank's published stipulations (1982) concerning the treatment of groups to be resettled.

More recent authors have pointed out that the World Bank learned from the mistakes of projects such as Transmigration V and greatly improved its social and environmental controls, especially during the 1990s. It has established a set of "Safeguard Policies" that set out wide ranging basic criteria that projects must meet to be acceptable. The policies are demanding, and as Mallaby observes: "Because of the combined pressures from Northern NGOs and shareholders, the Bank's project managers labor under "safeguard" rules covering ten sensitives issues...no other development lender is hamstrung in this way" (page 389). The ten policies cover: Environmental Assessment, Natural Habitats, Forests, Pest Management, Cultural Property, Involuntary Resettlement, Indigenous Peoples, Safety of Dams, Disputed Areas, and International Waterways.

The Independent Evaluation Group

The Independent Evaluation Group (IEG) (formerly known as the Operations Evaluation Department (OED)) plays an important check and balance role in the World Bank. Similar in its role to the US Government's Government Accountability Office (GAO), it is an independent unit of the World Bank that reports evaluation findings directly to the Bank's Board of Executive Directors. IEG evaluations provide an objective basis for assessing the results of the Bank's work, and ensuring accountability of World Bank management to the member countries (through the World Bank Board) in the achievement of its objectives.

Extractive Industries Review

After longstanding criticisms from civil society of the Bank's involvement in the oil, gas, and mining sectors, the World Bank in July 2001 launched an independent review called the Extractive Industries Review (EIR-not to be confused with Environmental Impact Report). The review was headed by an "Eminent Person", Dr. Emil Salim (former Environment Minister of Indonesia). Dr. Salim held consultations with a wide range of stakeholders in 2002 and 2003. The EIR recommendations were published in January 2004 in a final report entitled "Striking a Better Balance",.

The report concluded that fossil fuel and mining projects do not alleviate poverty, and recommended that World Bank involvement with these sectors be phased out by 2008 to be replaced by investment in renewable energy and clean energy. The World Bank published its Management Response to the EIR in September 2004 following extensive discussions with the Board of Directors.

The Management Response did not accept many of the EIR report's conclusions. However, the EIR served to alter the World Bank's policies on oil, gas and mining in important ways, as has been documented by the World Bank in a recent follow-up report. One area of particular controversy concerned the rights of indigenous peoples. Critics point out that the Management Response weakened a key recommendation that indigenous peoples and affected communities should have to provide 'consent' for projects to proceed-instead, there would be 'consultation'.. Following the EIR process, the World Bank issued a revised Policy on Indigenous Peoples.

Impact Evaluations

In recent years there has been an increased focus on measuring results of World Bank development assistance through impact evaluations. An impact evaluation assesses the changes in the well-being of individuals that can be attributed to a particular project, program or policy. Impact evaluations demand a substantial amount of information, time and resources. Therefore, it is important to select carefully the public actions that will be evaluated. One of the important considerations that could govern the selection of interventions (whether they be projects, programs or policies) for impact evaluation is the potential of evaluation results for learning. In general, it is best to evaluate interventions that maximize the possibility of learning from current poverty reduction efforts and provide insights for midcourse correction, as necessary.

Other Information

The World Bank provides summer internships to local DC students at its headquarters every year. This youth development program is a large investment in the city's youth and the World Bank partners with a local nonprofit, Urban Alliance Foundation, to provide this opportunity.

8

The World Economy

The world economy can be evaluated in various ways, depending on the model used, and this valuation can then be represented in various ways (for example, in 2006 US dollars). It is inseparable from the geography and ecology of Earth, and is therefore somewhat of a misnomer, since, while definitions and representations of the "world economy" vary widely, they must at a minimum exclude any consideration of resources or value based outside of the Earth.

For example, while attempts could be made to calculate the value of currently unexploited mining opportunities in unclaimed territory in Antarctica, the same opportunities on Mars would not be considered a part of the world economy-even if currently exploited in some way-and could be considered of latent value only in the same way as uncreated intellectual property, such as a previously unconceived invention. Beyond the minimum standard of concerning value in production, use, and exchange on the planet Earth, definitions, representations, models, and valuations of the world economy vary widely.

It is common to limit questions of the world economy exclusively to human economic activity, and the world economy is typically judged in monetary terms, even in cases in which there is no efficient market to help valuate certain goods or services, or in cases in which a lack of independent research or government cooperation makes establishing figures difficult. Typical examples are illegal drugs and prostitution, which by any standard are a part of the world economy, but for which there is by definition no legal market of any kind.

However, even in cases in which there is a clear and efficient market to establish a monetary value, economists do not typically use the current or official exchange rate to translate the monetary units of this market into a single unit for the world economy, since exchange rates typically do not closely reflect world-wide value, for example in cases where the volume or price of transactions is closely regulated by the government. Rather, market valuations in a local currency are typically translated to a single monetary unit using the idea of purchasing power. This is the method used below, which is used for estimating worldwide economic activity in terms of real US dollars. However, the world economy can be evaluated and expressed in many more ways. It is unclear, for example, how many of the world's 6.5 billion people have most of their economic activity reflected in these valuations.

ECONOMY-AN OVERVIEW

2005-2006

Global output (gross world product) (GWP) rose by 4.4% in 2005, led by China (9.3%), India (7.6%), and Russia (5.9%). The other 14 successor nations of the USSR and the other old Warsaw Pact nations again experienced widely divergent growth rates; the three Baltic nations continued as strong performers, in the 7% range of growth. Growth results posted by the major industrial countries varied from no gain for Italy to a strong gain by the United States (3.5%). The developing nations also varied in their growth results, with many countries facing population increases that erode gains in output. Externally, the nation-state, as a bedrock economic-political institution, is steadily losing control over international flows of people, goods, funds, and technology.

Internally, the central government often finds its control over resources slipping as separatist regional movements-typically based on ethnicity-gain momentum, e.g., in many of the successor states of the former Soviet Union, in the former Yugoslavia, in India, in Iraq, in Indonesia, and in Canada. Externally, the central government is losing decisionmaking powers to international bodies, notably the EU. In Western Europe, governments face the difficult political problem of channeling resources away from welfare programs in order to increase investment and strengthen incentives to seek employment. The addition of 80 million people each year to an already overcrowded globe is exacerbating the problems of pollution, desertification, underemployment, epidemics, and famine. Because of their own internal problems and priorities, the industrialized countries devote insufficient resources to deal effectively with the poorer areas of the world, which, at least from an economic point of view, are becoming further marginalized. The introduction of the euro as the common currency of much of Western Europe in January 1999, while paving the way for an integrated economic powerhouse, poses economic risks because of varying levels of income and cultural and political differences among the participating nations. The terrorist attacks on the US on 11 September 2001 accentuated a further growing risk to global prosperity, illustrated, for example, by the reallocation of resources away from investment to anti-terrorist programs. The opening of war in March 2003 between a US-led coalition and Iraq added new uncertainties to global economic prospects. After the coalition victory, the complex political difficulties and the high economic cost of establishing domestic order in Iraq became major global problems that continued through 2006.

STATISTICAL INDICATORS

Economy

GDP (GWP) (gross world product): (purchasing power parity exchange rates)-$59.38 trillion (2005 est.), $51.48 trillion (2004), $49 trillion (2002)

GDP (GWP) (gross world product) (IMF 179 countries): (market exchange rates)-$43.92 trillion (2005 est.), $40.12 trillion (2004), $32.37 trillion (2002)

GDP-real growth rate: 4.3% (2005 est.), 3.8% (2003), 2.7% (2001)

GDP-per capita: purchasing power parity-$9,300 (2005 est.), $8,200 (92) (2003), $7,900 (2002)

GDP-composition by sector: agriculture: 4% industry: 32% services: 64% (2004 est.)

Inflation rate (consumer prices): developed countries 1% to 4% typically; developing countries 5% to 60% typically; national inflation rates vary widely in individual cases, from declining prices in Japan to hyperinflation in several Third World countries (2003)

Derivatives outstanding notional amount: $273 trillion (end of June 2004), $84 trillion (end-June 1998)

Global debt issuance: $5.187 trillion (2004), $4.938 trillion (2003), $3.938 trillion (2002) (Thomson Financial League Tables)

Global equity issuance: $505 billion (2004), $388 billion (2003), $319 billion (2002) (Thomson Financial League Tables)

EMPLOYMENT

Unemployment rate: 30% combined unemployment and underemployment in many non-industrialized countries; developed countries typically 4%-12% unemployment

INDUSTRIES

Industries: dominated by the onrush of technology, especially in computers, robotics, telecommunications, and medicines and medical equipment; most of these advances take place in OECD nations; only a small portion of non-OECD countries have succeeded in rapidly adjusting to these technological forces; the accelerated deployment of new industrial (and agricultural) technology is complicating already grim environmental problems. Industrial production growth rate: 3% (2002 est.)

ENERGY

Yearly electricity-production: 15,850,000 GWh (2003 est.), 14,850,000 GWh (2001 est.)

Yearly electricity-consumption: 14,280,000 GWh (2003 est.), 13,930,000 GWh (2001 est.)

Oil-production: 79.65 million bbl/day (2003 est.), 75.46 million barrel/day (12,000,000 m^3/d) (2001)

Oil-consumption: 80.1 million bbl/day (2003 est.), 76.21 million barrel/day (12,120,000 m^3/d) (2001)

Oil-proved reserves: 1.025 trillion barrel (163 km^3) 37257

Natural gas-production: 2,569 km^3 (2001 est.)

Natural gas-consumption: 2,556 km^3 (2001 est.)

Natural gas-proved reserves: 161,200 km^3 (1 January 2002)

CROSS-BORDER

Yearly exports: $6.6 trillion (f.o.b., 2002 est.)

Exports-commodities: the whole range of industrial and agricultural goods and services

Exports-partners: US 17.4%, Germany 7.6%, UK 5.4%, France 5.1%, Japan 4.8%, China 4% (2002)

Yearly imports: $6.6 trillion (f.o.b., 2002 est.)

Imports-commodities: the whole range of industrial and agricultural goods and services

Imports-partners: US 11.2%, Germany 9.2%, China 7%, Japan 6.8%, France 4.7%, UK 4% (2002)

Debt-external: $2 trillion for less developed countries (2002 est.)

GIFT ECONOMY

Yearly economic aid-recipient: Official Development Assistance (ODA) $50 billion

COMMUNICATIONS

Telephones-main lines in use: 843,923,500 (2003)

1,263,367,600 (2005)

Telephones-mobile cellular: 2,168,433,600 (2005)

Internet Service Providers (ISPs): 10,350 (2000 est.)

Internet users: 1,091,730,861 (December 30, 2006 est.), 604,111,719 (2002 est.)

TRANSPORT

- Airports
    - Total: 49,973 (2004)

- Roadway
  - Total: 32,345,165 km
  - Paved: 19,403,061 km
  - Unpaved: 12,942,104 km (2002)
- Railways
  - Total: 1,122,650 km includes about 190,000 to 195,000 km of electrified routes of which 147,760 km are in Europe, 24,509 km in the Far East, 11,050 km in Africa, 4,223 km in South America, and 4,160 km in North America. And India alone has the length of 63,940 km (39,230 miles) of routes which makes it the largest rail network in the world.
  - Broad gauge: 251,153 km
  - Standard gauge: 710,754 km
  - Narrow gauge: 239,430 km
- Ports and harbors:: List of seaports

MILITARY

Military expenditures-dollar figure: aggregate real expenditure on arms worldwide in 1999 remained at approximately the 1998 level, about $750 billion (1999)

Military expenditures-percent of GDP: roughly 2% of gross world product (1999).

9

Economy of India

The economy of India is the fourth largest in the world as measured by purchasing power parity (PPP), with a gross domestic product (GDP) of US $3.666 trillion. When measured in USD exchange-rate terms, it is the twelth largest in the world, with a GDP of US $930.0 billion (2007). India is the second fastest growing major economy in the world, with a GDP growth rate of 9.2% at the end of the second quarter of 2006-2007. However, India's huge population results in a per capita income of $3400 at PPP and $714 at nominal. The World Bank classifies India as a low-income economy.

The economy is diverse and encompasses agriculture, handicrafts, textile, manufacturing, and a multitude of services. Although two-thirds of the Indian workforce still earn their livelihood directly or indirectly through agriculture, services are a growing sector and are playing an increasingly important role of India's economy. The advent of the digital age, and the large number of young and educated populace fluent in English, is gradually transforming India as an important 'back office' destination for global companies for the outsourcing of their customer services and technical support. India is a major exporter of highly-skilled workers in software and financial services, and software engineering.

India followed a socialist-inspired approach for most of its independent history, with strict government control over private sector participation, foreign trade, and foreign direct investment. However, since the early 1990s, India has gradually opened up its markets through economic reforms by reducing government controls on foreign trade and investment. The privatisation of publicly owned industries and the opening up of certain sectors to private and foreign interests has proceeded slowly amid political debate. India faces a burgeoning population and the challenge of reducing economic and social inequality. Poverty remains a serious problem, although it has declined significantly since independence, mainly due to the green revolution and economic reforms.

HISTORICAL OVERVIEW

India's economic history can be broadly divided into three eras, beginning with the pre-colonial period lasting up to the 17th century. The advent of British colonisation started the colonial period in the 17th century, which ended with the independence in 1947. The third period stretches from independence in 1947 until the present.

Pre-colonial

The citizens of the Indus Valley civilisation, a permanent and predominantly urban settlement that flourished between 2800 BC and 1800 BC, practised agriculture, domesticated animals, used uniform weights and measures, made tools and weapons, and traded with other cities. Evidence of well planned streets, a drainage system and water supply reveals their knowledge of urban planning, which included the world's first urban sanitation systems and the existence of a form of municipal government.

The 1872 census revealed that 91.3% of the population of the region constituting present-day India resided in villages, whose economies were largely isolated and self-sustaining, with agriculture the predominant occupation. This satisfied the food requirements of the village and provided raw materials for hand-based industries, such as textiles, food processing and crafts. Although many kingdoms and rulers issued coins, barter was prevalent. Villages paid a portion of their agricultural produce as revenue to the rulers, while its craftsmen received a part of the crops at harvest time for their services.

Religion, especially Hinduism, and the caste and the joint family systems, played an influential role in shaping economic activities. The caste system functioned much like medieval

European guilds, ensuring the division of labour, providing for the training of apprentices and, in some cases, allowing manufacturers to achieve narrow specialisation. For instance, in certain regions, producing each variety of cloth was the speciality of a particular sub-caste.

Superstitions about foreign travel among Hindus meant that a large part of India's foreign trade was conducted by foreigners and Muslims. Textiles such as muslin, Calicos, shawls, and agricultural products such as pepper, cinnamon, opium and indigo were exported to Europe, the Middle East and South East Asia in return for gold and silver.

Assessment of India's pre-colonial economy is mostly qualitative, owing to the lack of quantitative information. One estimate puts the revenue of Akbar's Mughal Empire in 1600 at £17.5 million, in contrast with the total revenue of Great Britain in 1800, which totalled £16 million. India, by the time of the arrival of the British, was a largely traditional agrarian economy with a dominant subsistence sector dependent on primitive technology. It existed alongside a competitively developed network of commerce, manufacturing and credit. After the fall of the Mughals and the rise of Maratha Empire, the Indian economy was plunged into a state of political instability due to internecine wars and conflicts.

Colonial

Colonial rule brought an institutional environment that guaranteed property rights among the colonizers, encouraged free trade, and created a single currency with fixed exchange rates, metric weights and measures, capital markets, a well developed system of railways and telegraphs, a civil service that aimed to be free from political interference, and a common-law, adversarial legal system. India's colonisation by the British coincided with major changes in the world economy-industrialisation, and significant growth in production and trade. However, at the end of colonial rule, India inherited an economy that was one of the poorest in the developing world, with industrial development stalled, agriculture unable to feed a rapidly growing population, one of the world's lowest life expectancies, and low rates of literacy.

An estimate by Cambridge University historian Angus Maddison reveals that India's share of the world income fell from 22.6% in 1700, comparable to Europe's share of 23.3%, to a low of 3.8% in 1952. While Indian leaders during the Independence struggle, and left-nationalist economic historians have blamed colonial rule for the dismal state of India's economy in its aftermath, a broader macroeconomic view of India during this period reveals that there were sectors of growth and decline, resulting from changes brought about by colonialism and a world that was moving towards industrialisation and economic integration.

Post-independence

Indian economic policy after independence was influenced by the colonial experience (which was seen by Indian leaders as exploitative in nature) and by those leaders' exposure to Fabian socialism. Policy tended towards protectionism, with a strong emphasis on import substitution, industrialisation, state intervention in labour and financial markets, a large public sector, business regulation, and central planning. Jawaharlal Nehru, the first prime minister, along with the statistician Prasanta Chandra Mahalanobis, carried on by Indira Gandhi formulated and oversaw economic policy. They expected favourable outcomes from this strategy, because it involved both public and private sectors and was based on direct and indirect state intervention, rather than the more extreme Soviet-style central command system. The policy of concentrating simultaneously on capital-and technology-intensive heavy industry and subsidising manual, low-skill cottage industries was criticised by economist Milton Friedman, who thought it would waste capital and labour, and retard the development of small manufacturerers.

India's low average growth rate from 1947-80 was derisively referred to as the Hindu rate of growth, because of the unfavourable comparison with growth rates in other Asian countries, especially the "East Asian Tigers". The economic reforms that caused a surge in economic growth after 1980 can be attributed to two stages of reform. The pro-business measures of 1980, initiated by Rajiv Gandhi, eased restrictions on capacity expansion for incumbents, removed price controls and reduced corporate taxes. The economic liberalisation of 1991, initiated by then Indian prime minister P. V. Narasimha Rao and his finance minister Manmohan Singh in response to a balance-of-payments crisis, did away with the Licence Raj (investment, industrial and import licensing) and ended many public monopolies, allowing automatic approval of foreign direct investment in many sectors. Since then, the overall direction of liberalisation has remained the same, irrespective of the ruling party, although no party has yet tried to take on powerful lobbies such as the trade unions and farmers, or contentious issues such as reforming labour laws and reducing agricultural subsidies.

FUTURE PROSPECTS

In 1999, Goldman Sachs has predicted that India's GDP in current prices will overtake France and Italy by 2020, Germany, UK and Russia by 2025 and Japan by 2035. By 2035 it is expected to reach as 3rd largest economy of the world behind US and China. Goldman Sachs has made these predictions based on India's expected growth rate of 5.3 to 6.1% in various periods,whereas India is registering more than 8% growth rate for the last 3 years. Economics experts and various studies conducted across the globe envisage India and China to rule the world in the 21st century. For over a century the United States has been the largest economy in the world but major developments have taken place in the world economy since then, leading to the shift of focus from the US and the rich countries of Europe to the two Asian giants-India and China.

The rich countries of Europe have seen the greatest decline in global GDP share by 4.9 percentage points, followed by the US and Japan with a decline of about 1 percentage point each. Within Asia, the rising share of China and India has more than made up the declining global share of Japan since 1990. During the seventies and the eighties, ASEAN countries and during the eighties South Korea, along with China and India, contributed to the rising share of Asia in world GDP.

According to some experts, the share of the US in world GDP is expected to fall (from 21 per cent to 18 per cent) and that of India to rise (from 6 per cent to 11 per cent in 2025), and hence the latter will emerge as the third pole in the global economy after the US and China. The basic idea is that income per capita was roughly similar prio to the industrial revolution with the regions that make up the boundaries of modern day China and India each had much larger economies than the west. Now with rapid growth in the developing world (except sub saharan africa) we are again going to have a situation of roughly similar standard of living in most of the world possibly within the next 50 years and China and India being over 3 times the size of any other country are probably gonna be the world's largest economy based on a average growth of 5% and a currency appreciation of 2% per annum vis a vis the USD.

By 2025 the Indian economy is projected to be about 60 per cent the size of the US economy. The transformation into a tri-polar economy will be complete by 2035, with the Indian economy only a little smaller than the US economy but larger than that of Western Europe. By 2035, India is likely to be a larger growth driver than the six largest countries in the EU, though its impact will be a little over half that of the US. India, which is now the fourth largest economy in terms of purchasing power parity, will overtake Japan and become third major economic power within 10 years.

GOVERNMENT INTERVENTION

State Planning and the Mixed Economy

After independence, India opted for a centrally planned economy to try to achieve an effective and equitable allocation of national resources and balanced economic development. The process of formulation and direction of the Five-Year Plans is carried out by the Planning Commission, headed by the Prime Minister of India as its chairperson.

India's mixed economy combines features of both capitalist market economy and the socialist command economy, but has shifted more towards the former over the past decade. The public sector generally covers areas which are deemed too important or not profitable enough to leave to the market, including such services as the railways and postal system. Since independence, there have been phases of nationalising such areas as banking and, more recently, of privatisation.

PUBLIC EXPENDITURE

India's public expenditure is classified as development expenditure, comprising central plan expenditure and central assistance and non-development expenditures; these categories can each be divided into capital expenditure and revenue expenditure. Central plan expenditure is allocated to development schemes outlined in the plans of the central government and public sector undertakings; central assistance refers to financial assistance and developmental loans given for plans of the state governments and union territories.

Non-development capital expenditure comprises capital defense expenditure, loans to public enterprises, states and union territories and foreign governments, while non-development revenue expenditure comprises revenue defence expenditure, administrative expenditure, subsidies, debt relief to farmers, postal deficit, pensions, social and economic services (education, health, agriculture, science and technology), grants to states and union territories and foreign governments.

India's non-development revenue expenditure has increased nearly fivefold in 2003-04 since 1990-91 and more than tenfold since 1985-1986. Interest payments are the single largest item of expenditure and accounted for more than 40% of the total non development expenditure in the 2003-04 budget. Defence expenditure increased fourfold during the same period and has been increasing due to growing tensions in the region, the expensive dispute with Pakistan over Jammu and Kashmir and an effort to modernise the military.

Administrative expenses are compounded by a large salary and pension bill, which rises periodically due to revisions in wages, dearness allowance etc. subsidies on food, fertilizers, education and petroleum and other merit and non-merit subsidies account are not only continuously rising, especially because of rising crude oil and food prices, but are also harder to rein in, because of political compulsions.

PUBLIC RECEIPTS

India has a three-tier tax structure, wherein the constitution empowers the union government to levy Income tax, tax on capital transactions (wealth tax, inheritance tax, gift tax), sales tax, service tax, customs and excise duties and the state governments to levy sales tax on intra-state sale of goods, tax on entertainment and professions, excise duties on manufacture of alcohol, stamp duties on transfer of property and collect land revenue (levy on land owned). The local governments are empowered by the state government to levy property tax, Octroi and charge users for public utilities like water supply, sewage etc. More than half of the revenues of the union and state governments come from taxes, of which half come from Indirect taxes. More than a quarter of the union government's tax revenues is shared with the state governments.

The tax reforms, initiated in 1991, have sought to rationalise the tax structure and increase compliance by taking steps in the following directions:

- Reducing the rates of individual and corporate income taxes, excises, customs and making it more progressive
- Reducing exemptions and concessions
- Simplification of laws and procedures
- Introduction of Permanent account number to track monetary transactions
- 21 of the 29 states introduced Value added tax (VAT) on April 1, 2005 to replace the complex and multiple sales tax system.

The non-tax revenues of the central government come from fiscal services, interest receipts, public sector dividends, etc., while the non-tax revenues of the States are grants from the central government, interest receipts, dividends and income from general, economic and social services.

Inter-State share in the federal tax pool is decided by the recommendations of the Finance Commission to the President.

GENERAL BUDGET

The Finance minister of India presents the annual union budget in the Parliament on the last working day of February. The budget has to be passed by the Lok Sabha before it can come into effect on April 1, the start of India's fiscal year. The

Union budget is preceded by an economic survey which outlines the broad direction of the budget and the economic performance of the country for the outgoing financial year. This economic survery involves all the various NGOs, women organizations, business people, old people associations etc.

India's union budget for 2005-06, had an estimated outlay of Rs.5,14,344 crores ($118 billion). Earnings from taxes amount to Rs. 2,73,466 crore ($63b). India's fiscal deficit amounts to 4.5% or 1,39,231 crore ($32b). The fiscal deficit is expected to be 2.8% of GDP, by March 2007.

CURRENCY SYSTEM

Rupee

The Rupee is the only legal tender accepted in India. The exchange rate as of 29 July 2006 is about 46.53 to a US dollar, 59.316 to a Euro, and 86.755 to a UK pound. This makes a crore rupees (Rs. 10,000,000) approximately equal to $214,915, □168,588, or £115,267. The Indian rupee is accepted as legal tender in the neighbouring Nepal and Bhutan, both of which peg their currency to that of the Indian rupee. The rupee is divided into 100 paise. The highest-denomination banknote is the 1,000 rupee note; the lowest-denomination coin in circulation is the 25 p coin.

Exchange Rates

Under the fixed exchange rate system, the value of the rupee was linked to the British pound sterling until 1946, and after independence, 30% of India's foreign trade was determined in pound sterling. In 1975, as per the floating exchange rate system, the value of the rupee was pegged to a basket of currencies and was tightly controlled by the Reserve Bank of India. In recent years its value has depreciated with respect to most currencies with the exception of the U.S. dollar.

Since liberalisation, the rupee is fully convertible on trade and current account. The former has enabled Indian businessmen and workers to convert their earnings abroad into rupee at market rates, while the latter has removed all restrictions on foreign exchange for current business transactions as well as travel, education, medical expenses, etc. India has committed to gradually move towards full convertibility, albeit with some restrictions on capital accounts, in order to encourage two-way flow of capital and investment.

DETERMINANTS

Demographics

India, with a population of 1.095 billion people, is the second most populous country in the world, accounting for one in six human beings of the Earth's population. Growth rate of population has decreased from a compound annual growth rate of 2.15 (1951-81) to 1.38% (2005-06), despite the decrease in the death rates owing to improvements in health care.

The large population puts further pressure on infrastructure and social services. A positive factor has been the large working-age population, which forms 45.33% of the population and is expected to increase substantially, because of the decreasing dependency ratio. Increased rates of literacy, better health care and self-sufficiency in food production in recent times have ensured that a large population has not caused any serious problems. The national labour market has been tightly regulated by successive governments ever since the Workmen's Compensation Act was passed in 1923.

GEOGRAPHY AND NATURAL RESOURCES

India's geography ranges from mountain ranges to deserts, plains, hills and plateaus, while its climate varies from tropical in the south to a more temperate climate in the north. India's total cultivable area is 1,269,219 km^2 (56.78% of total land area), which is decreasing due to constant pressure from an ever growing population and increased urbanisation.

India has a total water surface area of 314,400 km^2 and receives an average annual rainfall of 1,100 mm. Irrigation accounts for 92% of the water utilisation, and comprised 380 km^2 in 1974, and is expected to rise to 1,050 km^2 by 2025, with the balance accounted for by industrial and domestic consumers. India's inland water resources comprising rivers, canals, ponds and lakes and marine resources comprising the east and west coasts of the Indian ocean and other gulfs and bays provide employment to nearly 6 million people in the fisheries sector. India is the sixth largest producer of fish in the world and second largest in inland fish production. India's major mineral resources include Coal (fourth-largest reserves in the world), Iron ore, Manganese, Mica, Bauxite, Titanium ore, Chromite, Natural gas, Diamonds, Petroleum, Limestone and Thorium (world's largest along Kerala's shores). India's oil reserves, found in Bombay High off the coast of Maharashtra, Gujarat, and in eastern Assam meet 25% of the country's demand.

PHYSICAL INFRASTRUCTURE

Since independence, India has allocated nearly half of the total outlay of the five-year plans for infrastructural development. Much of the total outlay was spent on large projects in the area of irrigation, energy, transport, communications and social overheads. Development of infrastructure was completely in the hands of the public sector and was plagued by corruption, bureaucratic inefficiencies, urban-bias and an inability to scale investment.

India's low spending on power, construction, transportation, telecommunications and real estate, at $31 billion or 6% of GDP, compared to China's spending of $260 billion or 20% of its GDP in 2002 has prevented India from sustaining a growth rate of around 8%. This has prompted the government to partially open up infrastructure to the private sector allowing foreign investment which has helped in a sustained growth rate of above 8% for the past six quarters. India holds second position in the world in roadways' construction, more than twice that of China.

As of 15 January 2007, there were 2.10 million broadband lines in India. Low tele-density is the major hurdle for slow pickup in broadband services. Over 76% of the broadband lines were via DSL and the rest via cable modems.

POLITICS

India, a federal republic, has had stable democratic governments since independence. Politics is dominated by the centre-left Indian National Congress (INC), the right-wing Bharatiya Janata Party (BJP), the left-wing Communist Party of India (CPI) and CPI (Marxist) and various regional parties, which are either centre-right or centre-left. Despite the varied political spectrums they occupy, the necessity of forming coalitions for government formation, the growing middle class that generally favours liberalisation and tightening fiscal deficits, especially at the state levels, has meant that all political parties adopt a moderate view towards economic reforms.

FINANCIAL INSTITUTIONS

At the time of Independence, India inherited several institutions like the civil services, central bank, railways, etc., from her British rulers. Mumbai serves as the nation's commercial capital, with the Reserve Bank of India (RBI), Bombay Stock Exchange (BSE) and the National Stock Exchange (NSE) located here. The headquarters of many financial institutions are also located within the city.

The RBI, the country's central bank was established on 1 April 1935. It serves as the nation's monetary authority, regulator and supervisor of the financial system, manager of exchange control and as an issuer of currency. The RBI is governed by a central board, headed by a governor who is appointed by the Central government of India.

The BSE Sensex or the BSE Sensitive Index is a value-weighted index composed of 30 companies with April 1979 as the base year (100). These companies have the largest and most actively traded stocks and are representative of various sectors, on the Exchange. They account for around one-fifth of the market capitalisation of the BSE. The Sensex is generally regarded as the most popular and precise barometer of the Indian stock markets. Incorporated in 1992, the National Stock Exchange is one of the largest and most advanced stock markets in India. The NSE is the world's third largest stock exchange in terms of transactions. There are a total of 23 stock exchanges in India, but the BSE and NSE comprise 83% of the volumes. The Securities and Exchange Board of India (SEBI), established in 1992, regulates the stock markets and other securities markets of the country.

EARNING SECTORS

Agriculture

Given below is a chart of trend of output of cereals and major foodgrains as published by the Department of Food and Public Distribution with figures in tonnes.

Year	Cereals	Rice	Wheat	Coarsegrains	Pulses
2001-02	199,480,000	93,340,000	72,770,000	33,370,000	13,370,000
2004-05	192,730,000	87,800,000	73,030,000	31,880,000	13,670,000

India ranks second worldwide in farm output. Agriculture and allied sectors like forestry, logging and fishing accounted for 18.6% of the GDP in 2005, employed 60% of the total workforce and despite a steady decline of its share in the GDP, is still the largest economic sector and plays a significant role in the overall socio-economic development of India. Yields per unit area of all crops have grown since 1950, due to the special emphasis placed on agriculture in the five-year plans and steady improvements in irrigation, technology, application of modern agricultural practices and provision of agricultural credit and subsidies since the green revolution. However, international comparisons reveal that the average yield in India is generally 30% to 50% of the highest average yield in the world. The low productivity in India is a result of the following factors:

- Illiteracy, general socio-economic backwardness, slow progress in implementing land reforms and inadequate or inefficient finance and marketing services for farm produce.
- The average size of land holdings is very small (less than 20,000 m^2) and are subject to fragmentation, due to land ceiling acts and in some cases, family disputes. Such small holdings are often over-manned, resulting in disguised unemployment and low productivity of labour.
- Adoption of modern agricultural practices and use of technology is inadequate, hampered by ignorance of such practices, high costs and impracticality in the case of small land holdings.

- Irrigation facilities are inadequate, as revealed by the fact that only 53.6% of the land was irrigated in 2000-01, which result in farmers still being dependent on rainfall, specifically the Monsoon season. A good monsoon results in a robust growth for the economy as a whole, while a poor monsoon leads to a sluggish growth. Farm credit is regulated by NABARD, which is the statutory apex agent for rural development in the subcontinent.

Industry

India ranks fourteenth worldwide in factory output. Concerted efforts at industrialisation by the government, aiming at self-sufficiency in production and protection from foreign competition, for nearly four decades since independence, have encouraged a diverse (though small) industrial base.

They together account for 27.6% of the GDP and employ 17% of the total workforce. Economic reforms brought foreign competition, led to privatisation of certain public sector industries, opened up sectors hitherto reserved for the public sector and led to an expansion in the production of fast-moving consumer goods.

Post-liberalisation, the Indian private sector, which was usually run by oligopolies of old family firms and required political connections to prosper was faced with foreign competition, including the threat of cheaper Chinese imports. It has since handled the change by squeezing costs, revamping management, focusing on designing new products and relying on low labour costs and technology.

Six Indian companies have been listed in the Fortune Global 500 list for the year 2006. They are:

- Rank 153-Indian Oil Corporation Ltd.
- Rank 342-Reliance Industries Ltd.
- Rank 368-Bharat Petroleum Corporation Ltd.
- Rank 378-Hindustan Petroleum Corporation Ltd.
- Rank 402-Oil and Natural Gas Corporation Ltd.
- Rank 498-State Bank Of India Ltd.

Services

India ranks fifteenth worldwide in services' output. Still, this sector, providing employment to 23% of the work force, is the fastest growing sector, with a growth rate of 7.5% in 1991-2000 up from 4.5% in 1951-80. It has the largest share in the GDP, accounting for 53.8% in 2005 up from 15% in 1950. Business services (information technology, information technology enabled services, business process outsourcing) services are among the fastest growing sectors contributing to one third of the total output of services in 2000. The growth in the IT sector is attributed to increased specialisation, availability of a large pool of low cost, but highly skilled, educated and fluent English-speaking workers on the supply side and on the demand side, increased demand from foreign consumers interested in India's service exports or those looking to outsource their operations. India's IT industry, despite contributing significantly to its balance of payments, accounted for only about 1% of the total GDP or 1/50th of the total services. Excellent infrastructure in the service sector and the lowest communication cost has helped India to be a dominant player in these sectors.

Banking and Finance

The Indian money market is classified into: the organised sector (comprising private, public and foreign owned commercial banks and cooperative banks, together known as scheduled banks); and the unorganised sector (comprising individual or family owned indigenous bankers or money lenders and non-banking financial companies (NBFCs)). The unorganised sector and microcredit are still preferred over traditional banks in rural and sub-urban areas, especially for non-productive purposes, like ceremonies and short duration loans.

Prime Minister Indira Gandhi nationalised 15 banks in 1969, followed by six others in 1980, and made it mandatory for banks to provide 40% (since reduced to 10%) of their net credit to priority sectors like agriculture, small-scale industry, retail trade, small businesses, etc. to ensure that the banks fulfill their social and developmental goals. Since then, the number of bank branches has increased from 10,120 in 1969 to 98,910 in 2003 and the population covered by a branch decreased from 63,800 to 15,000 during the same period. The total deposits increased 32.6 times between 1971 to 1991 compared to 7 times between 1951 to 1971. Despite an increase of rural branches, from 1,860 or 22% of the total number of branches in 1969 to 32,270 or 48%, only 32,270 out of 5 lakh (500,000) villages are covered by a scheduled bank.

Since liberalisation, the government has approved significant banking reforms. While some of these relate to nationalised banks (like encouraging mergers, reducing government interference and increasing profitability and competitiveness), other reforms have opened up the banking and insurance sectors to private and foreign players.

SOCIO-ECONOMIC CHARACTERISTICS

Poverty

The recent economic developments have primarily helped upper-and middle-class Indians. While poverty in India has reduced significantly, 17.59% (over 300 million) of Indians still live below the national poverty line, although the UN Human Development Report 2006 indicates that nearly 80 percent of the populace live below $2 per day. Since the early 1950s, successive governments have implemented various schemes, under planning, to alleviate poverty, that have met with partial success.

All these programmes have relied upon the strategies of the Food for work programme and National Rural Employment Programme of the 1980s, which attempted to use the unemployed to generate productive assets and build rural infrastructure. In August 2005, the Indian parliament passed the Rural Employment Guarantee Bill, the largest programme of this type in terms of cost and coverage, which promises 100 days of minimum wage employment to every rural household in 200 of India's 600 districts. The question of whether economic reforms have reduced poverty or not has fuelled debates without generating any clear cut answers and has also put political pressure on further economic reforms, especially those involving the downsizing of labour and cutting agricultural subsidies.

Corruption

Corruption has been one of the pervasive problems affecting India. It takes the form of bribes, evasion of tax and exchange controls, embezzlement, etc. The economic reforms of 1991 reduced the red tape, bureaucracy and the Licence Raj that had strangled private enterprise and was blamed for the corruption and inefficiencies. Yet, a 2005 study by Transparency International (TI) India found that more than half of those surveyed had firsthand experience of paying bribe or peddling influence to get a job done in a public office.

The chief economic consequences of corruption are the loss to the exchequer, an unhealthy climate for investment and an increase in the cost of government-subsidised services. The TI India study estimates the monetary value of petty corruption in 11 basic services provided by the government, like education, healthcare, judiciary, police, etc., to be around Rs.21,068 crores. India still ranks in the bottom quartile of developing nations in terms of the ease of doing business, and compared to China, the average time taken to secure the clearances for a startup or to invoke bankruptcy is much greater.

The Right to Information Act (2005) and equivalent acts in the states, that require government officials to furnish information requested by citizens or face punitive action, computerisation of services and various central and state government acts that established vigilance commissions have considerably reduced corruption or at least have opened up avenues to redress grievances. The latest report by Transparency International puts India at 70th place and states that significant improvements was made by India in reducing corruption.

OCCUPATIONS AND UNEMPLOYMENT

Agricultural and allied sectors accounted for about 57% of the total workforce in 1999-2000, down from 60% in 1993-94. While agriculture has faced stagnation in growth, services have seen a steady growth. Of the total workforce, 8% is in the organised sector, two-thirds of which are in the public sector. The NSSO survey estimated that in 1999-2000, 106 million, nearly 10% of the population were unemployed and the overall unemployment rate was 7.32%, with rural areas doing marginally better (7.21%) than urban areas (7.65%).

Unemployment in India is characterised by chronic underemployment or disguised unemployment. Government schemes that target eradication of both poverty and unemployment, (Which in recent decades has sent millions of poor and unskilled people into urban areas in search of livelihoods.) attempt to solve the problem, by providing financial assistance for setting up businesses, skill honing, setting up public sector enterprises, reservations in governments, etc. The decreased role of the public sector after liberalisation has further underlined the need for focusing on better education and has also put political pressure on further reforms.

REGIONAL IMBALANCE

One of the critical problems facing India's economy is the sharp and growing regional variations among India's different states and territories in terms of per capita income, poverty, availability of infrastructure and socio-economic development.

The five-year plans have attempted to reduce regional disparities by encouraging industrial development in the interior regions, but industries still tend to concentrate around urban areas and port cities After liberalization, the more advanced states are better placed to benefit from them, with infrastructure like well developed ports, urbanisation and an educated and skilled workforce which attract manufacturing and service sectors. The union and state governments of backward regions are trying to reduce the disparities by offering tax holidays, cheap land, etc., and focusing more on sectors like tourism, which although being geographically and historically determined, can become a source of growth and is faster to develop than other sectors.

EXTERNAL TRADE AND INVESTMENT

Global Trade Relations

Until the liberalisation of 1991, India was largely and intentionally isolated from the world markets, to protect its fledging economy and to achieve self-reliance. Foreign trade was subject to import tariffs, export taxes and quantitative restrictions, while foreign direct investment was restricted by upper-limit equity participation, restrictions on technology transfer, export obligations and government approvals; these approvals were needed for nearly 60% of new FDI in the industrial sector. The restrictions ensured that FDI averaged only around $200M annually between 1985 and 1991; a large percentage of the capital flows consisted of foreign aid, commercial borrowing and deposits of non-resident Indians.

India's exports were stagnant for the first 15 years after independence, due to the predominance of tea, jute and cotton manufactures, demand for which was generally inelastic. Imports in the same period consisted predominantly of machinery, equipment and raw materials, due to nascent industrialisation. Since liberalisation, the value of India's international trade has become more broad-based and has risen to Rs. 63,080,109 crores in 2003-04 from Rs.1,250 crores in 1950-51. India's major trading partners are China, the US, the UAE, the UK, Japan and the EU. The exports during August 2006 were $10.3 billion up by 41.14% and import were $13.87 billion with an increase of 32.16% over the previous year.

India is a founding-member of General Agreement on Tariffs and Trade (GATT) since 1947 and its successor, the World Trade Organization. While participating actively in its general council meetings, India has been crucial in voicing the concerns of the developing world. For instance, India has continued its opposition to the inclusion of such matters as labour and environment issues and other non-tariff barriers into the WTO policies.

Balance of Payments

Since independence, India's balance of payments on its current account has been negative. Since liberalisation in the 1990s (precipitated by a balance of payment crisis), India's exports have been consistently rising, covering 80.3% of its imports in 2002-03, up from 66.2% in 1990-91. Although India is still a net importer, since 1996-97, its overall balance of payments (i.e., including the capital account balance), has been positive, largely on account of increased foreign direct investment and deposits from non-resident Indians; until this time, the overall balance was only occasionally positive on account of external assistance and commercial borrowings. As a result, India's foreign currency reserves stood at $141bn in 2005-06.

India's reliance on external assistance and commercial borrowings has decreased since 1991-92, and since 2002-03, it has gradually been repaying these debts. Declining interest rates and reduced borrowings decreased India's debt service ratio to 14.1% in 2001-02, from 35.3% in 1990-91.

Foreign Direct Investment in India

As the fourth-largest economy in the world, India is undoubtedly one of the most preferred destinations for foreign direct investments (FDI); India has strength in information technology and other significant areas such as auto components, chemicals, apparels, pharmaceuticals and jewellery. India has always held promise for global investors, but its rigid FDI policies were a significant hindrance in this regard. However, as a result of a series of ambitious and positive economic reforms aimed at deregulating the economy and stimulating foreign investment, India has positioned itself as one of the front-runners of the rapidly growing Asia Pacific Region. India has a large pool of skilled managerial and technical expertise. The size of the middle-class population at 300 million exceeds the population of both the US and the EU, and represents a powerful consumer market.

India's recently liberalised FDI policy (2005) allows up to a 100% FDI stake in ventures. Industrial policy reforms have substantially reduced industrial licensing requirements, removed restrictions on expansion and facilitated easy access to foreign technology and foreign direct investment FDI. The upward moving growth curve of the real-estate sector owes some credit to a booming economy and liberalized FDI regime. In March 2005, the government amended the rules to allow 100 per cent FDI in the construction business. This automatic route has been permitted in townships, housing, built-up infrastructure and construction development projects including housing, commercial premises, hotels, resorts, hospitals, educational institutions, recreational facilities, and city-and regional-level infrastructure.

NATIONAL STOCK EXCHANGE OF INDIA

The National Stock Exchange of India (NSE), is one of the largest and most advanced stock markets in the World. The NSE is the world's third largest stock exchange in terms of transactions. It is located in Mumbai, the financial capital of India. The NSE VSAT terminals, 2799 in total (31st December 2005), cover 320 cities in India

Origins

The National Stock Exchange of India was promoted by leading Financial institutions at the behest of the Government of India, and was incorporated in November 1992 as a tax-paying company. In April 1993, it was recognized as a stock exchange under the Securities Contracts (Regulation) Act, 1956. NSE commenced operations in the Wholesale Debt Market (WDM) segment in June 1994. The Capital Market (Equities) segment of the NSE commenced operations in November 1994, while operations in the Derivatives

Innovations

NSE has remained in the forefront of modernization of India's capital and financial markets, and its pioneering efforts include:

- Being the first national, anonymous, electronic limit order book (LOB) exchange to trade securities in India. Since the success of the NSE, existent market and new market structures have followed the "NSE" model.
- Setting up the first clearing corporation "National Securities Clearing Corporation Ltd." in India. NSCCL was a landmark in providing novation on all spot equity market (and later, derivatives market) trades in India.
- Co-promoting and setting up of National Securities Depository Limited, first depository in India.
- Setting up of S&P CNX Nifty.

- NSE pioneered commencement of Internet Trading in February 2000, which led to the wide popularization of the NSE in the broker community.
- Being the first exchange that, in 1996, proposed exchange traded derivatives, particularly on an equity index, in India. After four years of policy and regulatory debate and formulation, the NSE was permitted to start trading equity derivatives three days after the BSE.
- Being the first exchange to trade ETFs (exchange traded funds) in India.

Markets

Currently, NSE has the following major segments of the capital market:

- Equity
- Futures and Options
- Retail Debt Market
- Wholesale Debt Market

Indices

NSE also set up as index services firm known as India Index Services & Products Limited (IISL) and has launched several stock indices, including:

- S&P CNX Nifty
- CNX Nifty Junior
- CNX 100 (= S&P CNX Nifty + CNX Nifty Junior)
- S&P CNX 500 (= CNX 100 + 400 major players across 72 industries)
- CNX Midcap (introduced on 18 July 2005 replacing CNX Midcap 200)

Certifications

NSE also conducts online examination and awards certification, under its programmes of NSE's Certification in Finanacial Markets (NCFM). Currently, certifications are available in 9 modules, covering different sectors of financial and capital markets. Branches of the NSE are located throughout India.

RESERVE BANK OF INDIA

The Reserve Bank of India (RBI) is the central bank of India, and was established on April 1, 1935 in accordance with the provisions of the Reserve Bank of India Act, 1934. Since its inception, it has been headquartered in Mumbai. Though originally privately owned, RBI has been fully owned by the Government of India since nationalization in 1949. RBI is governed by a central board (headed by a Governor) appointed by the Central Government. The current governor of RBI is Dr.Y.Venugopal Reddy (who succeeded Dr. Bimal Jalan on September 6, 2003). RBI has 22 regional offices across India. The Reserve Bank of India was set up on the recommendations of the Hilton Young Commission. The commission submitted its report in the year 1926, though the bank was not set up for nine years.

Board of Directors

On June 27,2006, the Union Government of India reconstituted the Central Board of Directors of the Reserve Bank of India (RBI) with 13 members, including Azim Premji and Kumar Mangalam Birla. The other members of the board are:

- Suresh Tendulkar, Economist and Member, Prime Minister's Economic Advisory Council (to represent Eastern Area Local Board)
- U. R. Rao, former Chairman, ISRO and Chairman Research Council, Physical Research Laboratory, Department of Space (to represent Northern Area Local Board)
- Lakshmi Chand, IAS (Retd.) (to represent Southern Area Local Board)
- Shashi Rekha Rajagopalan, Consultant, Co-operatives
- Suresh Kumar Neotia, Chairman, Ambuja Cement
- A. Vaidyanathan, Madras Institute of Development Studies

- Man Mohan Sharma, FRS, Former Director, Mumbai University Institute of Chemical Technology
- D. Jayavarthanavelu, Chairman and Managing Director, Laxmi Machine Works Ltd.

Those who were renominated to the board include

- Y. H. Malegam, Chartered Accountant, (to represent Western Area Local Board),
- H. P. Ranina, Supreme Court Advocate,
- Ashok S. Ganguly, Member, Investment Commission and Chairman, ICICI OneSource.

The retiring Directors include

- Narayan Murthy
- Mihir Rakshit
- K. Madhava Rao
- V. S. Vyas
- K.P. Singh
- Amrita Patel
- Suresh Krishna.

On 1 July, 2006 in an attempt to enhance the quality of customer service and strengthen the grievance redressal mechanism, the Reserve Bank of India constituted a new department-Customer Service Department (CSD).

Main Objectives

Monetary Authority

- Formulates, implements and monitors the monetary policy.
- Objective: maintaining price stability and ensuring adequate flow of credit to productive sectors.

Regulator and Supervisor of the Financial System

- Prescribes broad parameters of banking operations within which the country's banking and financial system functions.

- *Objective*: Maintain public confidence in the system, protect depositors' interest and provide cost-effective banking services to the public. The Banking Ombudsman Scheme has been formulated by the Reserve Bank of India (RBI) for effective redressal of complaints by bank customers

Manager of Exchange Control

- Manages the Foreign Exchange Management Act, 1999.
- *Objective:* To facilitate external trade and payment and promote orderly development and maintenance of foreign exchange market in India.

Issuer of Currency

- Issues and exchanges or destroys currency and coins not fit for circulation.
- *Objective:* To give the public adequate quantity of supplies of currency notes and coins and in good quality.

Developmental Role

- Performs a wide range of promotional functions to support national objectives.

Related Functions

- Banker to the Government: performs merchant banking function for the central and the state governments; also acts as their banker.
- Banker to banks: maintains banking accounts of all scheduled banks.
- Owner and operator of the depository (SGL) and exchange (NDS) for government bonds.

There is now an international consensus about the need to focus the tasks of a central bank upon central banking. RBI is far out of touch with such a principle, owing to the sprawling mandate described above.

Major Liabilities of Commercial Banks

Figures below are in millions of Indian Rupees.

Year	Deposits and other Accounts	Bills Payable
1950	9,983	173
1955	11,592	262
1960	20,218	317
1965	32,897	446
1970	64,793	923
1975	156,665	2,254
1980	439,869	10,995
1985	1,032,134	24,556
1990	1,820,468	38,656
1995	3,984,352	116,622
2000	4,45,666	150,444
2005		

Major Assets of Commercial Banks

Figures below are in millions of Indian Rupees.

Year	Investments	Advances
1950	4,330	5,353
1955	4,600	7,037
1960	7,241	12,458
1965	9,884	21,954
1970	18,148	46,850
1975	45,999	106,167
1980	126,642	272,673
1985	303,378	623,553
1990	687,151	1,095,412
1995	1,750,206	2,243,308
2000	1,750,206	2,243,308
2005		

Tarapore Committee

The Tarapore committee is a committee setup by the Reserve Bank of India under the chairmanship of former RBI deputy governor S S Tarapore to "lay the roadmap" to capital account convertibility. The five-member committee recommended a three-year timeframe for complete convertibility by 1999-2000.

In March 2006, the Finance Minister of India, P Chidambaram said that the Central government was "within striking distance" of implementing the committee's report.

INDIAN RUPEE

The rupee (Hindi: *Rupiyah*) is the currency of India. The issuance of the currency is controlled by the Reserve Bank of India. The ISO 4217 code for the Indian rupee is INR.

In most parts of India, the rupee is known as the rupee, roopayi, rupaye, rubai or one of the other terms derived from the Sanskrit rupyakam, raupya meaning silver; rupyakam meaning (coin) of silver. However, in the Bengali and Assamese languages, spoken in Assam, Tripura, Orissa and West Bengal, the rupee is known as a Taka, and is written as such on Indian banknotes. The modern rupee is subdivided into 100 paise (singular paisa). As is standard in Indian English, large values of Indian rupees are counted in terms of thousands, lakh (100 thousand, in digits 1,00,000), crore (100 lakhs, in digits 1,00,00,000) and arawb (100 crore, in digits 1,00,00,00,000). The use of million or billion, as is standard in American or British English, is far less common. For example, the amount INR 1,25,84,729.25 is spoken as one crore twenty-five lakhs eighty-four thousand seven hundred twenty-nine rupees and twenty-five paise.

History

India was one of the earliest issuers of coins (circa 6th Century BC). The first "rupee" is believed to have been introduced by Sher Shah Suri (1486-1545), based on a ratio of 40 copper pieces (paisa) per rupee. Among the earliest issues of paper rupees were those by the Bank of Hindustan (1770-1832), the General Bank of Bengal and Bihar

(1773-75, established by Warren Hastings) and the Bengal Bank (1784-91), amongst others.

During British rule, and the first decade of independence, it was subdivided into 16 annas. Each anna was subdivided into 4 paise (also written pice) or 12 pies. Until 1815, the Madras Presidency also issued a currency based on the fanam, with 12 fanams equal to the rupee.

Historically, the rupee, derived from the Sanskrit word raupya, which means silver, was a silver coin. This had severe consequences in the nineteenth century, when the strongest economies in the world were on the gold standard. The discovery of vast quantities of silver in the U.S. and various European colonies resulted in a decline in the relative value of silver to gold. Suddenly the standard currency of India could not buy as much from the outside world. This event was known as "the fall of the rupee."

In 1898, the rupee was tied to the gold standard through the British pound by pegging the rupee at a value of 1 shillings 4 pence (i.e., 15 rupees = 1 pound). In 1920, the rupee was increased in value to 2 shillings (10 rupees = 1 pound). However, in 1927, the peg was once more reduced, this time to 1 shilling 6 pence (13 rupees = 1 pound). This peg was maintained until 1966, when the rupee was devalued and pegged to the U.S. dollar at a rate of 7.5 rupees = 1 dollar (at the time, the rupee became equal to 11.4 British pence). This peg lasted until the U.S. dollar devalued in 1971. The Indian rupee replaced the Danish Indian rupee in 1845, the French Indian rupee in 1954 and the Portuguese Indian escudo in 1961. Following independence in 1947, the Indian rupee replaced all the currencies of the previously autonomous states. Some of these states had issued rupees equal to those issued by the British (such as the Travancore rupee). Other currencies included the Hyderabad rupee and the Kutch kori.

In 1957, decimalisation occurred and the rupee was divided into 100 naye paise (Hindi for "new paise"). In 1964, the initial "naye" was dropped. Many still refer to 25, 50 and 75 paise as 4, 8 and 12 annas respectively, not unlike the usage of "bit" in American English for ½ dollar.

International Use

With Partition, the Pakistani rupee came into existence, initially using Indian coins, and Indian currency notes simply overstamped with Pakistan. In previous times, the Indian rupee was regarded as an official currency of other countries, including Kuwait, Bahrain, Qatar, the Trucial States (now the UAE), and Malaysia. The Gulf rupee, also known as the Persian Gulf rupee (XPGR), was introduced by the Indian government as a replacement for the Indian rupee for circulation exclusively outside the country with the Reserve Bank of India Amendment Act, May 1, 1959. This creation of a separate currency was an attempt to reduce the strain put on India's foreign reserves by gold smuggling. After India devalued the rupee on June 6, 1966, those countries still using it-Oman, Qatar and what is now the United Arab Emirates (known as the Trucial States until 1971)-replaced the Gulf rupee with their own currencies. Kuwait and Bahrain had already done so in 1961 and 1965 respectively.

The Indian rupee is also linked with the Bhutanese Ngultrum. The Indian rupee is also accepted in towns of Nepalese side of Nepal-India border and some Indian shops in the United Kingdom.

Regal Issues, 1862-1947

In 1862, coins were introduced which are referred to as Regal issues. They bore the portrait of Queen Victoria and the designation "India". Denominations were 1/12 anna, ½ pice, ¼ and ½ anna (all in copper), 2 annas, ¼, ½ and 1 rupee (silver) and 5 and 10 rupees and 1 mohur (gold). The gold denominations ceased production in 1891 whilst no ½ anna coins wereissued dated later than 1877.

In 1906, bronze replaced copper for the lowest three denominations and in 1907, a cupro-nickel 1 anna was introduced. In 1918 and 1919, cupro-nickel 2, 4 and 8 annas were introduced, although the 4 and 8 annas coins were only issued until 1921 and did not replace their silver equivalents. Also in 1918 and 1919, the Bombay mint struck gold sovereigns and 15 rupee coins identical in size to the sovereigns as an emergency measure due to the First World War.

In the early 1940s, several changes were implemented. The 1/12 anna and ½ pice ceased production, the ¼ anna was changed to a bronze, holed coin, cupro-nickel and nickel-brass ½ anna coins were introduced, nickel-brass was used to produce some 1 and 2 annas coins, and the composition of the silver coins was reduced from 91.7% to 50%. The last of the regal issues were cupro-nickel ¼, ½ and 1 rupee pieces minted in 1946 and 1947.

Independent Issues, Predecimal, 1950-1957

Indias first coins after independence were issued in 1950. They were 1 pice, ½, 1 and 2 annas, ¼, ½ and 1 rupee denominations. The sizes and compositions were the same as the final Regal issues, except for the 1 pice, which was bronze but not holed.

Independent Issues, Decimal, 1957-

The first decimal issues of India consisted of 1, 2, 5, 10, 25 and 50 naye paise and 1 rupee. The 1 naya paisa was bronze, the 2, 5 and 10 naye paise were cupro-nickel and the 25 and 50 naye paise and 1 rupee were nickel. In 1964, the word naya(e) was removed from all the coins. Between 1964 and 1967, aluminium 1, 2, 3, 5 and 10 paise were introduced. In 1968, nickel-brass 20 paise were introduced, replaced by aluminium coins in 1982. Between 1972 and 1975, cupro-nickel replaced nickel in the 25 and 50 paise and the 1 rupee. In 1982, cupro-nickel 2 rupees coins were introduced. In 1988, stainless steel 10, 25 and 50 paise were introduced, followed by 1 rupee coins in 1992. Also in 1992, the 5 rupee coin was introduced.

The coins commonly in circulation are 25 and 50 paise, 1, 2 and 5 rupees. 5, 10, and 20 paise coins, although valid, have become increasingly rare in regular usage.

SECURITIES AND EXCHANGE BOARD OF INDIA

Securities and Exchange Board of India (SEBI) is a board (autonomous body) created by the Government of India in 1988 and given statutory form in 1992 with the SEBI Act 1992 with its head office at Mumbai. It is chaired by Mr. M. Damodaran a respected turnaround civil servant credited with turning around large public sector companies from near death scenarios including the famous Unit Trust of India. Below the Board, headed by the Chairman, the staff/officers of the organization are led by Executive Directors.

Sebi has three functions rolled into one body: legislative, judicial and executive. It drafts rules in its legislative capacity, it conducts enquiries and enforcement action in its executive function and it passes rulings and orders in its judicial capacity. Though this makes it exceedingly powerful, there is an appeals process to create accountability.

Sebi has had a mixed history in terms of its success as a regulator. Though it has pushed systemic reforms aggressively and successively (e.g. the quick movement towards making the markets electronic and paperless), it seems to lack the legal expertise needed to sustain prosecutions/enforcement actions. It has often received flak from the appellate body known as the Securities Appellate Tribunal (SAT). From the SAT, an appeal lies straight to the Supreme Court of India.

Functions

Its main functions are:

- helping the business in stock exchanges and any other securities markets,
- registering and regulating the working of stock brokers, sub-brokers, share transfer agents, bankers to an issue, trustees of trust deeds, registrars to an issue, merchant bankers, underwriters, portfolio managers, investment advisers and such other intermediaries who may be associated with securities markets in any manner.
- registering and regulating the working of the depositories, participants, custodians of securities, foreign institutional investors, credit rating agencies and such other intermediaries as the Board may, by notification, specify in this behalf.
- registering and regulating the working of venture capital funds and collective investment schemes including mutual funds;

- promoting and regulating self-regulatory organisations;
- prohibiting fraudulent and unfair trade practices relating to securities markets;
- promoting investors' education and training of intermediaries of securities markets;
- prohibiting insider trading in securities;
- regulating substantial acquisition of shares and takeover of companies;
- calling for information from undertaking inspection, conducting inquiries and audits of the stock exchanges, mutual funds and other persons associated with the securities market and intermediaries and self-regulatory organisations in the securities market;
- calling for information and record from any bank or any other authority or board or corporation established or constituted by or under any Central, State or Provincial Act in respect of any transaction in securities which is under investigation or inquiry by the Board;19
- performing such functions and exercising such powers under the provisions of Securities Contracts (Regulation) Act, 1956, as may be delegated to it by the Central Government;
- levying fees or other charges for carrying out the purpose of this section;
- conducting research for the above purposes;
- calling from or furnishing to any such agencies, as may be specified by the Board, such information as may be considered necessary by it for the efficient discharge of its functions
- performing such other functions as may be prescribed.

NATIONAL THERMAL POWER CORPORATION

National Thermal Power Corporation is the largest power generation company in India. The Forbes Global 2000 ranking for 2005 ranks it as the 5th leading company in India and the 486th leading company in the world. It is a public listed (Bombay

Stock Exchange) Indian public sector company, with majority shares owned by the Government of India. At present, Government of India holds 89.5% of the total equity shares of the company and the balance 10.5% is held by FIIs, Domestic Banks, Public and others. NTPC ranks amongst the top five companies, in terms of market capitalisation.

NTPC's core business is engineering, construction and operation of power generating plants and also providing consultancy to power utilities in India and abroad. As on date the installed capacity of NTPC is 26, 404 MW through its 14 coal based (21,395 MW), 7 gas based (3,955 MW) and 4 Joint Venture Projects (1,054 MW).

NTPC's share on 31 Mar 2006 in the total installed capacity of the country was 19.51% and it contributed 27.68% of the total power generation of the country during 2005-06. Thus, every fourth home in India is enlightened by NTPC. A total of 170.88 BUs of electricity was produced across all the stations of the company in the financial year 2005-2006. The Net Profit after Tax on March 31, 2006 was INR 58, 202 million. Net Profit after Tax for the quarter ended June 30, 2006 was INR 15528 million, which is 18.65% more than the same quarter in the previous financial year (2004-2005) where the profit was INR 13087 million.

Pursuant to special resolution passed by the Shareholders at the Company's Annual General Meeting held on September 23, 2005 and the approval of the Central Government under section 21 of the Companies Act, 1956, the name of the Company "National Thermal Power Corporation Limited" has been changed to "NTPC Limited" with effect from October 28, 2005.

The company, which has completed its thirty years of existence on November 7, 2005, has made its foray into hydro-power and is planning to go into nuclear too).

OIL INDIA

Oil India, (OIL) is a large natural gas and petroleum company in India under the administrative control of the Ministry of Petroleum and Natural Gas of the Government of India. OIL is engaged in the business of exploration, development and production of crude oil and natural gas, transportation of crude oil and production of liquid petroleum gas.

OIL is the pioneer in exploration and production of hydrocarbons in India, and traces its roots back to Oil India Private Ltd., formed in 1959 with The Burmah Oil Company Ltd. holding two-thirds of equity and Government of India holding one-third. Oil India Private evolved into Oil India Ltd., which was an equal partnership between Burmah Oil and Government of India. In 1983 the company became a public sector undertaking of the Government of India.

The Company has over 100,000 square kilometers of license areas for oil and gas exploration. It has emerged as a consistently profitable international company with exploration blocks as far as Libya and sub-Saharan Africa.

10

Purchasing Power Parity and GDP

ORIGIN AND DEVELOPMENT

Purchasing power parity (PPP) theory was developed by Gustav Cassel in 1920. It is the method of using the long-run equilibrium exchange rate of two currencies to equalize the currencies' purchasing power. It is based on the law of one price, the idea that, in an efficient market, identical goods must have only one price. Purchasing power parity is often called absolute purchasing power parity to distinguish it from a related theory relative purchasing power parity, which predicts the relationship between the two countries' relative inflation rates and the change in the exchange rate of their currencies.

A purchasing power parity exchange rate equalizes the purchasing power of different currencies in their home countries for a given basket of goods. These special exchange rates are often used to compare the standards of living of two or more countries. The adjustments are meant to give a better picture than comparing gross domestic products (GDP) using market exchange rates. This type of adjustment to an exchange rate is controversial because of the difficulties of finding comparable baskets of goods to compare purchasing power across countries.

Market exchange rates fluctuate widely, but many believe that PPP exchange rates reflect the long run equilibrium value. The distortions caused by using market rates are accentuated because prices of non-traded goods and services are usually lower in poorer economies. For example, a U.S. dollar exchanged and spent in the People's Republic of China will buy much more than a dollar spent in the United States.

The differences between PPP and market exchange rates can be significant. For example, the World Bank's World Development Indicators 2005 estimates that one United States dollar is equivalent to approximately 1.8 Chinese yuan by purchasing power parity in 2003.. However, based on nominal exchange rates, one U.S. dollar is currently equal to 7.9 yuan. This discrepancy has large implications; for instance, GDP per capita in the People's Republic of China is about US$1,800, while on a PPP basis it is about US$7,204. This is frequently misused to assert that China is the world's second largest economy, but such a calculation would be invalid under the PPP theory. At the other extreme, Japan's nominal GDP per capita is around US$37,600, but its PPP figure is only US$30,615.

Estimation of purchasing power parity is complicated by the fact that countries do not simply differ in a uniform price level; rather, the difference in food prices may be greater than the difference in housing prices, while also less than the difference in entertainment prices. People in different countries typically consume different baskets of goods. It is necessary to compare the cost of baskets of goods and services using a price index. This is a difficult task because purchasing patterns and even the goods available to purchase differ across countries. Thus, it is necessary to make adjustments for differences in the quality of goods and services. Additional statistical difficulties arise with multilateral comparisons when (as is usually the case) more than two countries are to be compared. When PPP comparisons are to be made over some interval of time, proper account needs to be made of inflationary effects.

Explanation

For a U.S. dollar to buy as much in the UK as in the U.S., as is assumed under the law of one price, the price of a basket of goods in pounds in the UK (denoted as: £P) times the spot exchange rate (denoted as: $/£) should equal the price of the same basket in the U.S. priced in dollars (denoted as: $P).

£P ($/£)= $P

This implies that the exchange rate that equalizes the value of a dollar of purchasing power (the PPP exchange rate) is:

($/£)= $P/£P

If the actual spot rate is greater, it suggests that the £ is over-valued against the $. If the actual spot rate is less, it suggest that the $ is overvalued against the £. For example if a "representative" consumption basket costs $1,500 in the U.S. and £1,000 in the UK the PPP exchange rate would be $1.50/£. If the actual spot rate was $1.80/£ this would indicate that the pound is overvalued by 20%, or equivalently the dollar is undervalued by 16.7%.

PPP EQUALIZATION AND THE LAW OF ONE PRICE

The law of one price states that differing prices of a traded good will tend to equalize in the absence of tariffs, other barriers to trade and prohibitively high shipping rates. The law of one price can also be stated as: "In an efficient market all identical goods must have only one price." The naïve PPP hypothesis is that free trade of goods should revert exchange rates to their PPP values. However, econometric analysis rejects this hypothesis, and gives a better prediction of the PPP/exchange rate relationship (the CPI) based on relative GDPs. Neo-classical economics includes Balassa-Samuelson effect theory, which explains the PPP model adjustment giving the equilibrium CPIs.

BIG MAC INDEX

An entertaining example of one measure of PPP is the Big Mac index popularised by The Economist, which looks at the prices of a Big Mac burger in McDonald's restaurants in different countries. If a Big Mac costs US$4 in the U.S. and GBP£3 in Britain, the PPP exchange rate would be £3 for $4. The Big Mac Index is presumably useful because it is based on a well-known good whose final price, easily tracked in many countries, includes input costs from a wide range of sectors in the local economy, such as agricultural commodities (beef, bread, lettuce, tomatoes), labor (blue and white collar), advertising, rent and real estate costs, transportation, etc.

Examples

West and Central African Franc

In 2003, the U.S. Dollar bought on average about 550 CFA franc. Because of a difference in purchasing power within some of the regions using the CFA franc, their purchasing power parity exchange rate differed greatly (lower implies a stronger currency): Cameroon 240, Central African Republic 166, Chad 172, Republic of the Congo 677, Equatorial Guinea 114, Gabon 413, Benin 273, Burkina Faso 167.

GDP of China

The CIA misuses the purchase power parity (PPP) method in its calculations of Gross National Product. By this measure the People's Republic of China has the second largest economy in the world, at $8.182 trillion (2005 est.) (CIA methodology for PPP). However, the empirical foundation for all PPP estimates for China is weak, since no comprehensive survey of Chinese prices has ever been carried out by the International Comparison Project. Moreover, PPP measures the urban consumer basket of goods, which is a very small part of the economy of China. Prices behind existing PPP estimates are few, out of date and may be unrepresentative of today's price structure.

However, the World Bank's World Development Indicators 2005 estimates that one United States dollar is equivalent to approximately 1.8 Chinese yuan by purchasing power parity in 2003.

NEED FOR PPP ADJUSTMENTS TO GDP

Using market exchange rates to compare countries' standard of living or per capita Gross Domestic Product can give a very misleading picture. The exchange rate only reflects traded goods in contrast to non-traded ones. Also, currencies are traded for purposes other than trade in goods and services, e.g., to buy capital assets whose prices vary more than those of physical goods. Also, different interest rates, speculation, hedging or interventions by central banks can influence the foreign-exchange market.

THE PPP METHOD IS USED AS AN ALTERNATIVE

For example, if the value of the Mexican peso falls by half compared to the U.S. dollar, the Mexican Gross Domestic Product measured in dollars will also halve. However, this exchange rate results from international trade and financial markets. It does not necessarily mean that Mexicans are any poorer; if incomes and prices measured in pesos stay the same, they will be no worse off assuming that imported goods are not essential to the quality of life of individuals. Measuring income in different countries using PPP exchange rates helps to avoid this problem.

PPP exchange rates are especially useful when official exchange rates are artificially manipulated by governments. Countries with strong government control of the economy sometimes enforce official exchange rates that make their own currency artificially strong. By contrast, the currency's black market exchange rate is artificially weak. In such cases a PPP exchange rate is likely the most realistic basis for economic comparison.

DIFFICULTIES

The main reasons why PPP does not perfectly reflect standards of living are:

- PPP numbers can vary with the specific basket of goods used, making it a rough estimate.
- Preferences and choices can vary from country to country. Goods then differ in their contribution to welfare.
- International competitiveness is mainly affected by the exchange rate and not by PPP.
- Differences in quality of goods are not sufficiently reflected in PPP.
- The price of a product within one currency-zone may vary drastically (for example, the average price of a can of soda is drastically lower in Lexington, Kentucky than in New York, New York. This is even more noticeable within the Eurozone.
- Imported goods are purchased at market exchange rates, and thus a country that has to import all of its food would appear better off than it actually is if the PPP is used as the measurement of well-being.

PPP calculations are often used to measure poverty rates.

RANGE AND QUALITY OF GOODS

The goods that the currency has the "power" to purchase are a basket of goods of different types:

1. Local, non-tradable goods and services (like electric power) that are produced and sold domestically.
2. Tradable goods such as non-perishable commodities that can be sold on the international market (e.g. diamonds).

The more a product falls into category 1 the further its price will be from the currency exchange rate. (Moving towards the PPP exchange rate.) Conversely, category 2 products tend to trade close to the currency exchange rate.

More processed and expensive products are likely to be tradable, falling into the second category, and drifting from the PPP exchange rate to the currency exchange rate. Even if the PPP "value" of the Chinese currency is five times stronger than the currency exchange rate, it won't buy five times as much of internationally traded goods like steel, cars and microchips, but non-traded goods like housing, services ("haircuts"), and domestically produced rice. The relative price differential between tradables and non-tradables from high-income to low-income countries is a consequence of the Balassa-Samuelson effect, and gives a big cost advantage to labour intensive production of tradable goods in low income countries (like China), as against high income countries (like Switzerland). The corporate cost advantage is nothing more sophisticated than access to cheaper workers, but because the pay of those workers goes further in low-income countries than high, the relative pay differentials (inter-country) can be sustained for longer than would be the case otherwise. (This is another way of saying that the wage rate is based on average local productivity, and that this is below the per capita productivity that factories selling tradable goods to international markets can achieve. This is sometimes called exploitation.) An equivalent cost benefit comes from non-traded goods that can be sourced locally (nearer the PPP-exchange rate than the nominal exchange rate in which receipts are paid). These act as a relatively cheaper factor of production than is available to factories in richer countries.

DIFFICULTIES WITH PPP COMPARISONS IN WELFARE ECONOMICS

While using PPP exchange rates for income comparison is an improvement over using market exchange rates, it is still imperfect, and comparisons using the PPP method can still be misleading. Comparing standards of living using the PPP method implicitly assumes that the real value placed on goods is the same in different countries. In reality, what is considered a luxury in one culture could be considered a necessity in another. The PPP method does not account for this. (This is not primarily a flaw in the exchange rate methodology, as cultural and interpersonal differences in utility functions are a more fundamental microeconomic problem.)

A PPP exchange rate varies depending on the choice of goods used for the index (CPI). Hence, it is possible to deliberately or accidentally bias a PPP exchange rate by the choice of a bundle. Indeed, it may be hard to construct equivalent representative bundles for the consumption habits of very different societies. PPP could also have difficulty accounting for differences in quality between goods in one country and equivalent goods in another.

Even if a good PPP is used, GDP per capita is still a measure of the economic output of the whole economy, not a direct measure of the mean or median person's quality of life. Other factors such as the standards of homes and schools, access to public services, the extent of pollution, and strength of consumer protection laws are hard to quantify and generally not fully reflected in the GDP. Even a PPP-adjusted measure of GDP per capita must be used with caution, for all the usual reasons that the GDP figure itself is limited (for instance, its inability to capture the surplus between subjective value and payment price).

For example, in 2002, the nominal GDP per capita in Japan was about US$40,000, while the equivalent PPP into a U.S. goods basket was estimated at $27,000. In the U.S., GDP per capita was about $36,400 (nominal and real if based on 2002 dollars). This means that the average U.S. citizen could enjoy slightly more consumption than the average Japanese (vastly more if private saving is removed from consumption income).

However, it does not necessarily follow, that this implies a "higher standard of living" in the sense of "enjoying life" more; the U.S. has higher crime rates and less social cohesion than Japan, while Japan has much less physical space per person and arguably less individual freedom. Ultimately, the quality of life will depend on subjective judgement and individual preferences.

While per-capita income does not take into account inequalities in wealth distribution, neither does the PPP-scaled income.

CLARIFICATION TO PPP NUMBERS OF THE IMF

The GDP number for all reporting areas are one number in the reporting areas local currency. Therefore, in the local currency the PPP and market (or government) exchange rate is always 1.0 to its own currency, so the PPP and market exchange rate GDP number is always per definition the same for any duration of time, anytime, in that area's currency. The only time the PPP exchange rate and the market exchange rate can differ is when the GDP number is converted into another currency.

Only because of different base numbers (because of for example "current" or "constant" prices, or an annualized or averaged number) are the USD to USD PPP exchange rate not 1.0, see the IMF data here:. The PPP exchange rate is 1.023 from 1980 to 2002, and the "constant" and "current" price is the same in 2000, because that's the base year for the "constant" (inflation adjusted) currency.

GROSS DOMESTIC PRODUCT

A region's gross domestic product,or GDP, is one of several measures of the size of its economy. The GDP of a country is defined as the market value of all final goods and services produced within a country in a given period of time. It is also considered the sum of value added at every stage of production of all final goods and services produced within a country in a given period of time. Until the 1980s the term GNP or gross national product was used in the United States. The two terms

GDP and GNP are almost identical. The most common approach to measuring and understanding GDP is the expenditure method:

GDP = consumption + investment + government spending + (exports-imports)

"Gross" means depreciation of capital stock is not included. With depreciation, with net investment instead of gross investment, it is the net domestic product. Consumption and investment in this equation are the expenditure on final goods and services. The exports minus imports part of the equation (often called cumulative exports) then adjusts this by subtracting the part of this expenditure not produced domestically (the imports), and adding back in domestic production not consumed at home (the exports).

Economists (since Keynes) have preferred to split the general consumption term into two parts; private consumption, and public sector (or government) spending. Two advantages of dividing total consumption this way in theoretical macroeconomics are:

- Private consumption is a central concern of welfare economics. The private investment and trade portions of the economy are ultimately directed (in mainstream economic models) to increases in long-term private consumption.
- If separated from endogenous private consumption, government consumption can be treated as exogenous, so that different government spending levels can be considered within a meaningful macroeconomic framework.

THE COMPONENTS

Each of the variables C, I, G and NX (where GDP = C + I + G + NX as above):

- C is private consumption in the economy. This includes most personal expenditures of households such as food, rent, medical expenses and so on but does not include new housing.

- I is defined as business investments in capital. Examples of investment by a business include construction of a new mine, purchase of software, or purchase of machinery and equipment for a factory. Spending by households on new houses is also included in Investment. 'Investment' in GDP is meant very specifically as non-financial product purchases. Buying financial products is classed as saving in macroeconomics, as opposed to investment (which, in the GDP formula is a form of spending). The distinction is (in theory) clear: if money is converted into goods or services, without a repayment liability it is investment. For example, if you buy a bond or a share, the ownership of the money has only nominally changed hands, and this transfer payment is excluded from the GDP sum. Although such purchases would be called investments in normal speech, from the total-economy point of view, this is simply swapping of deeds, and not part of the real economy or the GDP formula.
- G is the sum of government expenditures on final goods and services. It includes salaries of public servants, purchase of weapons for the military, and any investment expenditure by a government. It does not include any transfer payments, such as social security or unemployment benefits. The relative size of government expenditure compared to GDP as a whole is critical in the theory of crowding out, and the Keynesian cross.
- X is gross export. GDP captures the amount a country produces, including goods and services produced for overseas consumption, therefore exports are added.
- M is gross import. Imports are subtracted since imported goods will be included in the terms G, I, or C, and must be deducted to avoid counting foreign supply as domestic.
- NX are "net exports" in the economy: gross exports-gross imports. There is a fixed relation: NX = X-M.

It is important to understand the meaning of each variable precisely in order to:

- Read national accounts.
- Understand Keynesian or neo-classical macroeconomics.

Examples of GDP Component Variables

Examples of C, I, G, & NX: If you spend money to renovate your hotel so that occupancy rates increase, that is private investment, but if you buy shares in a consortium to do the same thing it is saving. The former is included when measuring GDP (in I), the latter is not. However, when the consortium conducted its own expenditure on renovation, that expenditure would be included in GDP.

If the hotel is your private home your renovation spending would be measured as Consumption, but if a government agency is converting the hotel into an office for civil servants the renovation spending would be measured as part of public sector spending (G).

If the renovation involves the purchase of a chandelier from abroad, that spending would also be counted as an increase in imports, so that NX would fall and the total GDP is unaffected by the purchase. (This highlights the fact that GDP is intended to measure domestic production rather than total consumption or spending. Spending is really a convenient means of estimating production.)

If you are paid to manufacture the chandelier to hang in a foreign hotel the situation would be reversed, and the payment you receive would be counted in NX (positively, as an export). Again, we see that GDP is attempting to measure production through the means of expenditure; if the chandelier you produced had been bought domestically it would have been included in the GDP figures (in C or I) when purchased by a consumer or a business, but because it was exported it is necessary to 'correct' the amount consumed domestically to give the amount produced domestically. (As in Gross Domestic Product.).

GDP Income Account

Another way of measuring GDP is to measure the total income payable in the GDP income accounts. This should provide the same figure as the expenditure method described above.

The formula for GDP measured using the income approach, called GDP(I), is:

GDP = Compensation of employees + Gross operating surplus + Gross mixed income + Taxes less subsidies on production and imports

- Compensation of employees (COE) measures the total renumeration to employees for work done. It includes wages and salaries, as well as employer contributions to social security and other such programs.
- Gross operating surplus (GOS) is the surplus due to owners of incorporated businesses. Often called profits, although only a subset of total costs are subtracted from gross output to calculate GOS.
- Gross mixed income (GMI) is the same measure as GOS, but for unincorporated businesses. This often includes most small businesses.

The sum of COE, GOS and GMI is called total factor income, and measures the value of GDP at factor (basic) prices. The difference between basic prices and final prices (those used in the expenditure calculation) is the total taxes and subsidies that the Government has levied or paid on that production. So adding taxes less subsidies on production and imports converts GDP at factor cost to GDP(I).

Another formula can be written as this:

GDP = R + I + P + SA + W

R = rents

I = interests

P = profits

SA = statistical adjustments (corporate income taxes, dividends, undistributed corporate profits)

W = wages

Measurement

International Standards

The international standard for measuring GDP is contained in the book System of National Accounts (1993), which was prepared by representatives of the International Monetary Fund,

European Union, Organisation for Economic Cooperation and Development, United Nations and World Bank. The publication is normally referred to as SNA93, to distinguish it from the previous edition published in 1968 (called SNA68).

SNA93 sets out a set of rules and procedures for the measurement of national accounts. The standards are designed to be flexible, to allow for differences in local statistical needs and conditions.

National Measurement

Within each country GDP is normally measured by a national government statistical agency, as private sector organisations normally do not have access to the information required (especially information on expenditure and production by governments).

- *Argentina:* Instituto Nacional de Estadística y Censos (INDEC)
- *Australia:* Australian Bureau of Statistics (ABS).
- *Austria:* Statistik Austria.
- *Bangladesh:* Bangladesh Bureau of Statistics
- *Brazil:* Instituto Brasileiro de Geografia e Estatística (IBGE).
- *Chile:* Instituto Nacional de Estadísticas (INE).
- *Colombia:* Departamento Administrativo Nacional de Estadistica (DANE).
- *Canada:* Statistics Canada (StatCan).
- *France:* Institut National de la Statistique et des Etudes Economiques (INSEE).
- *Iceland:* Statistics Iceland.
- *India:* Government of India Ministry of Statistics and Programme Implementation.
- *Japan:* Ministry of Economy, Trade and Industry (METI).
- *Korea (South):* National Stastical Office, Republic of Korea (NSO).

- *Mexico:* Instituto Nacional de Geografía, Estadística e Informática (INEGI).
- *The Netherlands:* Centraal Bureau voor de Statistiek (Statistics Netherlands).
- *Pakistan:* Federal Bureau of Statistics.
- *Poland:* Glowny Urzad Statystyczny
- *Russia:* Federal Service of State Statistics (Rosstat).
- *United Kingdom:* Office for National Statistics (ONS).
- *United States:* Bureau of Economic Analysis (BEA).
- *Jamaica:* Statistical Institute of Jamaica (STATIN)

GDP can measure spending on all goods and services. GDP can also measure all income earned.

Interest Rates

Net interest expense is a transfer payment in all sectors except the financial sector. Net interest expenses in the financial sector is seen as production and value added and is added to GDP.

CROSS-BORDER COMPARISON

The level of GDP in different countries may be compared by converting their value in national currency according to either

- current currency exchange rate: GDP calculated by exchange rates prevailing on international currency markets
- purchasing power parity exchange rate: GDP calculated by purchasing power parity (PPP) of each currency relative to a selected standard (usually the United States dollar).

The relative ranking of countries may differ dramatically between the two approaches.

- The current exchange rate method converts the value of goods and services using global currency exchange rates. This can offer better indications of a country's international purchasing power and relative economic strength. For instance, if 10% of GDP is being spent on buying hi-tech foreign arms, the number of weapons purchased is entirely governed by current exchange rates, since arms are a traded product bought on the international market (there is no meaningful 'local' price distinct from the international price for high technology goods).

- The purchasing power parity method accounts for the relative effective domestic purchasing power of the average producer or consumer within an economy. This can be a better indicator of the living standards of less-developed countries because it compensates for the weakness of local currencies in world markets. The PPP method of GDP conversion is most relevant to non-traded goods and services.

There is a clear pattern of the purchasing power parity method decreasing the disparity in GDP between high and low income (GDP) countries, as compared to the current exchange rate method. This finding is called the Penn effect.

GDP and Standard of Living

GDP per capita is often used as an indicator of standard of living in an economy. While this approach has advantages, many criticisms of GDP focus on its use as a sole indicator of standard of living. The major advantages to using GDP per capita as an indicator of standard of living are that it is measured frequently, widely and consistently; frequently in that most countries provide information on GDP on a quarterly basis (which allows a user to spot trends more quickly), widely in that some measure of GDP is available for practically every country in the world (allowing crude comparisons between the standard of living in different countries), and consistently in that the technical definitions used within GDP are relatively consistent between countries, and so there can be confidence that the same thing is being measured in each country.

The major disadvantage of using GDP as an indicator of standard of living is that it is not, strictly speaking, a measure of standard of living. GDP is intended to be a measure of particular types of economic activity within a country. Nothing about the definition of GDP suggests that it is necessarily a measure of standard of living. For instance, in an extreme example, a country which exported 100 per cent of its production would still have a high GDP, but a very poor standard of living.

The argument in favour of using GDP is not that it is a good indicator of standard of living, but rather that (all other things being equal) standard of living tends to increase when GDP per capita increases. This makes GDP a proxy for standard of living, rather than a direct measure of it. GDP per capita can also be seen as a proxy of labor productivity. As the productivity of the workers increases, employers must compete for them by paying higher wages. Conversely, if productivity is low, then wages must be low or the businesses will not be able to make a profit. There are a number of controversies about this use of GDP.

Criticisms and Limitations

GDP is widely used by economists to follow how the economy is moving, as its variations are relative quickly identified. However, its value as an indicator for the standard of living is considered to be limited. An alternative for this purpose is the United Nations' Human Development Index in which the GDP is a contributing factor in its calculation. Criticisms of how the GDP is used include:

- GDP does not take into account the black market, where the money spent isn't registered, and the non-monetary economy, where no money comes into play at all, resulting in inaccurate or abnormally low GDP figures. For example, in countries with major business transactions occurring informally, portions of local economy are not easily registered. Bartering may be more prominent than the use of money, even extending to services (I helped you build your house ten years ago, so now you help me).
- This mainstream economic analysis ignores the environment, subsistence production and domestic work. The current system counts oil spills and wars as contributors to economic growth, while child-rearing

and housekeeping are deemed valueless. The work of New Zealand economist, Marilyn Waring, has highlighted that if a concerted attempt to factor in unpaid work were made, then it would in part, undo the injustices of unpaid (and in some cases, slave) labour, and also provide the political transparency and accountability necessary for democracy. Also, when GDP is used as a measure of success over time, the amount of housework that was done 50 years ago compared to the present time is much greater. Thus, comparing GDP over time cannot take into account the changes in society and lifestyle.

- It ignores volunteer, unpaid work. For example, Linux contributes nothing to GDP, but it was estimated that it would have cost more than a billion US dollars for a commercial company to develop.
- Very often different calculations of GDP are confused among each other. For cross-border comparisons one should especially regard whether it is calculated by purchasing power parity (PPP) method or current exchange rate method.
- GDP counts work that produces no net change or that results from repairing harm. For example, rebuilding after a natural disaster or war may produce a considerable amount of economic activity and thus boost GDP, but it would have been far better if the disaster had never occurred in the first place. The economic value of health care is another classic example-it may raise GDP if many people are sick and they are receiving expensive treatment, but it is not a desirable situation. Alternative economic measures, such as the standard of living or discretionary income per capita better measure the human utility of economic activity.
- Quality of life-human happiness-is determined by many other things than physical goods and services. Even the alternative economic measures of standard of living and discretionary income do not take these factors into account.

- As the single most important figure in statistics it is subject to fraud, such as the usage of hedonic price indexing on official GDP numbers in the US, thereby creating investments out of nothing while statistically dampening inflation.
- Cross border trade within companies distorts the GDP and is done frequently to escape high taxation. Examples include the German Ebay that evades German tax by doing business in Switzerland, and American companies that have founded holdings in Ireland to "buy" their own products for cheap from their continental factories (without shipping) and selling them for profit via Ireland- thereby reducing their taxes and increasing Irish GDP.
- People may buy cheap, low-durability goods over and over again, or they may buy high-durability goods less often. It is possible that the monetary value of the items sold in the first case is higher than that in the second case, in which case a higher GDP is simply the result of greater inefficiency and waste. (This is not always the case; durable goods are often more difficult to produce than flimsy goods, and consumers have a financial incentive to find the cheapest long-term option. With goods that are undergoing rapid change, such as in fashion or high technology, the short lifespan may increase customer satisfaction by allowing them to have newer products.)
- If a nation does not spend, but saves and invests overseas, its GDP will be diminished in comparison to one that spends borrowed money; thus accumulated savings and debt are not taken into account so long as adequate financing continues.
- GDP does not measure the sustainability of growth. A country may achieve a temporarily high GDP by over-exploiting natural resources or by misallocating investment. For example, the large deposits of phosphates gave the people of Nauru one of the highest per capita incomes on earth, but since 1989 their standard of living has declined sharply as the supply has run out. Oil-rich states can sustain high GDPs

without industrializing, but this high level would no longer be sustainable if the oil runs out. Economies experiencing an economic bubble, such as a housing bubble or stock bubble, or a low private-saving rate tend to appear to grow faster due to higher consumption, mortgaging their futures for present growth. Economic growth at the expense of environmental degradation can end up costing dearly to clean up; GDP does not account for this.

- As a measure of actual sale prices, GDP does not capture the economic surplus between the price paid and subjective value received, and can therefore underestimate aggregate utility.
- The annual growth of real GDP is adjusted by using the "GDP deflator", which tends to underestimate the objective differences in the quality of manufactured output over time. (The deflator is explicitly based on subjective experience when measuring such things as the consumer benefit received from computer-power improvements since the early 1980s). Therefore the GDP figure may underestimate the degree to which improving technology and quality-level are increasing the real standard of living.
- GDP does not take disparity in incomes between the rich and poor into account.

The limits of GDP (or GNP, a slightly different notion) can be summed up in the words of two critics. Robert Kennedy said:

The gross national product includes air pollution and advertising for cigarettes and ambulances to clear our highways of carnage. It counts special locks for our doors and jails for the people who break them. GNP includes the destruction of the redwoods and the death of Lake Superior. It grows with the production of napalm, and missiles and nuclear warheads... it does not allow for the health of our families, the quality of their education, or the joy of their play. It is indifferent to the decency of our factories and the safety of our streets alike. It does not include the beauty of our poetry or the strength of our marriages, or the intelligence of our public debate or the integrity of our public officials. It measures everything, in short, except that which makes life worthwhile.

The second critic, Simon Kuznets the inventor of the GDP, in his very first report to the US Congress in 1934 said:

...the welfare of a nation can scarcely be inferred from a measure of national income. If the GDP is up, why is America down? Distinctions must be kept in mind between quantity and quality of growth, between costs and returns, and between the short and long run. Goals for more growth should specify more growth of what and for what.

Some economists have attempted to create a replacement for GDP called the Genuine Progress Indicator (GPI), which attempts to address many of the above criticisms. Many nations calculate a national wealth, a sum of all assets in a nation, but this again does not account for future obligations such as environmental degradation, asset bubbles, and debt. Other nations such as Bhutan have advocated gross national happiness as a standard of living. (Bhutan claims to be the world's happiest nation.)

11

Exchange Rate

In finance, the exchange rate (also known as the foreign-exchange rate, forex rate or FX rate) between two currencies specifies how much one currency is worth in terms of the other. For example an exchange rate of 120 Japanese yen (JPY, ¥) to the United States dollar (USD, $) means that JPY 120 is worth the same as USD 1. The foreign exchange market is one of the largest markets in the world. By some estimates, about 2 trillion USD worth of currency changes hands every day.

The spot exchange rate refers to the current exchange rate. The forward exchange rate refers to an exchange rate that is quoted and traded today but for delivery and payment on a specific future date.

EXCHANGE RATE QUOTATIONS

An exchange rate quotation is given by stating the number of units of a price currency that can be bought in terms of 1 unit currency. For example, in a quotation that says the EUR/USD exchange rate is 1.2 (USD per EUR), the price currency is USD and the unit currency is EUR.

Quotes using a country's home currency as the price currency (e.g., £0.574744 = $1 in the UK) are known as direct quotation or price quotation (from that country's perspective) and are used by most countries.

Quotes using a country's home currency as the unit currency (e.g., $1.73990 = £1 in the UK) are known as indirect quotation or quantity quotation and are used in British newspapers and are also common in Australia, New Zealand and Canada.

- direct quotation: 1 foreign currency unit = x home currency units
- indirect quotation: 1 home currency unit = x foreign currency units

Note that, using direct quotation, if the home currency is strengthening (i.e., appreciating, or becoming more valuable) then the exchange rate number decreases. Conversely if the foreign currency is strengthening, the exchange rate number increases and the home currency is depreciating.

When looking at a currency pair such as EUR/USD, many times the first component (EUR in this case) will be called the base currency. The second is called the counter currency. For example: EUR/USD = 1.2836, means EUR is the base and USD the counter, so 1 EUR = 1.2836 USD.

Currency pair are given with four digits except au JPY with two digits (EURUSD: 1.2836-EURJPY: 150.17)

Free or Pegged

If a currency is free-floating, its exchange rate is allowed to vary against that of other currencies and is determined by the market forces of supply and demand. Exchange rates for such currencies are likely to change almost constantly as quoted on financial markets, mainly by banks, around the world. A movable or adjustable peg system is a system of fixed exchange rates,but with a provision for the devaluation of a currency. For example, between 1994 and 2005, the Chinese yuan (CNY, ¥) was pegged to the United States dollar at ¥8.2768 to $1. The Chinese were not the only country to do this; from the end of World War II until 1970, Western European countries all maintained fixed exchange rates with the US dollar based on the Bretton Woods system.

Nominal and Real Exchange Rates

- The nominal exchange rate is the rate at which an organization can trade the currency of one country for the currency of another.
- The real exchange rate (RER) is an important concept in economics, though it is quite difficult to grasp

concretely. It is defined by the model: RER = e(P/P*), where 'e' is the exchange rate, as the number of foreign currency units per home currency unit; where P is the price level of the home country; and where P* is the foreign price level.

Unfortunately, this compact and simple model for RER calculations is only a theoretical ideal. In practical usage, there are many foreign currencies and price level values to take into consideration. Correspondingly, the model calculations become increasingly more complex. Furthermore, the model is based on purchasing power parity (PPP), which implies a constant RER. The empirical determination of a constant RER value could never be realised, due to limitations on data collection. PPP would imply that the RER is the rate at which an organization can trade goods and services of one economy (e.g. country) for those of another. For example, if the price of a good increases 10% in the UK, and the Japanese currency simultaneously appreciates 10% against the UK currency, then the price of the good remains constant for someone in Japan. The people in the UK, however, would still have to deal with the 10% increase in domestic prices. It is also worth mentioning that government-enacted tariffs can affect the actual rate of exchange, helping to reduce price pressures. More recent approaches in modelling the RER employ a set of macroeconomic variables, such as relative productivity and the real interest rate differential.

FLUCTUATIONS IN EXCHANGE RATES

A market based exchange rate will change whenever the values of either of the two component currencies change. A currency will tend to become more valuable whenever demand for it is greater than the available supply. It will become less valuable whenever demand is less than available supply (this does not mean people no longer want money, it just means they prefer holding their wealth in some other form, possibly another currency).

Increased demand for a currency is due to either an increased transaction demand for money, or an increased speculative demand for money. The transaction demand for money is highly correlated to the country's level of business activity, gross domestic product (GDP), and employment levels. The more people there are out of work, the less the public as a whole will spend on goods and services. Central banks typically have little difficulty adjusting the available money supply to accommodate changes in the demand for money due to business transactions.

The speculative demand for money is much harder for a central bank to accommodate but they try to do this by adjusting interest rates. An investor may choose to buy a currency if the return (that is the interest rate) is high enough. The higher a country's interest rates, the greater the demand for that currency. It has been argued that currency speculation can undermine real economic growth, in particular since large currency speculators may deliberately create downward pressure on a currency in order to force that central bank to sell their currency to keep it stable (once this happens, the speculator can buy the currency back from the bank at a lower price, close out their position, and thereby take a profit).

In choosing what type of asset to hold, people are also concerned that the asset will retain its value in the future. Most people will not be interested in a currency if they think it will devalue. A currency will tend to lose value, relative to other currencies, if the country's level of inflation is relatively higher, if the country's level of output is expected to decline, or if a country is troubled by political uncertainty.

For example, when Russian President Vladimir Putin dismissed his Government on February 24, 2004, the price of the ruble dropped. When China announced plans for its first manned space mission, synthetic futures on Chinese yuan jumped (since China's currency is officially pegged, synthetic markets have emerged that can behave as if the yuan were floating).

Like the stock exchange, money can be made or lost on the foreign exchange market by investors and speculators buying and selling at the right times. Currencies can be traded at spot and foreign exchange options markets. The spot market represents current exchange rates, whereas options are derivatives of exchange rates.

FOREIGN EXCHANGE MARKETS

The foreign exchange markets are usually highly liquid as the world's main international banks provide a market around-the-clock. The Bank for International Settlements reported that global foreign exchange market turnover daily averages in April was $650 billion in 1998 (at constant exchange rates) and increased to $1.9 trillion in 2004 (Triennial Central Bank Survey of Foreign Exchange and Derivatives Market Activity 2004-Final Results). The biggest foreign exchange trading centre is London, followed by New York and Tokyo.

CUSTOMER SERVICE

Definition

Customer service is the provision of service to customers before, during and after a purchase.

Its importance varies by product, industry and customer. As an example, an expert customer might require less pre-purchase service (i.e., advice) than a novice customer. In many cases, customer service is more important if the purchase relates to a "service" as opposed to a "product".

Customer service may be provided by a person (e.g., sales and service representative), or by automated means called self-service. Examples of self service are Internet sites.

Customer service is normally an integral part of a company's customer value proposition.

Implementation of Customer Service

Customer service may be employed to generate such competitive advantage as a particular service proposition can be harder to copy for competitors.

The implementation of a particular customer service proposition must consider several elements of the organization, including

- culture
- hiring
- training

- incentives
- processes
- support technology

Competitive Advantage

A company may attempt to differentiate itself from its competition through the provision of better customer service. The consistent delivery of superior service requires the careful design and execution of a whole system of activities that includes people, technology, and processes.

Role of Technology

Technology has made available a wide range of customer service tools. They range from support websites and the ability to have live chats with technical staff to databases tracking individual customers' preferences, pattern of buying, payment methods etc., and tailoring products and service responses based on this advanced data. Specialist software that is designed for the tracking of service levels and for helping recognize areas for improvement are often integrated into other enterprise operational software tools such as ERP software.

Accountability

Customers tend to be more forgiving of organizations who acknowledge and apologize for their mistakes rather than denying them. Taking responsibility for mistakes and correcting them is considered an important aspect of good customer service.

12

Major Sectors of an Economy

PRIVATE SECTOR

The private sector of a nation's economy consists of all that is outside the state. It includes a variety of entities such as for-profit and non-profit enterprises, corporations, banks (other than central banks), any other non-governmental organizations, as well as individuals not employed by the state.

Capitalism revolves primarily around the private sector controlling industry.

PUBLIC SECTOR

The public sector is the part of economic and administrative life that deals with the delivery of goods and services by and for the government, whether national, regional or local/ municipal.

Examples of public sector activity range from delivering social security, administering urban planning and organising national defences. The organization of the public sector (public ownership) can take several forms, including:

- Direct administration funded through taxation; the delivering organisation generally has no specific requirement to meet commercial success criteria, and production decisions are determined by government.
- Publicly owned corporations (in some contexts, especially manufacturing, "State-owned enterprises"); which differ from direct administration in that they have greater commercial freedoms and are expected to operate

according to commercial criteria, and production decisions are not generally taken by government (although goals may be set for them by government).

- Partial outsourcing (of the scale many businesses do, e.g. for IT services), is considered a public sector model.

A borderline form is:

- Complete outsourcing or contracting out, with a privately owned corporation delivering the entire service on behalf of government. This may be considered a mixture of private sector operations with public ownership of assets, although in some forms the private sector's control and/or risk is so great that the service may no longer be considered part of the public sector.

The decision about what are proper matters for the public sector as opposed to the private sector is probably the single most important dividing line among socialist, liberal, conservative, and libertarian political philosophy, with (broadly) socialists preferring greater state involvement, libertarians favoring minimal state involvement, and conservatives and liberals favouring state involvement in some aspects of the society but not others.

VOLUNTARY SECTOR

The voluntary sector of a nation's economy consists of those entities which are not for profit and yet, at the same time, are not agencies of the state-e.g. charities, volunteer community centres and religious organizations. They may, in some countries, be subject to state scrutiny if they wish to qualify for charitable status. In Japan since the 1980s, the third sector refers to joint corporations invested both by the public sector and private one.

Voluntary sector organisations form part of The Third Sector, which although still ill-defined, also includes organisations such as Co-Operatives, Trade Unions and Universities. In many countries there are also hybrid organisations which engage in social enterprise and which fall into the Third Sector categorisation. These are essentially not-for-profit bodies which have a profit generating arm to cover operational expenses.

The UK government sees the Third Sector as "the place between State and (the)private sector": see Cabinet Office-Office of the Third Sector Organisations within the Third Sector have social goals that are their main reason for being. The term 'voluntary sector' is restrictive to the extent that it excludes certain activities such as social enterprise, and social entrepreneurship, both of which are ways of addressing social problems.

PRIVATIZATION

Privatization (alternately "denationalization" or "disinvestment") is the transfer of property or responsibility from the public sector (government) to the private sector (business). The term can refer to partial or complete transfer of any property or responsibility held by government. A similar transfer in the opposite direction could be referred to the nationalization or municipalization of some property or responsibility.

The term also has been used to describe an unrelated, nongovernmental interaction involving the buyout, by the majority owner, of all shares of a holding company's stock-privatizing a publicly traded stock.

TYPES OF PRIVATIZATION

There are three main methods of privatization:

- Share Issue privatization (SIP)-selling shares on the stock market
- Asset Sale privatization-selling the entire firm or part of it to a strategic investor, usually by auction or using Treuhand model
- Voucher privatization-shares of ownership are distributed to all citizens, usually for free or at a very low price.

Share issue privatization is the most common type.

Share issue can broaden and deepen domestic capital markets, boosting liquidity and potentially economic growth, but if the capital markets are insufficiently developed it may be difficult to find enough buyers, and transaction costs (eg underpricing required) may be higher. For this reason, many some governments elect for listings in the more developed and liquid markets such as Euronext, the London, New York or Hong Kong Stock Exchanges are popular because they are highly developed and sophisticated.

As a result of higher political and currency risk deterring foreign investors, asset sales are more common in developing countries.

Voucher privatization has mainly been used in the transition economies of Central and Eastern Europe-countries such as Russia, Poland and Czechoslovakia (Czech Republic and Slovakia)

A very substantial benefit to share or asset sale privatizations is that bidders compete to offer the state the highest price, creating revenues for the state to redistribute in addition to new tax revenue. Voucher privatisations, on the other hand, would be a genuine return of the assets into the hands of the general population, and create a real sense of participation and inclusion. Vouchers, like all other private property, could then be sold on if preferred.

Pro-Privatization and Anti-Privatization Arguments

Pro-Privatization

Proponents of privatization believe that private market actors can more efficiently deliver many goods or service than government due to free market competition. In general, over time this will lead to lower prices, improved quality, more choices, less corruption, less red tape, and quicker delivery. Many proponents do not argue that everything should be privatized; the existence of problems such as market failures and natural monopolies may limit this. However, a small minority thinks that everything can be privatized, including the state itself.

The basic economic argument given for privatization is that governments have few incentives to ensure that the enterprises they own are well run. One problem is the lack of comparison in state monopolies. It is difficult to know if an enterprise if efficient or not without competitors to compare against. Another is that the central government administration, and the voters who elect them, have difficulty evaluating the efficeny of numerous and very different enterprises. A private owner, often specialising and gaining great knowledge about a certain industrial sector, can evaluate and then reward or punish the management in much fewer enterprises much more efficiently. Also, governments can raise money by taxation or simply printing money should revenues be insufficient, unlike a private owner.

It there are both private and state owned enterprises competing against each other, then the state owned may borrow money more cheaply from the debt markets than private enterprises, since the state owned enterprises are ulitmately backed by the taxation and printing press power of the state, gaining an unfair advantage.

Privatizing a non-profitable company which was state-owned may force the company to raise prices in order to become profitable. However, this would remove the need for the state to provide tax money in order to cover the losses.

- *Performance:* State-run industries tend to be bureaucratic. A political government may only be motivated to improve a function when its poor performance becomes politically sensitive, and such an improvement is easily reversed by another regime.
- *Improvements:* Conversely, the government may put off improvements due to political sensitivity and special interests-even in cases of companies that are run well and better serve their customers' needs.
- *Corruption:* A monopolized function is prone to corruption; decisions are made primarily for political reasons, personal gain of the decision-maker (i.e. "graft"), rather than economic ones.
- *Accountability:* Managers of privately owned companies are accountable to their owners/shareholders and to the consumer, and can only exist and thrive where needs are met.
- *Civil Liberty Concerns:* A company controlled by the State may have access to information or assets which

may be used against dissidents or any individuals who disagree with their policies.

- *Goals:* A political government tends to run an industry or company for political goals rather than economic ones.
- *Capital:* Privately held companies can more easily raise investment capital in the financial markets, investment decisions are governed by market interest rates. State-owned industries have to compete with demands from other government departments and special interests.
- *Security:* Governments have had the tendency to "bail out" poorly run businesses when, economically, it may be better to let the business fold, often due to the sensitivity of job losses.
- *Lack of Market Discipline:* Poorly managed state companies are insulated from the same discipline as private companies, which could go bankrupt, have their management removed, or be taken over by competitors.
- *Natural Monopolies:* The existence of natural monopolies does not mean that these sectors must be state owned. Governments can enact or are armed with anti-trust legislation and bodies to deal with anti-competitive behaviour of all companies public or private.
- *Concentration of Wealth:* Ownership of and profits from successful enterprises tend to be dispersed and diversified. The availability of more investment vehicles stimulates to capital markets and promotes job creation.
- *Political Influence:* Nationalized industries are prone to interference from politicians for political or populist reasons. Examples include making an industry buy supplies from local producers (when that may be more expensive than buying from abroad), forcing an industry to freeze its prices/fares to satisfy the electorate or control inflation, increasing its staffing to reduce unemployment, or moving its operations to marginal constituencies.
- *Profits:* Private companies make a profit by enticing consumers to buy their products in preference to their

competitors'. Private corporations exist to serve exactly the needs of their clients; their clients' propensity to pay is usually correlated with how well they serve the needs. Corporations of different sizes may target different market niches in order to focus on marginal groups and satisfy their demand.

Anti-Privatization

Opponents of privatization dispute the claims concerning the alleged lack of incentive for governments to ensure that the enterprises they own are well run, on the basis of the idea that governments are proxy owners answerable to the people. It is argued that a government which runs nationalized enterprises poorly will lose public support and votes, while a government which runs those enterprises well will gain public support and votes. Thus, democratic governments do have an incentive to maximize efficiency in nationalized companies, due to the pressure of future elections.

Opponents of certain privatizations believe certain parts of the social terrain should remain closed to market forces in order to protect them from the unpredictability and ruthlessness of the market (such as private prisons, basic health care, and basic education). Another view is that some of the utilities which government provides benefit society at large and are indirect and difficult to measure or unable to produce a profit, such as defense. Still another is that natural monopolies are by definition not subject to competition and better administrated by the state.

The controlling ethical issue in the anti-privatization perspective is the need for responsible stewardship of social support missions. Market interactions are all guided by self-interest, and successful actors in a healthy market must be committed to charging the maximum price that the market will bear. Privatization opponents believe that this model is not compatible with government missions for social support, whose primary aim is delivering affordability and quality of service to society.

Many privatization opponents also warn against the practice's inherent tendency toward corruption. As many areas which the government could provide are essentially profitless, the only way private companies could, to any degree, operate them would be through contracts or block payments. In these cases, the private firm's performance in a particular project would be removed from their performance, and embezzlement and dangerous cost cutting measures might be taken to maximize profits.

Some would also point out that privatizing certain functions of government might hamper coordination, and charge firms with specialized and limited capabilities to perform functions which they are not suited for. In rebuilding a war torn nation's infrastructure, for example, a private firm would, in order to provide security, either have to hire security, which would be both necessarily limited and complicate their functions, or coordinate with government, which, due to a lack of command structure shared between firm and government, might be difficult. A government agency, on the other hand, would have the entire military of a nation to draw upon for security, whose chain of command is clearly defined. Opponents would say that this is a false assertion: numerous books refer to poor organisation between government departments (for example the Hurricane Katrina incident).

Furthermore, opponents of privatization argue that it is undesirable to transfer state-owned assets into private hands for the following reasons:

- *Performance:* A democratically elected government is accountable to the people through a legislature, Congress or Parliament, and is motivated to safeguarding the assets of the nation. The profit motive may be subordinated to social objectives.
- *Improvements:* the government is motivated to performance improvements as well run businesses contribute to the State's revenues.
- *Corruption:* Government ministers and Civil servants are bound to uphold the highest ethical standards, and standards of probity are guaranteed through codes of conduct and declarations of interest. However, the selling process could lack transparency, allowing the purchaser and civil servants controlling the sale to gain personally.

- *Accountability:* The public does not have any control or oversight of private companies.
- *Civil Liberty Concerns:* A democratically elected government is accountable to the people through Parliament, and can intervene when civil liberties are threatened.
- *Goals:*The government may seek use state companies as instruments to further social goals for the benefit of the nation as a whole.
- *Capital:* Governments can raise money in the financial markets most cheaply to re-lend to State-owned enterprises.
- *Lack of Market Discipline:* Governments have chosen to keep certain companies/industries under public ownership because of their strategic importance or sensitive nature.
- *Cuts in Essential Services:* If a government-owned company providing an essential service (such as water supply) to all citizens is privatized, its new owner(s) could lead to the abandoning of the social obligation to those who are less able to pay, or to regions where this service is unprofitable.
- *Natural Monopolies:* Privatization will not result in true competition if a natural monopoly exists.
- *Concentration of Wealth:* Profits from successful enterprises end up in private, often foreign, hands instead of being available for the common good.
- *Political Influence:* Governments may more easily exert pressure on state-owned firms to help implementing Government policy.
- *Downsizing:* Private companies often face a conflict between profitability and service levels, and could over-react to short-term events. A state-owned company might have a longer-term view, and thus be less likely to cut back on maintenance or staff costs, training etc, to stem short term losses.

- *Profit:* Private companies do not have any goal other than to maximize profits. A private company will serve the needs of those who are most willing (and able) to pay, as opposed to the needs of the majority, and are thus anti-democratic

Outcomes

Nellis and Kikeri have shown that in competitive industries with well-informed consumers, privatization consistently improves efficiency. Such efficiency gains mean a one-off increase in GDP, but through improved incentives to innovate and reduce costs also tend to raise the rate of economic growth. The type of industries to which this generally applies include manufacturing and retailing. Although typically there are social costs associated with these efficiency gains, many economists argue that these can be dealt with by appropriate government support through redistribution and perhaps retraining.

In sectors that are natural monopolies or public services, the results of privatization are much more mixed, as a private monopoly behaves much the same as a public one in liberal economic theory. In general, if the performance of an existing public sector operation is sufficiently bad, privatization (or threat thereof) has been known to improve matters. Indeed, Megginson & Netter showed that the greatest gains from privatization are achieved in the pre-privatization period as reforms are made to prepare for the transfer to private hands. Changes may include, inter alia, the imposition of related reforms such as greater transparency and accountability of management, improved internal controls, regulatory systems, and better financing, rather than privatization itself.

Regarding political corruption, it is a controversial issue whether the size of the public sector per se results in corruption. The Nordic countries have low corruption but large public sectors. However, these countries score high on the Ease of Doing Business Index, due to good and often simple regulations, and for political rights and civil liberites, showing high government accountability and transparency. One should also notice the successful, corruption-free privatizations and restructuring of government enterprises in the Nordic countries.

For example, dismantling telecommunications monopolies have resulted in several new players entering the market and intense competetion with price and service.

Also regarding corruption, the sales themselves give a large opportunity for grand corruption. Privatizations in Russia and Latin America were accompanied by large scale corruption during the sale of the state owned companies. Those with political connections unfairly gained large wealth, which has discredited privatization in these regions. While media have reported widely the grand corruption that accompanied the sales, studies have argued that in addition to increased operating efficiency, daily petty corruption is, or would be, larger without privatization, and that corruption is more prevalent in non-privatized sectors. Furthermore, there is evidence to suggest that extralegal and unofficial activities are more prevalent in countries that privatized less.

ALTERNATIVES TO PRIVATIZATION

Municipalization

Transferring control of a nationalized business to municipal government is an alternative sometimes proposed to privatization.

Sub-contracting

It is possible that national services may sub-contract or out-source functions to private enterprises. A notable example of this is in the United Kingdom, where many municipalities have contracted out their garbage collection or administration of parking fines by tender to private companies.

In addition, the British government is debating the possibility of involving the private sector more in the workings of the NHS, principally by referring patients to private surgeries to ease the load on existing NHS human resources, and covering the cost of this.

Part Ownership

An enterprise may be privatized, with a number of shares in the company being retained by the state. This is a particularly notable phenomenon in Germany, where the state owns around a third of Deutsche Telekom. As of 2005, the state of North Rhine-Westphalia is also planning to buy shares in the energy company E.ON in an attempt to control spiralling costs.

Whilst partial privatization could be an alternative, it is more often a stepping stone to full privatization. It can offer the business a smoother transition period during which it can gradually adjust to market competition. Some state-owned companies are so large that there is the risk of sucking liquidity from the rest of the market, even in the most liquid marketplaces, and thus must be sold off bit by bit. The first tranche of a multi-step privatization would also in the first instance establish a valuation for the enterprise to mitigate complaints of under-pricing.

NOTABLE PRIVATIZATIONS

Privatization programmes have been undertaken in many countries across the world, falling into three major groups. The first is privatization programmes conducted by transition economies in Central and Eastern Europe after 1989 in the process of instituting a market economy. The second is privatization programmes carried out in developing countries under the influence of international financial institutions such as the World Bank and IMF. The third is privatization programmes carried out by developed country governments, the most comprehensive probably being those of New Zealand and the United Kingdom in the 1980s and 1990s.

Privatization has been notably successful in telecommunications in Europe because genuine competition has arisen: the former state-owned enterprises lost their monopolies due to legislation and technological change, competitors entered the market, and prices for broadband access and telephone calls fell dramatically.

One example of failed privatizations of natural monopolies may be the privatization of British railways. The UK railroad track-owning company Railtrack, in effect a natural monopoly, has been effectively repossessed by the British government. Train operation remains in the hands of private operators with franchises awarded by the Department for Transport (except for Merseyrail the franchise of which is awarded by Merseyside Passenger Transport Executive).

There are various precedents in history which some would claim as examples in which improper privatization, or the failure of government to conduct certain functions, caused various complications.

1. In the reconstruction of Iraq, the government decided to contract out many different reconstruction functions to private firms. Shortly thereafter, those firms have been accused of cutting corners and being generally ineffective in reconstructing the country. Halliburton, in particular, was accused of, among other things, skimping on the cost of providing meals to soldiers. Various other complaints include the lagging reconstruction of water and electricity utilities, and providing defective equipment to soldiers.
2. Many, such as Dick Polman of The Philadelphia Inquirer, noted that prior to Hurricane Katrina, the government had "privatized many of FEMA's basic functions". The uncoordinated action between private emergency relief agencies, as well as the military (which would often turn back relief trucks) resulting in the poor response to the storm that many would claim was a result of this privatization.

Negative Popular Responses to Privatization

Privatization proposals in key public service sectors such as water and electricity are in many cases strongly opposed by opposition political parties and civil society groups. Usually campaigns involve demonstrations and political means; sometimes they may become violent (eg Cochabamba Riots of 2000 in Bolivia; Arequipa, Peru, June 2002). Opposition is often strongly supported by trade unions. Opposition is usually strongest to water privatization-as well as Cochabamba (2000), recent examples include Ghana and Uruguay (2004). In the latter case a civil-society-initiated referendum banning water privatization was passed in October 2004.

13

International Trade

International trade is the exchange of goods and services across international boundaries or territories. In most countries, it represents a significant share of GDP. While international trade has been present throughout much of history, its economic, social, and political importance has been on the rise in recent centuries. Industrialization, advanced transportation, globalization, multinational corporations, and outsourcing are all having a major impact. Increasig international trade is the primary meaning of "globalization".

International trade is also a branch of economics, which, together with international finance, forms the larger branch of international economics.

INTERNATIONAL TRADE THEORY

Several different models have been proposed to predict patterns of trade and to analyze the effects of trade policies such as tariffs.

Ricardian Model

The Ricardian model focuses on comparative advantage and is perhaps the most important concept in international trade theory. In a Ricardian model, countries specialize in producing what they produce best. Unlike other models, the Ricardian framework predicts that countries will fully specialize instead of producing a broad array of goods. Also, the Ricardian model does not directly consider factor endowments, such as the relative amounts of labor and capital within a country.

Heckscher-Ohlin Model

The Heckscher-Ohlin model was produced as an alternative to the Ricardian model of basic comparative advantage. Despite its greater complexity it did not prove much more accurate in its predictions. However from a theoretical point of view it did provide an elegant solution by incorporating the neoclassical price mechanism into international trade theory.

The theory argues that the pattern of international trade is determined by differences in factor endowments. It predicts that countries will export those goods that make intensive use of locally abundant factors and will import goods that make intensive use of factors that are locally scarce. Empirical problems with the H-O model, known as the Leontief paradox, were exposed in empirical tests by Wassily Leontief who found that the United States tended to export labor intensive goods despite having a capital abundance.

Specific Factors

In this model, labour mobility between industries is possible while capital is immobile between industries in the short-run. The specific factors name refers to the given that in the short-run specific factors of production, such as physical capital, are not easily transferable between industries. The theory suggests that if there is an increase in the price of a good, the owners of the factor of production specific to that good will profit in real terms. Additionally, owners of opposing specific factors of production (i.e. labour and capital) are likely to have opposing agendas when lobbying for controls over immigration of labour. Conversely, both owners of capital and labour profit in real terms from an increase in the capital endowment. This model is ideal for particular industries. This model is ideal for understanding income distribution but awkward for discussing the pattern of trade.

Gravity Model

The Gravity model of trade presents a more empirical analysis of trading patterns rather than the more theoretical models discussed above. The gravity model, in its basic form, predicts trade based on the distance between countries and the interaction of the countries' economic sizes. The model mimics the Newtonian law of gravity which also considers distance and physical size between two objects. The model has been proven to be empirically strong through econometric analysis. Other factors such as income level, diplomatic relationships between countries, and trade policies are also included in expanded versions of the model.

REGULATION OF INTERNATIONAL TRADE

Traditionally trade was regulated through bilateral treaties between two nations. For centuries under the belief in Mercantilism most nations had high tariffs and many restrictions on international trade. In the 19th century, especially in Britain, a belief in free trade became paramount and this view has dominated thinking among western nations for most of the time since then. In the years since the Second World War multilateral treaties like the GATT and World Trade Organization have attempted to create a globally regulated trade structure.

Free trade is usually most strongly supported by the most economically powerful nations in the world, though they often engage in selective protectionism for those industries which are politically important domestically, such as the protective tariffs applied to agriculture and textiles by the United States and Europe. The Netherlands and the United Kingdom were both strong advocates of free trade when they were economically dominant, today the United States, the United Kingdom, Australia and Japan are its greatest proponents. However, many other countries (such as India, China and Russia) are increasingly becoming advocates of free trade as they become more economically powerful themselves. As tariff levels fall there is also an increasing willingness to negotiate non tariff measures, including foreign direct investment, procurement and trade facilitation. The latter looks at the transaction cost associated with meeting trade and customs procedures.

Traditionally agricultural interests are usually in favour of free trade while manufacturing sectors often support protectionism. This has changed somewhat in recent years, however. In fact, agricultural lobbies, particularly in the United

States, Europe and Japan, are chiefly responsible for particular rules in the major international trade treaties which allow for more protectionist measures in agriculture than for most other goods and services. During recessions there is often strong domestic pressure to increase tariffs to protect domestic industries. This occurred around the world during the Great Depression leading to a collapse in world trade that many believe seriously deepened the depression.

The regulation of international trade is done through the World Trade Organization at the global level, and through several other regional arrangements such as MERCOSUR in South America, NAFTA between the United States, Canada and Mexico, and the European Union between 27 independent states. The 2005 Buenos Aires talks on the planned establishment of the Free Trade Area of the Americas (FTAA) failed largely due to opposition from the populations of Latin American nations. Similar agreements such as the MAI (Multilateral Agreement on Investment) have also failed in recent years.

RISKS IN INTERNATIONAL TRADE

The risks that exist in international trade can be divided into two major groups:

Economic Risks

- Risk of insolvency of the buyer,
- Risk of protracted default-the failure of the buyer to pay the amount due within six months after the due date
- Risk of non-acceptance
- Surrendering economic sovereignty

Political Risks

- Risk of cancellation or non-renewal of export or import licences
- War risks
- Risk of expropriation or confiscation of the importer's company

- Risk of the imposition of an import ban after the shipment of the goods
- Transfer risk-imposition of exchange controls by the importer's country or foreign currency shortages
- Surrendering political sovereignty

FOREIGN DIRECT INVESTMENT

Foreign direct investment (FDI) is defined as a long-term investment by a foreign direct investor in an enterprise resident in an economy other than that in which the foreign direct investor is based. The FDI relationship, consists of a parent enterprise and a foreign affiliate which together form a transnational corporation (TNC). In order to qualify as FDI the investment must afford the parent enterprise control over its foreign affiliate. The UN defines control in this case as owning 10% or more of the ordinary shares or voting power of an incorporated firm or its equivalent for an unincorporated firm.

History

Types of FDI

- *Greenfield Investment:* Direct investment in new facilities or the expansion of existing facilities. Greenfield investments are the primary target of a host nation's promotional efforts because they create new production capacity and jobs, transfer technology and know-how, and can lead to linkages to the global marketplace. However, it often does this by crowding out local industry; multinationals are able to produce goods more cheaply (because of advanced technology and efficient processes) and uses up resources (labor, intermediate goods, etc). Another downside of greenfield investment is that profits from production do not feed back into the local economy, but instead to the multinational's home economy. This is in contrast to local industries whose profits flow back into the domestic economy to promote growth.
- *Mergers and Acquisitions:* Transfers of existing assets from local firms to foreign firms takes place; the primary

type of FDI. Cross-border mergers occur when the assets and operation of firms from different countries are combined to establish a new legal entity. Cross-border acquisitions occur when the control of assets and operations is transferred from a local to a foreign company, with the local company becoming an affiliate of the foreign company. Unlike greenfield investment, acquisitions provide no long term benefits to the local economy--even in most deals the owners of the local firm are paid in stock from the acquiring firm, meaning that the money from the sale could never reach the local economy. Nevertheless, mergers and acquisitions are a significant form of FDI and until around 1997, accounted for nearly 90% of the FDI flow into the United States.

- *Horizontal Foreign Direct Investment:* Investment in the same industry abroad as a firm operates in at home.
- *Vertical Foreign Direct Investment:* Takes two forms:
  (1) *Backward Vertical FDI:* Where an industry abroad provides inputs for a firm's domestic production process
  (2) *Forward Vertical FDI:* In which an industry abroad sells the outputs of a firm's domestic production

Types of FDI based on the Motives of the Investing Firm

FDI can also be categorized based on the motive behind the investment from the perspective of the investing firm:

- *Resource Seeking:* Investments which seek to acquire factors of production that are more efficient than those obtainable in the home economy of the firm. In some cases, these resources may not be available in the home economy at all (e.g. cheap labor and natural resources). This typifies FDI into developing countries, for example seeking natural resources in the Middle East and Africa, or cheap labor in Southeast Asia and Eastern Europe.
- *Market Seeking:* Investments which aim at either penetrating new markets or maintaining existing ones. FDI of this kind may also be employed as defensive strategy; it is argued that businesses are more likely to

be pushed towards this type of investment out of fear of losing a market rather than discovering a new one. This type of FDI can be characterized by the foreign Mergers and Acquisitions in the 1980's by Accounting, Advertising and Law firms.

- *Efficiency Seeking:* Investments which firms hope will increase their efficiency by exploiting the benefits of economies of scale and scope, and also those of common ownership. It is suggested that this type of FDI comes after either resource or market seeking investments have been realized, with the expectation that it further increases the profitability of the firm. Typically, this type of FDI is mostly widely practiced between developed economies; especially those within closely integrated markets (e.g. the EU).

ECONOMIC INEQUALITY

Economic inequality refers to disparities in the distribution of economic assets and income. The term typically refers to inequality among individuals and groups within a society, but can also refer to inequality among nations. There is debate as to what equality should mean. Some think in terms of equality of opportunity and others in terms of equality of outcome.

Economic inequality has existed in a wide range of societies and historical periods; its nature, cause and importance are open to broad debate. A country's economic structure or system (for example, capitalism or socialism), ongoing or past wars, and differences in individuals' abilities to create wealth are all involved in the creation of economic inequality. Numerical indexes measuring economic inequality among individuals compares the well-being and numbers of the rich with those of the poor. Inequality is most often measured using the Gini coefficient (defined based on the Lorenz curve).

Economic inequality among different individuals or social groups is best measured within a single country. This is because country-specific factors tend to obscure inter-country comparisons of individuals' incomes. A single nation will have more or less inequality depending on the social and economic structure of that country.

Causes of Inequality

There are many reasons for economic inequality within societies. These causes are often inter-related, non-linear, and complex. Acknowledged factors that impact economic inequality include the labour market, innate ability, education, race, gender, culture, wealth condensation, and development patterns.

The Labour Market

A major cause of economic inequality within modern market economies is the determination of wages by the market. In this view, inequality is caused by the differences in the supply and demand for different types of work.

A job where there are many willing workers (high supply) but only a small number of positions (low demand) will result in a low wage for that job. This is because competition between workers drives down the wage. An example of this would be low-skill jobs such as dish-washing or customer service. Because of the persistence of unemployment in market economies and the fact that these jobs require very little skill results in a very high supply of willing workers. Contrary wise, there is a limited number of jobs available. Competition amongst workers tend to drive down the wage since if any one worker demands a higher wage the employer can simply hire another employee at an equally low wage.

A job where there are few willing workers (low supply) but a large demand for the skills these workers have will results in high wages for that job. This is because competition between employers will drive up the wage. An example of this would be high-skill jobs such as engineers, professional athletes, or capable CEOs. Competition amongst employers tend to drive up wages since if any one employer demands a low wage, the worker can simply quit and easily find a new job at a higher wage.

While the above examples tend to identify skill with high demand and wages, this is not necessarily the case. For example, highly skilled computer programmers in western countries have seen their wages suppressed by competition from computer programmers in India who are willing to accept a lower wage.

The final results amongst these supply and demand interactions is a gradation of different wages representing income inequality within society.

Innate Ability

Many people believe that there is a correlation between differences in innate ability, such as intelligence, strength, or charisma, and an individual's wealth. Relating these innate abilities back to the labour market suggests that such abilities are in high demand relative to their supply and hence play a large role in increasing the wage of those who have them. Contrariwise, such innate abilities might also affect an individuals ability to operate within society in general, regardless of the labour market.

Various studies have been conducted on the correlation between IQ scores and wealth income. The book titled "IQ and the Wealth of Nations", written by Dr. Richard Lynn, examines this relationship with limited success; other peer-reviewed research papers have also been criticised harshly. Without further research on the topic, incorporating statistical models that are universally accepted, it is fairly difficult to come towards an objective conclusion regarding any relationship between intelligence and wealth or income.

Education

One important factor in the creation of inequality is variation in individuals' access to education. Education, especially in an area where there is a high demand for workers, creates high wages for those with this education. Contrariwise, those who are unable to afford an education generally receive much lower wages.

Many economists believe that a major reason the world has experienced increasing levels of inequality since the 1980s is an increase in the demand for highly skilled workers in high tech industries. They believe that this has resulted in an increase in wages for those with an education, but has not increased the wages of those without an education, leading to greater inequality.

Gender, Race, and Culture

The existence of different genders, races and cultures within a society is also thought to contribute to economic inequality. Scientists such as Richard Lynn argue that there are innate group differences in ability that are partially responsible for producing race and gender group differences in wealth.

The idea of the gender gap tries to explain differences in income between genders. Culture and religion are thought to play a role in creating inequality by either encouraging or discouraging wealth-acquiring behavior, and by providing a basis for discrimination. In many countries individuals belonging to certain racial and ethnic minorities are more likely to be poor. Proposed causes include cultural differences amongst different races, an educational achievement gap, and racism.

Development Patterns

Simon Kuznets argued that levels of economic inequality are in large part the result of stages of development. Kuznets saw a curve-like relationship between level of income and inequality, now known as Kuznets curve. According to Kuznet, countries with low levels of development have relatively equal distributions of wealth. As a country develops, it acquires more capital, which leads to the owners of this capital having more wealth and income and introducing inequality. Eventually, through various possible redistribution mechanisms such as trickle down effects and social welfare programs, more developed countries move back to lower levels of inequality. Kuznets demonstrated this relationship using cross-sectional data. However, more recent testing of this theory with superior panel data has shown it to be very weak.

Wealth Condensation

Wealth condensation is a theoretical process by which, under certain conditions, newly-created wealth concentrates in the possession of already-wealthy individuals or entities. This is reflected in the common saying 'the rich get richer and the poor get poorer'. According to this theory, those who already hold wealth have the means to invest in new sources of creating wealth or to otherwise leverage the accumulation of wealth, thus are the beneficiaries of the new wealth. Over time, wealth condensation can significantly contribute to the persistence of inequality within society. As an example of wealth condensation, truck drivers who own their own trucks often make more money than those who do not, since the owner of a truck can escape the rent charged to drivers by owners (even taking into account maintenance and other costs). Hence, a truck driver who has wealth to begin with can afford to buy his own truck in order to make more money. A truck driver who does not own his own truck makes a lesser wage and is therefore stuck in a Catch-22, unable to buy his own truck to increase his income.

As another example of wealth condensation, savings from the upper-income groups tend to accumulate much faster than saving from the lower-income groups. Upper-income groups can save a significant portion of their incomes. On the other hand, lower-income groups barely make enough to cover their consumptions, hence only capable of saving a fraction of their incomes or even none. Assuming both groups earn the same yield rate on their savings, the return on upper-income groups' savings are much greater than the lower-income groups' savings because upper-income groups have a much larger base. Related to wealth condensation are the effects of intergenerational inequality. The rich tend to provide their offspring with a better education, increasing their chances of achieving a high income. Furthermore, the wealthy often leave their offspring with a hefty inheritance, jump-starting the process of wealth condensation for the next generation.

Mitigating Factors

There are many factors that tend to constrain the amount of economic inequality within society. These factors may be divided into two general classes: government sponsored, and market driven. The relative merits and effectiveness of each approach is a subject of heated debate. Proponents of government sponsored approaches to reducing economic inequality generally believe that economic inequality represents a fundamental injustice, and that it is the right and duty of the government to correct this injustice. Government sponsored approaches to reducing economic inequality include:

- Mass education-to increase the supply of skilled labor and decrease the wage of skilled labor to reduce income inequality;
- Progressive taxation, where the rich are taxed more than the poor-to reduce the amount of income inequality in society.
- Minimum wage legislation-to raise the income of the poorest working group.
- The Nationalization or subsidization of essential goods and services such as food, healthcare, education, and housing-to reduce the amount of inequality in society-by providing goods and services that everyone needs cheaply or freely, governments can effectively increase the disposable income of the poorer members of society.

Proponents of free markets do not generally see economic inequality in a free market as fundamentally unjust. Market-driven reductions in economic inequality are therefore incidental to economic freedom. Nevertheless there are some market forces which work to reduce economic inequality:

- In a market-driven economy, too much economic disparity could generate pressure for its own removal. In an extreme example, if one person owned everything, that person would immediately (in a market economy) have to hire people to maintain their property, and that person's wealth would immediately begin to dissipate. (García-Peñalosa 2006)
- By a concept known as the "decreasing marginal utility of wealth", a wealthy person will tend not to value their last dollar as much as a poor person, since a poor person's dollars are more likely to be spent for essentials. This could tend to move wealth from the rich to the poor. A derogatory term for this is the "trickle down effect".

Effects of Inequality

Social Cohesion

Research has shown a clear link between income inequality and social cohesion. In more equal societies, people are much more likely to trust each other, measures of social capital suggest greater community involvement, and homicide rates are consistently lower.

One of the earliest writers to note the link between economic equality and social cohesion was Alexis de Tocqueville in his Democracy in America. Writing in 1831:

Among the new objects that attracted my attention during my stay in the United States, none struck me with greater force than the equality of conditions. I easily perceived the enormous influence that this primary fact exercises on the workings of society. It gives a particular direction to the public mind, a particular turn to the laws, new maxims to those who govern, and particular habits to the governed... It creates opinions, gives rise to sentiments, inspires customs, and modifies everything it does not produce... I kept finding that fact before me again and again as a central point to which all of my observations were leading.

In a 2002 paper, Eric Uslaner and Mitchell Brown showed that there is a high correlation between the amount of trust in society and the amount of income equality. They did this by comparing results from the question "would others take advantage of you if they got the chance?" in U.S General Social Survey and others with statistics on income inequality.

Robert Putnam, professor of political science at Harvard, established links between social capital and economic inequality. His most important studies (Putnam, Leonardi, and Nanetti 1993, Putnam 2000) established these links in both the United States and in Italy. On the relationship of inequality and involvement in community he says:

Community and equality are mutually reinforcing... Social capital and economic inequality moved in tandem through most of the twentieth century. In terms of the distribution of wealth and income, America in the 1950s and 1960s was more egalitarian than it had been in more than a century... Those same decades were also the high point of social connectedness and civic engagement. Record highs in equality and social capital coincided. Conversely, the last third of the twentieth century was a time of growing inequality and eroding social capital... The timing of the two trends is striking: somewhere around 1965-70 America reversed course and started becoming both less just economically and less well connected socially and politically. (Putnam 2000 pp 359)

In addition to affecting levels of trust and civic engagement, inequality in society has also shown to be highly correlated with crime rates. Most studies looking into the relationship between crime and inequality have concentrated on homicides-since homicides are almost identically defined across all nations and jurisdictions. There have been over fifty studies showing tendencies for violence to be more common in societies where income differences are larger. Research has been conducted comparing developed countries with undeveloped countries, as well as studying areas within countries. Daly et al. 2001 found that among U.S States and Canadian Provinces there is a ten-fold difference in homicide rates related to inequality. They estimated that about half of all variation in homicide rates can be accounted for by differences in the amount of inequality in each province or state. Fajnzylber et al. (2002) found a similar relationship worldwide. Among comments in academic literature on the relationship between homicides and inequality are:

- The most consistent finding in cross-national research on homicides has been that of a positive association between income inequality and homicides. (Neapolitan 1999 pp 260)
- Economic inequality is positively and significantly related to rates of homicide despite an extensive list of conceptually relevant controls. The fact that this relationship is found with the most recent data and using a different measure of economic inequality from previous research, suggests that the finding is very robust. (Lee and Bankston 1999 pp 50)

Population Health

Recently, there has been increasing interest from epidemiologists on the subject of economic inequality and its relation to the health of populations. There is a very robust correlation between socioeconomic status and health. This correlation suggests that it is not only the poor who tend to be sick when everyone else is healthy, but that there is a continual gradient, from the top to the bottom of the socioeconomic ladder, relating status to health. This phenomenon is often called the "SES Gradient". Lower socioeconomic status has been linked to chronic stress, heart disease, ulcers, type 2 diabetes, rheumatoid arthritis, certain types of cancer, and premature aging.

There is debate regarding the cause of the SES Gradient. A number of researchers, see a definite link between economic status and mortality due to the greater economic resources of the wealthy, but they find little correlation due to social status differences.

Other researchers such as Richard Wilkinson, J. Lynch, and G.A. Kaplan have found that socioeconomic status strongly affects health even when controlling for economic resources and access to health care. Most famous for linking social status with health are the Whitehall studies-a series of studies conducted on civil servants in London. The studies found that although all civil servants in England have the same access to health care, there was a strong correlation between social status and health. The studies found that this relationship remained strong even when controlling for health-affecting habits such as exercise, smoking and drinking. Furthermore, it has been noted that no amount of medical attention will help decrease the likelihood of somcone getting type 2 diabetes or rheumatoid arthritis-yet both are more common among populations with lower socioeconomic status. Lastly, it has been found that amongst the wealthiest quarter of countries on earth (a set stretching from Luxembourg to Slovakia) there is no relation between a country's wealth and general population health-suggesting that past a certain level, absolute levels of wealth have little impact on population health, but relative levels within a country do.

The concept of psychosocial stress attempts to explain how psychosocial phenomena such as status and social stratification can lead to the many diseases associated with the SES Gradient. Higher levels of economic inequality tend to intensify social hierarchies and generally degrade the quality of social relations-leading to greater levels of stress and stress-related diseases. Richard Wilkinson found this to be true not only for the poorest members of society, but also for the wealthiest. Economic inequality is bad for everyone's health.

The effects of inequality on health are not limited to human populations. David H. Abbott at the Wisconsin National Primate Research Center found that among many primate species, less egalitarian social structures correlated with higher levels of stress hormones among socially subordinate individuals.

Utility, Economic Welfare, and Distributive Efficiency

Economic inequality is thought to reduce distributive efficiency within society. That is to say, inequality reduces the sum total of personal utility because of the decreasing marginal utility of wealth. For example, a house may provide less utility to a single millionaire as a summer home than it would to a homeless family of five. The marginal utility of wealth is lowest among the richest. In other words, an additional dollar spent by a poor person will go to things providing a great deal of utility to that person, such as basic necessities like food, water, and healthcare; meanwhile, an additional dollar spent by a much richer person will most likely go to things providing relatively less utility to that person, such as luxury items. From this standpoint, for any given amount of wealth in society, a society with more equality will have higher aggregate utility. Some studies (Layard 2003;Blanchard and Oswald 2000, 2003) have found evidence for this theory, noting that in societies where inequality is lower, population-wide satisfaction and happiness tend to be higher.

Economist Arthur Cecil Pigou discussed the impact of inequality in The Economics of Welfare. He wrote:

Nevertheless, it is evident that any transference of income from a relatively rich man to a relatively poor man of similar temperament, since it enables more intense wants, to be satisfied at the expense of less intense wants, must increase the aggregate sum of satisfaction. The old "law of diminishing utility" thus leads securely to the proposition: Any cause which increases the absolute share of real income in the hands of the poor, provided that it does not lead to a contraction in the size of the national dividend from any point of view, will, in general, increase economic welfare.

In addition to the argument based on diminishing marginal utility, Pigou makes a second argument that income generally benefits the rich by making them wealthier than other people, whereas the poor benefit in absolute terms. Pigou writes: Now the part played by comparative, as distinguished from absolute, income is likely to be small for incomes that only suffice to provide the necesaries and primary comforts of life, but to be large with large incomes. In other words, a larger proportion of the satisfaction yielded by the incomes of rich people comes from their relative, rather than from their absolute, amount. This part of it will not be destroyed if the incomes of all rich people are diminished together. The loss of economic welfare suffered by the rich when command over resources is transferred from them to the poor will, therefore, be substantially smaller relatively to the gain of economic welfare to the poor than a consideration of the law of diminishing utility taken by itself suggests.--Arthur Cecil Pigou in The Economics of Welfare

Schmidtz (2006) argues that maximizing the sum of individual utilities does not necessarily imply that the maximum social utility is achieved. For example: A society that takes Joe Rich's second unit of corn is taking that unit away from someone who... has nothing better to do than plant it and giving it to someone who... does have something better to do with it. That sounds good, but in the process, the society takes seed corn out of production and diverts it to food, thereby cannibalizing itself.

Economic Incentives

Many people accept inequality as a given, and argue that the prospect of greater material wealth provides incentives for competition and innovation within an economy.

Some modern economic theories, such as the neoclassical school, have suggested that a functioning economy requires a certain level of unemployment. These theories argue that unemployment benefits must be below the wage level to provide an incentive to work, thereby mandating inequality. Other theories, including socialism and Keynesianism, dispute this alleged positive role of unemployment. Many economists believe that one of the main reasons that inequality might induce economic incentive is because material wellbeing and conspicuous consumption are related to status. In this view, high stratification of income (high inequality) creates high amounts of social stratification, leading to greater competition for status. One of the first writers to note this relationship was Adam Smith who recognized "regard" as one of the major driving forces behind economic activity. From The Theory of Moral Sentiments in 1759:

What is the end of avarice and ambition, of the pursuit of wealth, of power, and pre-eminence? Is it to supply the necessities of nature? The wages of the meanest labourer can supply them... Why should those who have been educated in the higher ranks of life, regard it as worse than death, to be reduced to live, even without labour, upon the same simple fare with him, to dwell under the same lowly roof, and to be clothed in the same humble attire?

From whence, then, arises that emulation which runs through all the different ranks of men, and what are the advantages which we propose by that great purpose of human life which we call bettering our condition? To be observed, to be attended to, to be taken notice of with sympathy, complacency, and approbation, are all the advantages which we can propose to derive from it. It is the vanity, not the ease, or the pleasure, which interests us (Theory of Moral Sentiments, Part I, Section III, Chapter II).

Modern sociologists and economists such as Juliet Schor and Robert H. Frank have studied the extent to which economic activity is fueled by the ability of consumption to represent social status. Schor, in The Overspent American, argues that the increasing inequality during the 1980s and 1990s strongly accounts for increasing aspirations of income, increased consumption, decreased savings, and increased debt. In Luxury Fever Robert H. Frank argues that people's satisfaction with their income is much more strongly affected by how it compares with others than its absolute level.

ECONOMIC GROWTH

Several recent economists have investigated the relationship between inequality and economic growth using econometrics.

In their study for the World Institute for Development Economics Research, Giovanni Andrea Cornia and Julius Court (2001) reach policy conclusions as to the optimal distribution of income. They conclude that too much equality negatively impacts growth due to "incentive traps, free-riding, labour shirking, and high supervision costs". They also claim that high levels of inequality negatively impacts growth, due to "incentive traps, erosion of social cohesion, social conflicts, and uncertain property rights". They advocate for policies which put equality at the low end of this "efficient" range.

Robert Barro wrote a paper arguing that inequality reduces growth in poor countries and promotes growth in rich ones. A number of other researchers have derived conflicting results, some concluding there is a negative effect of inequality on growth and others a positive. Patrizio Pagano used Granger causality, a technique that can determine two way interaction between two variables, to attempt to explain these previous findings. Pagano's research suggested that inequality had a negative effect on growth while growth increased inequality. The two-way interaction largely explains the contradiction in past research.

PERSPECTIVES REGARDING ECONOMIC INEQUALITY

There are various schools of thought regarding economic inequality.

Marxism

Marxism favors an eventual communist society where distribution is based on an individual's needs rather than his ability to produce, social class, inheritance, or other such factors. In such a system inequality would be low or non-existent assuming everyone had the same "needs".

Liberalism

Classical liberals and libertarians generally do not take a stance on wealth inequality, but believe in equality under the law regardless of whether it leads to unequal wealth distribution. Ludwig von Mises explains: The liberal champions of equality under the law were fully aware of the fact that men are born unequal and that it is precisely their inequality that generates social cooperation and civilization. Equality under the law was in their opinion not designed to correct the inexorable facts of the universe and to make natural inequality disappear. It was, on the contrary, the device to secure for the whole of mankind the maximum of benefits it can derive from it. Henceforth no man-made institutions should prevent a man from attaining that station in which he can best serve his fellow citizens.

Libertarian Robert Nozick argued that government redistributes wealth by force (usually in the form of taxation), and that the ideal moral society would be one where all individuals are free from force. However, Nozick recognized that some modern economic inequalities were the result of forceful taking of property, and a certain amount of redistribution would be justified to compensate for this force but not because of the inequalities themselves. John Rawls argued in A Theory of Justice that inequalities in the distribution of wealth are only justified when they improve society as a whole, including the poorest members. Rawls does not discuss the full implications of his theory of justice. Some see Rawls's argument as a justification for capitalism since even the poorest members of society theoretically benefit from increased innovations under capitalism; others believe only a strong welfare state can satisfy Rawls's theory of justice.

Classical liberal Milton Friedman believed that if government action is taken in pursuit of economic equality that political freedom would suffer. In a famous quote, he said:

A society that puts equality before freedom will get neither. A society that puts freedom before equality will get a high degree of both.

Arguments based on Social Justice

Patrick Diamond and Anthony Giddens (professors of Economics and Sociology, respectively) hold that

pure meritocracy is incoherent because, without redistribution, one generation's successful individuals would become the next generation's embedded caste, hoarding the wealth they had accumulated.

They also state that social justice requires redistribution of high incomes and large concentrations of wealth in a way that spreads it more widely, in order to "recognise the contribution made by all sections of the community to building the nation's wealth." (Patrick Diamond and Anthony Giddens, 27 June 2005, New Statesman)

Claims Economic Inequality Weakens Societies

In most western democracies, the desire to eliminate or reduce economic inequality is generally associated with the political left. The main practical argument in favor of reduction is the idea that economic inequality reduces social cohesion and increases social unrest, thereby weakening the society.

There is evidence that this is true and it is intuitive, at least for small face-to-face groups of people. Alberto Alesina, Rafael Di Tella, and Robert MacCulloch find that inequality negatively affects happiness in Europe but not in the United States.

It has also been argued that economic inequality invariably translates to political inequality, which further aggravates the problem.

The main disagreement between the western democratic left and right, is basically a disagreement on the importance of each effect, and where the proper balance point should be. Both sides generally agree that the causes of economic inequality based on non-economic differences (race, gender, etc.) should be minimized. There is strong disagreement on how this minimization should be achieved.

Arguments that Inequality is not a Primary Concern

The acceptance of economic inequality is generally associated with the political right. One argument in favor of the acceptance of economic inequality is that, as long as the cause is mainly due to differences in behavior, the inequality provides incentives that push the society towards economically healthy and efficient behavior. Capitalists see orderly competition and individual initiative as crucial to economic prosperity and accordingly believe that economic freedom is more important than economic equality.

Another argument is that more inequality does not necessarily mean more poverty, and that although poverty is bad, inequality is not bad in itself. Thus, a policy can be considered good if it makes some wealthy people more wealthy without making anyone more poor, even though it increases the total amount of inequality.

A third argument is that capitalism, especially free market capitalism, results in voluntary transactions among parties. Since the transactions are voluntary, each party at least believes they benefit from the transaction. According to the subjective theory of value, both parties will indeed benefit the transaction (assuming there is no fraud or extortion involved).

14

Green Revolution

The term Green Revolution is used to describe the transformation of agriculture in many developing nations that led to significant increases in agricultural production between the 1940s and 1960s. This transformation occurred as the result of programs of agricultural research, extension, and infrastructural development largely funded by the Rockefeller Foundation, the Ford Foundation, and national governments. The term "Green Revolution" was first used in 1968 by former USAID director William Gaud, who stated, "[The rapid spread of modern wheat and rice varieties throughout Asia] and other developments in the field of agriculture contain the makings of a new revolution... I call it a Green Revolution based on the application of science and technology.

The Green Revolution has had major social and ecological impacts, which have drawn intense praise and equally intense criticism.

History

Green Revolution in Mexico

The Green Revolution began in 1943 with the establishment of the Office of Special Studies. The venture was a collaboration between the Rockefeller Foundation and the presidential administration of Camacho in Mexico. While Camacho's predecessor Cárdenas promoted peasant subsistence agriculture through policies of land reform, Camacho's primary goal for Mexican agriculture was to aid in the nation's industrial development and economic growth. US Vice President Henry Wallace, who was instrumental in convincing the Rockefeller

Foundation to work with the Mexican government in agricultural development, saw Camacho's ambitions as beneficial to US economic and military interests.

J. George Harrar, who would later become president of the Rockefeller Foundation, headed the Office of Special Studies. Its lead scientists included Norman Borlaug, Edwin Wellhausen, and William Colwell. Researchers from both the United States and Mexico were involved in this program. The main initiative of the Office was the development of high-yielding maize and wheat varieties. Borlaug received the 1970 Nobel Peace Prize for his work on wheat breeding.

The Mexican national government invested heavily in rural infrastructure development, and the adoption of new seed varieties became widespread. Mexico became self-sufficient in wheat production by 1951 and began to export wheat thereafter.

INTERNATIONAL SPREAD OF THE GREEN REVOLUTION

With the experience of agricultural development judged as a success by many of the powerholders involved, the Rockefeller Foundation sought to spread the Green Revolution to other nations. The Office of Special Studies in Mexico became an informal international research institution in 1959, and in 1963 it formally became CIMMYT (The International Maize and Wheat Improvement Center).

The second nation to which the Green Revolution spread was India. The Ford Foundation had a presence in the nation, and their social scientists had decided that the technological development of agriculture was important to the future of India. At the same time Chidambaram Subramaniam, the former Indian Minister of Steel and Mines, became Minister of Food and Agriculture. The Foundation and Indian government collaborated to import a huge amount of wheat seed from CIMMYT. India then began its own Green Revolution program of plant breeding, irrigation development, and financing of agrochemicals. By the late 1970s, the Green Revolution raised rice yields in India by 30 percent and bought India the vital time to curb its population growth without suffering a recurrence of the devastating famines of the 1940s.

The Rockefeller and Ford Foundation jointly established IRRI (The International Rice Research Institute) in the Philippines in 1961. HYVs (high yielding varieties) spread throughout that country, Indonesia, Pakistan, Sri Lanka, and other non-Soviet bloc countries throughout Latin American, Asia, and North Africa. USAID became involved in subsidizing rural infrastructure development and fertilizer shipments.

AGRICULTURAL PRODUCTION AND FOOD SECURITY

Technologies

The projects within the Green Revolution spread technologies that had already existed, but had not been widely used outside of industrialized nations. These technologies included pesticides, irrigation projects, and synthetic nitrogen fertilizer.

The novel technological development of the Green Revolution was the production of what some referred to as "miracle seeds.". Scientists created strains of maize, wheat, and rice that are generally referred to as HYVs or "high yielding varieties." HYVs have an increased nitrogen-absorbing potential compared to other varieties. Since cereals that absorbed extra nitrogen would typically lodge, or fall over before harvest, semi-dwarfing genes were bred into their genomes. Norin 10 wheat, a variety developed by Orville Vogel from Japanese dwarf wheat varieties, was instrumental in developing Green Revolution wheat cultivars. IR8, the first widely implemented HYV rice to be developed by IRRI, was created through a cross between an Indonesian variety named "Peta" and a Chinese variety named "Dee Geo Woo Gen."

With the availability of molecular genetics in Arabidopsis and rice the mutant genes responsible (reduced height(rht), gibberellin insensitive (gai1) and slender rice (slr1)) have been cloned and identified as cellular signalling components of gibberellic acid, a phytohormone involved in regulating stem growth via its effect on cell division. Stem growth in the mutant background is significantly reduced leading to the dwarf phenotype. Photosynthetic investment in the stem is reduced dramatically as the shorter plants are inherently more stable mechanically. Assimilates become redirected to grain production, amplifying in particular the effect of chemical fertilisers on commercial yield.

HVs significantly outperform traditional varieties in the presence of adequate irrigation, pesticides, and fertilizers. In the absence of these inputs, traditional varieties may outperform HYVs. One criticism of HYVs is that they were developed as F1 hybrids, meaning they need to be purchased by a farmer every season rather than saved from previous seasons, thus increasing a farmer's cost of production.

Production Increases

Cereal production more than doubled in developing nations between the years 1961-1985 Yields of rice, maize, and wheat increased steadily during that period. The production increases can be attributed roughly equally to irrigation, fertilizer, and seed development, at least in the case of Asian rice.

Some, however, have challenged the purported production increases of Green Revolution agriculture. Miguel A. Altieri, for example, writes that the comparison between traditional systems of agriculture and Green Revolution has been unfair, because Green Revolution agriculture produces monocultures of cereal grains, while traditional agriculture usually incorporates polycultures. Additionally, some traditional systems of agriculture that were displaced by the Green Revolution such as the chinampas in Mexico or raised-field rice farming in Asia are known to be very highly-productive.

Effects on Food Security

The effects of the Green Revolution on global food security are difficult to understand because of the complexities involved in food systems.

The major purported achievement of the Green Revolution has been that the production increases have helped to avoid widespread famine. It is also often claimed that Green Revolution agriculture is responsible for feeding billions of people. These assertions generally assume some variation of the Malthusian principle of population. Malthusianism has been evident throughout the history of the Green Revolution. The team sent to survey Mexican agriculture in 1941 for the

Rockefeller Foundation cited the high birth rate and relative inadequacy of its agriculture as a cause for concern. In 1959 the Ford Foundation carried out a study in India that stated the nation's population would outstrip its food supply by 1966, although validity of its methodology was a subject of criticism. At Borlaug's Nobel acceptance speech he stated, "...we are dealing with two opposing forces, the scientific power of food production and the biologic power of human reproduction."

The world population has grown by about four billion since the beginning of the Green Revolution and most believe that, without the Revolution, there would be yet greater famine and malnutrition than the UN presently attributes to the planet Earth (approximately 850 million people suffering from chronic malnutrition in 2005). The average person in the developing world consumes about 25% more calories per day now than before the Green Revolution.

Increasing food production however is not synonymous with increasing food security, and is only part of a larger equation. For example, Amartya Sen's work has found that large historic famines have not been caused by decreases in food supply, but by socioeconomic dynamics and a failure of public action. There are several claims about how the Green Revolution may have decreased food security for some people. One such claim involves the shift of subsistence-oriented cropland to cropland oriented towards production of grain for export and/or animal feed. For example, the Green Revolution replaced much of the land used for pulses that fed Indian peasants for wheat, which did not make up a large portion of the peasant diet. Also, the pesticides involved in rice production eliminated fish and weedy green vegetables from the diets of Asian rice farmers.

Social Changes

Political Impacts

There is a significant amount of evidence suggesting that the Green Revolution had the effect of weakening socialist movements in many nations. In countries like India, Mexico, and the Philippines, technological solutions were sought as an alternative to expanding agrarian reform initiatives, the latter of which were often linked to socialist politics.

Socioeconomic Impacts

The transition from traditional agriculture in which inputs were generated on-farm to Green Revolution agriculture, which required the purchase of inputs, lead to the widespread establishment of rural credit institutions. Smaller farmers often went into debt, which in many cases result in a loss of rights to their farmland. The increased level of mechanization on larger farms made possible by the Green Revolution removed an important source of employment from the rural economy. Because wealthier farmers had better access to credit and land, the Green Revolution increased class disparities. Because some regions were able to adopt Green Revolution agriculture more readily than others (for political or geographical reasons), interregional economic disparities increased as well. The new economic difficulties of smallholder farmers and landless farm workers led to increased rural-urban migration. The increase in food production led to a decrease in food prices for urban dwellers, and the increase in urban population increased the potential for industrialization. However, industry was unable to absorb all of the displaced agricultural labor and some cities grew at unsustainable rates.

Globalization

In the most basic sense, the Green Revolution was a product of globalization as evidenced in the creation of international agricultural research centers that shared information, and with transnational funding from groups like the Rockefeller Foundation, Ford Foundation, and USAID. Additionally, the inputs required in Green Revolution agriculture created new markets for seed and chemical corporations, many of which were based in the United States. For example, Standard Oil of New Jersey established hundreds of distributors in the Philippines to sell agricultural packages composed of HYV seed, fertilizer, and pesticides.

ECOLOGICAL CHANGE

Pesticides

Green Revolution agriculture increased the use of pesticides, which were necessary to limit the high levels of pest damage that inevitably occur in monocultures. Organochlorides, a chemical group of pesticides including DDT and dieldrin that spread with the Green Revolution, does not easily break down in the environment and therefore accumulates through the food chain and spread throughout ecosystems. Other problems with pesticides include the poisoning of farm workers, the contamination of water, and the evolution of resistance in pest organism populations.

Water Issues

Irrigation projects have created significant problems of salinization, waterlogging, and lowering of water tables in certain areas.

BIODIVERSITY

The spread of Green Revolution agriculture affected both agricultural biodiversity and wild biodiversity. There is little argument that the Green Revolution acted to reduce agricultural biodiversity, as it relied upon just a few varieties of each crop. This has led to concerns about the susceptibility of a food supply to pathogens that cannot be controlled by agrochemicals, as well as the permanent loss of many valuable genetic traits bred into cereal varieties over thousands of years. To address these concerns, massive seed banks such as CGIAR's International Plant Genetic Resources Institute have been established.

There are varying opinions about the effect of the Green Revolution on wild biodiversity. One hypothesis speculates that by increasing production per unit of land area, agriculture did not need to expand into new, uncultivated areas to feed a growing human population. A counterhypothesis speculates that biodiversity was sacrificed because traditional systems of agriculture that were displaced have often incorporated practices to preserve wild biodiversity, and because the Green Revolution expanded agricultural development into new areas where it was once unprofitable or too arid.

Nevertheless, the world community has clearly acknowledged the negative impacts of agricultural expansion as the 1992 Rio Treaty, signed by 189 nations, has generated numerous national Biodiversity Action Plans which assign significant biodiversity loss to agriculture's expansion into new domains (Whether the habitat used was an arid region or an uninhabited bog, biotic impacts can be extensive.)

LEGACY OF THE GREEN REVOLUTION

IRRI and CIMMYT became a part of the CGIAR which was established in 1971. Since that time, CGIAR has added many research centers throughout the world.

CGIAR has responded, at least in part, to criticisms of Green Revolution methodologies. This began in the 1980s, and mainly was a result of pressure from donor organizations. Methods like Agroecosystem Analysis and Farming System Research have been adopted to gain a more holistic view of agriculture. Methods like Rapid Rural Appraisal and Participatory Rural Appraisal have been adopted to help scientists understand the problems faced by farmers and even give farmers a role in the development process.

15

Economic History of India

Economic history of India, in the sense of the meaning of the term economic in its current sense, is at least 5000 years old.

INDUS VALLEY CIVILIZATION

The Indus Valley civilization, the first known permanent and predominantly urban settlement that flourished between 2800 BC to 1800 BC boasted of an advanced and thriving economic system. Its citizens practiced agriculture, domesticated animals, made sharp tools and weapons from copper, bronze and tin and traded with other cities. Evidence of well laid streets, layouts, drainage system and water supply in the valley's major cities, Harappa, Mohenjo-daro and Rakhigarhi reveals their knowledge of urban planning.

ANCIENT AND MEDIEVAL CHARACTERISTICS

Much of India's population resided in villages, whose economy was largely isolated and self-sustaining. Agriculture was the predominant occupation of the populace and satisfied a village's food requirements besides providing raw materials for hand based industries like textile, food processing and crafts. Besides farmers, other classes of people were barbers, carpenters, doctors (Ayurvedic practitioners), goldsmiths, weavers, etc.

Religion

Religion, especially Hinduism, played an influential role in shaping economic activities. The system of castes and sub-castes, despite its social fallbacks, functioned much like medieval European guilds, ensuring division of labour and provided for training of apprentices. The caste system restricted people from changing one's occupation and aspiring to an upper caste's lifestyle. Thus, a barber could not become a goldsmith and even a highly skilled carpenter could not aspire to the lifestyle or privileges enjoyed by a Kshatriya (person of a warrior class). This barrier to mobility on labour restricted economic prosperity to a few castes.

Pilgrimage towns like Allahabad, Benares, Nasik, Puri, etc., mostly centred around rivers, developed into centres of trade and commerce. Religious functions, festivals and the practice of taking a pilgrimage resulted in a flourishing pilgrimage economy.

Family Business

In the joint family system, members of a family pooled their resources to maintain the family and invest in business ventures. The system ensured younger members were trained and employed in the family business and the older and disabled persons would be supported by the family. The system, by preventing the agricultural land from being split ensured higher yield because of the benefits of scale. The system curbed members from taking initiative because of the support system and family or work discords intertwined, leading to sub-division and fragmentation of land which lead to lower yield and productivity.

Organizational Entities

Along with the family-run business and individually owned business enterprises, ancient India possessed a number of other forms of engaging in business or collective activity, including the gana, pani, puga, vrata, sangha, nigama and sreni. Nigama, pani and sreni refer most often to economic organizations of merchants, craftspeople and artisans, and perhaps even para-military entities. In particular, the sreni was a complex organizational entity that shares many similarities with modern corporations, which were being used in India from around the 8th century BC until around the 10th century AD. The use of such entities in ancient India was widespread including virtually every kind of business, political and municipal activity.

The sreni was a separate legal entity which had the ability to hold property separately from its owners, construct its own rules for governing the behavior of its members, and for it to contract, sue and be sued in its own name. Some ancient sources have rules for lawsuits between two or more sreni and some sources make reference to a government official (Bhandagarika) who worked as an arbitrator for disputes amongst sreni from at least the 6th century BC onwards. There were between 18 to 150 sreni at various times in ancient India covering both trading and craft activities. This level of specialization of occupations is indicative of a developed economy in which the sreni played a critical role. Some sreni could have over 1000 members as there were apparently no upper limits on the number of members. The sreni had a considerable degree of centralized management. The headman of the sreni represented the interests of the sreni in the king's court and in many official business matters. The headman could also bind the sreni in contracts, set the conditions of work within the sreni, often received a higher salary, and was the administrative authority within the sreni. The headman was often selected via an election by the members of the sreni, who could also be removed from power by the general assembly. The headman often ran the enterprise with two to five executive officers, who were also elected by the assembly.

Italic text "Coinage" Punch marked Silver Ingots, in circulation around 5th century BC and the first metallic coins were minted around 6th century BC by the Mahajanapadas of the Gangetic plains were the earliest traces of coinage in India. While India's many kingdoms and rulers issued coins, barter was still widely prevalent. Villages paid a portion of their agricultural produce as revenue while its craftsmen received a stipend out of the crops at harvest time for their services. Each village, as an economic unit was mostly self-sufficient.

MAURYA EMPIRE

During the Maurya Empire (c. 321-185 BC), there were a number of important changes and developments to the Indian economy. It was the first time most of India was unified under one ruler. With an empire in place, the trade routes throughout India became more secure thereby reducing the risk associated with the transportation of goods. The empire spent considerable resources building roads and maintaining them throughout India.

The improved infrastructure combined with increased security, greater uniformity in measurements, and increasing usage of coins as currency enhanced trade. During this time, the Arthasastra ("science of state") was written by the Maurya prime minister and Takshashila University professor Chanakya. The Arthasastra is one of the most important ancient texts on economics, politics and administration. It was a treatise on how to maintain and expand power, obtain material gain, and administer an empire. It covers both theory and implementation and contains many clear and detailed rules regarding the governing of an empire.

The economic situation in the Maurya Empire is comparable to the Roman Empire several centuries later, which both had extensive trade connections and both had organizations similar to corporations. While Rome had organizational entities which were largely used for public state-driven projects, Mauryan India had numerous private commercial entities which existed purely for private commerce. This was due to the Mauryas having to contend with pre-existing sreni hence they were more concerned about keeping the support of these pre-existing private commercial entities, while the Romans did not have such pre-existing entities to contend with hence they were able to prevent such entities from developing.

Exports

Surplus of Indian manufactures, like the muslin of Dacca, calicos of Bengal, shawls of Kashmir, other textiles and handicrafts, agricultural products like pepper, cinnamon, opium and indigo were exported to Europe, Middle East and South East Asia in return for gold and silver. Superstitions about sea faring may have existed among some Hindu groups, which meant that part of India's foreign trade may have been carried out by foreigners.

GDP Estimates

According to economic historian Angus Maddison in his book The World Economy: A Millennial Perspective, India had the world's largest economy in the 1st century and 11th century, with a 32.9% share of world GDP in the 1st century and 28.9% in 1000 CE. However, it must be noted that Maddison in his work was comparing geographic regions before 1500 and the comparisons between India and China were between geographic locations that included those countries. In 1700, when most of India was ruled by the Mughal Empire, it had a 24.4% share of world GDP, the largest at the time, which fell drastically to 3.8% by 1952. Another estimate of India's pre-colonial economy puts the revenue of Akbar's Mughal empire in 1600 at £17.5 million, in contrast to the entire treasury of Great Britain in 1800, which totalled £16 million.

BRITISH RULE

The British colonial rule created an institutional environment that did stabilize the law and order situation to a large extent. The British stifled the trade with rest of the world. They concentrated on exploiting the resources of India to their advantage. They created a well developed system of railways, telegraphs and a modern legal system. The infrastructure the British created was mainly geared towards the exploitation of resources of India. The British focus on their own interests created a situation in which India could not benefit from major changes in the world economy-industrialisation, growth in trade and production, and new thinking on economic policies followed by states. By the end of the colonial rule India inherited an economy that was one of the poorest in the world and totally stagnant, with industrial development stalled, agriculture unable to feed a rapidly accelerating population, who were subject to frequent famines, had one of the world's lowest life expectancy, suffered from pervasive malnutrition and was largely illiterate. The British rule ruined India economically.

GDP Estimates

An estimate by Cambridge historian Angus Maddison reveals that, India's share of the world income, reduced from

24.4% in 1700, comparable to Europe's share of 23.3 %, to a low of 3.8% in 1952. While Indian leaders during the Independence struggle and left-nationalist economic historians have blamed the colonial rule for the dismal state of India's economy, a broader macroeconomic view of India during this period reveals that there were segments of both growth and decline, resulting from changes brought about by colonialism and a world that was moving towards industrialisation and economic integration.

Price of Silver-Rate of Exchange: 1871-72 to 1892-93

Period	Price of Silver (in pence per Troy ounce)	Rupee exchange rate (in pence)
1871-1872	60½	23 ⅛
1875-1876	56¾	21 ⅝
1879-1880	51¼	20
1883-1884	50½	19½
1887-1888	44¾	18 ⅞
1890-1891	47 11/16	18 ⅛
1891-1892	45	16¾
1892-1893	39	15

Source: B.E. Dadachanji. History of Indian Currency and Exchange, 3rd enlarged ed.

Bombay: D.B. Taraporevala Sons & Co, 1934), p.15.

The Fall of the Rupee

After its victory in the Franco-Prussian War (1870-71), Germany extracted a huge indemnity from France of £200,000,000, and then moved to join Britain on a gold standard for currency. France, the U.S. and other industrialising countries followed Germany in adopting a gold standard throughout the 1870s. At the same time, other countries, such as Japan, which did not have the necessary access to gold or those, such as India, which were subject to imperial policies that determined that they did not move to a gold standard, remained mostly on a silver standard. A huge divide between silver-based and gold-based economies resulted. The worst affected were economies with silver standard that traded mainly with economies with gold standard. With discovery of more and more silver reserves, those currencies based on gold continued to rise in value and those based on silver were declining due to demonetization of silver. For India which carried out most of its trade with gold based countries, especially Britain, the impact of this shift was profound. As the price of silver continued to fall, so too did the exchange value of the rupee, when measured against sterling.

POST-INDEPENDENCE TO 1979

At independence the economy was predominantly agrarian. Most of the population was employed in agriculture, and most of those people were very poor, existing by cropping their own small plots or supplying labor to other farms. Landownership, land rental, and sharecropping rights were complex, involving layers of intermediaries.

Moreover, the structural economic problems inherited at independence were exacerbated by the costs associated with the partition of British India, which had resulted in about 12 million to 14 million refugees fleeing past each other across the new borders between India and Pakistan. The settlement of refugees was a considerable financial strain.

Partition also divided complementary economic zones. Under the British, jute and cotton were grown in the eastern part of Bengal, the area that became East Pakistan (after 1971, Bangladesh), but processing took place mostly in the western part of Bengal, which became the Indian state of West Bengal in 1947. As a result, after independence India had to employ land previously used for food production to cultivate cotton and jute for its mills.

India's leaders--especially the first prime minister, Jawaharlal Nehru, who introduced the five-year plans--agreed that strong economic growth and measures to increase incomes and consumption among the poorest groups were necessary goals for the new nation. Giving utmost importance to the economy, Jawaharlal appointed R. K. Shanmukham Chetty, a person who did not participate in the mainstream Indian Independence Movement as the finance minister, since he believed that more than ideology, having right person in the right job was important. Government was assigned an important role in the process of alleviating poverty, and since 1951 a series of plans have guided the country's economic development. Although there was considerable growth in the 1950s, the long-term rates of growth were less positive than India's politicians desired and less than those of many other Asian countries.

Since 1950, India ran into trade deficits that increased in magnitude in the 1960s. The Government of India had a budget deficit problem and therefore could not borrow money from abroad or from the private sector, which itself had a negative savings rate. As a result, the government issued bonds to the RBI, which increased the money supply, leading to inflation. In 1966, foreign aid, which was hitherto a key factor in preventing devaluation of the rupee was finally cut off and India was told it had to liberalise its restrictions on trade before foreign aid would again materialise.

The response was the politically unpopular step of devaluation accompanied by liberalisation. The Indo-Pakistani War of 1965 led the US and other countries friendly towards Pakistan to withdraw foreign aid to India, which further necessitated devaluation. Defence spending in 1965/1966 was 24.06% of total expenditure, the highest in the period from 1965 to 1989. This accompanied by the drought of 1965/1966 lead to a severe devaluation of the rupee. In 1950, Japan produced about 60% of the output of India. By 1975, India produced just over 20% of the output of Japan. Current GDP per capita grew 33% in the Sixties reaching a peak growth of 142% in the Seventies, decelerating sharply back to 41% in the Eighties and 20% in the Nineties.

From FY 1951 to FY 1979, the economy grew at an average rate of about 3.1 percent a year in constant prices, or at an annual rate of 1.0 percent per capita. During this period, industry grew at an average rate of 4.5 percent a year, compared with an annual average of 3.0 percent for agriculture. Many factors contributed to the slowdown of the economy after the mid-1960s, but economists differ over the relative importance of those factors. Structural deficiencies, such as the need for institutional changes in agriculture and the inefficiency of much of the industrial sector, also contributed to economic stagnation. Wars with China in 1962 and with Pakistan in 1965 and 1971; a flood of refugees from East Pakistan in 1971; droughts in 1965, 1966, 1971, and 1972; currency devaluation in 1966; and the first world oil crisis, in 1973-1974, all jolted the economy.

POST LIBERALISATION

Initial Period

As late as 1991, India still had a fixed exchange rate system, where the rupee was pegged to the value of a basket of currencies of major trading partners. India started having balance of payments problems since 1985, and by the end of 1990, it was in a serious economic crisis. The government was close to default and its foreign exchange reserves had reduced to the point that India could barely finance three weeks' worth of imports. The Government of India headed by Chandrashekher decided to usher in a slew of reforms that are collectively termed as liberalisation in the Indian media with Manmohan Singh whom he appointed as a special economical advisor. This event marked a tremendous shift in India's economy since independence-it assumed an outward-shift of encouraging exports instead of the inward focus that stressed on import substitution till then.

The reforms brought changes in three broad areas, collectively known as liberalisation, privatisation and globalisation. Liberalisation did away with regulatory hurdles and minimised licensing requirements. Privatisation reduced the role of the state and public sector in business. Globalisation made it easier for the MNCs to operate in India. This policy was later continued by Prime minister P. V. Narasimha Rao, and he was ably supported by his finance minister Manmohan Singh and other officials such as C. Rangarajan, Montek Singh Ahluwalia, Shankar Acharya and Y. Venugopal Reddy. The initial period culminated in 1996 with the government getting voted out of power. This brought coalition politics to centre-stage and the pace of reforms slackened.

UF Rule

The Union budget presented by United Front Finance Minister P. Chidambaram (1996-1998) was praised for its increase of reforms and pro-growth policies, but India's economy was hampered by the 1997 Asian Economic Crisis in Thailand, Indonesia, Singapore, Malaysia, Hong Kong, Japan and South Korea, as well as the fragile nature of the ruling UF coalition.

It should be noted that despite the economic and political adversities, India's economy did not decline-it maintained a slow growth of GDP and a falling value of its currency. However, rising prices of common products like onions and slow reduction in employment created much public consternation.

NDA Rule

National Democratic Front led by BJP, was in helm of economic affairs from 1998-2004. During this period there were two finance ministers, viz., Yashwant Sinha (1998-2003) and Jaswant Singh (2003-2004). The main economic achievement of the government was the universal license in telecom field, which allows CDMA license holders to provide GSM services and vice versa. NDA started off the Golden Quadrilateral road network connecting main metros of Delhi, Chennai, Mumbai and Kolkata.

The project, still under construction, was one of the most ambitious infrastructure projects of independent India. Simultaneously, North-South and East-West highway projects were planned and construction was started. Education for all is still an unrealised dream in India. This was made a fundamental right by amending the constitution of India and huge amount of money was pumped into the project under the name of Sarva Shiksha Abhiyan. This project met with limited success.

MACRO-ECONOMIC TREND

This is a chart of trend of gross domestic product and foreign trade of India at market prices estimated by Ministry of Statistics and Programme Implementation with figures in millions of Indian Rupees.

Year	Gross Domestic Product	Exports	Imports	US Dollar Exchange in (Rs.)	Inflation Index (2000=100)
1950	99,340			4.79	
1955	108,730			4.79	
1960	171,670			4.77	
1965	276,680			4.78	
1970	456,770			7.56	
1975	832,690			8.39	
1980	1,380,334	90,290	135,960	7.86	18
1985	2,729,350	149,510	217,540	12.36	28
1990	5,542,706	406,350	486,980	17.50	42
1995	11,571,882	1,307,330	1,449,530	32.42	69
2000	20,791,898	2,781,260	2,975,230	44.94	100
2005	34,195,278			44.09	121

Note: 1: Lawrence H. Officer, "Exchange rate between the United States dollar and forty other countries, 1913-1999." Economic History Services, EH.Net, 2002.

For purchasing power parity comparisons, the US Dollar is exchanged at 9.46 Rupees only.

Despite steady growth and continuous reforms since the Nineties, Indian economy is still mired in bureaucratic hurdles from coast to coast. This was confirmed by a World Bank report published in late 2006 ranking Pakistan (at 74th) well ahead of India (at 134th) based on ease of doing business

AGRICULTURE IN INDIA

Agriculture in India is one of the most prominent sectors in its economy. Agriculture and allied sectors like forestry, logging and fishing accounted for 18.6% of the GDP in 2005 and employed 60% of the country's population. It accounts for 8.56% of India's exports. About 43 % of India's geographical area is used for agricultural activity. Despite a steady decline of its share in the GDP, agriculture is still the largest economic sector and plays a significant role in the overall socioeconomic development of India.

The monsoons play a critical role in the Indian sub-continent's agriculture in determining whether the harvest will be bountiful, average, or poor in any given year. The entire rainfall in the sub-continent is concentrated in the few monsoon months. Agriculture in India is constitutionally the responsibility of the states rather than the central government. The central government's role is in formulating policy and providing financial resources for agriculture.

The government administers prices of essential commodities to protect farmers interests. It also administers other commodities which are produced by government-controlled companies, like petroleum, coal, nitrogenous fertilizers, etc. Other than these, most agricultural commodity markets operate under the normal forces of demand and supply.

History of Indian Agriculture

Evidence of the presence of wheat and some legumes in the 6th millennium BCE have been found in the Indus Valley. Oranges were cultivated in the same millennium. The crops grown in the valley around 4000 BCE were typically wheat, peas, sesame seed, barley, dates and mangoes. By 3500 BCE cotton growing and cotton textiles were quite advanced in the valley.

By 3000 BCE farming of rice had started. Other monsoon crops of importance of the time was cane sugar. By 2500 BCE, rice was an important component of the staple diet in Mohenjodaro near the Arabian Sea.

The Indus Plain had rich alluvial deposits which came down the Indus River in annual floods. This helped sustain farming that formed basis of the Indus Valley Civilization at Harappa. The people built dams and drainage systems for the crops.

By 2000 BCE tea, bananas and apples were being cultivated in India. There was coconut trade with East Africa in 200 BCE. By 500 CE, eggplants were being cultivated.

Agricultural Movements

Green Revolution

After independence, considering India's growing population, the government took steps to increase the food production. Yields per unit area of all crops have grown since 1950. The 1970s saw a huge increase in India's wheat production. This is known as the Green Revolution in the country. Reasons for the growth are the special emphasis placed on agriculture and steady improvements in irrigation, technology, application of modern agricultural practices and provision of agricultural credit and subsidies. Prof. Shireesh is known as the "Father of the Green Revolution".

Operation Flood

Operation Flood was the name of a rural development programme started by the National Dairy Development Board (NDDB) in 1970 with the objective of creating a nationwide milk grid. This movement followed the and helped in alleviating poverty and famine levels from dangerous proportions in India during the era. It resulted in India becoming the largest producer of milk and milk products, so it is also called the White Revolution of India.

Production

India is the largest producer in the world of milk, cashew nuts, coconuts, tea, ginger, turmeric and black pepper. It also has the world's largest cattle population (193 million). India ranks second worldwide in farm output. It is the second largest producer of wheat, sugar, groundnut and inland fish. It is the third largest producer of tobacco and rice. India accounts for 10 per cent of the world fruit production with first rank in the production of banana and sapota. Given below is a chart of trend of output of cereals and major foodgrains as published by the Department of Food and Public Distribution with figures in tonnes.

Year	Cereals	Rice	Wheat	Coarsegrains	Pulses
2001-02	199,480,000	93,340,000	72,770,000	33,370,000	13,370,000
2004-05	192,730,000	87,800,000	73,030,000	31,880,000	13,670,000

Despite high growth, international comparisons reveal that the average yield in India is generally 30% to 50% of the highest average yield in the world. The low productivity in India is a result of the following factors:

- Illiteracy, general socioeconomic backwardness, reforms and inadequate or inefficient finance and marketing services for farm produce.
- The average size of land holdings is very small (less than 20,000 m²) and are subject to fragmentation, due to land ceiling acts and in some cases, family disputes. Such small holdings are often over-manned, resulting in disguised unemployment and low productivity of labour.
- Adoption of modern agricultural practices and use of technology is inadequate, hampered by ignorance of such practices, high costs and impracticality in the case of small land holdings.
- Irrigation facilities are inadequate, as revealed by the fact that only 53.6% of the land was irrigated in 2000-01, which result in farmers still being dependent on rainfall, specifically the Monsoon season. A good monsoon results in a robust growth for the economy as a whole, while a poor monsoon leads to a sluggish growth. Farm credit is regulated by NABARD, which is the statutory apex agent for rural development in the subcontinent.

In the last few decades several farmers have committed suicide especially in the states of Andhra Pradesh, Maharashtra, Karnataka, and Kerala. Combating this has become a major challenge for these governments. Some of the causes for the deaths include indebtedness of small and marginal farmers and repeated crop failures.

Agriculture in the Indian States

Agriculture is the main component for most of the state economies in India.

Historically, the Punjab region (the five rivers region) has been one of the most fertile regions on earth. The region is ideal for wheat-growing. Punjab is called the "Granary of India" or

"India's bread-basket". It produces 60% of India's wheat, and 40% of India's rice. The south Indian states of Andhra Pradesh, Tamil Nadu and Karnataka are also major producers of rice, Tamil Nadu being India's second biggest producer of rice. These states are mostly irrigated by the rivers Krishna, Godavari and Cauvery.

Haryana is self-sufficient in food production and the second largest contributor to India's central pool of food grains. Haryana contributed significantly to the Green Revolution in India in the 1970s. The National Dairy Research Institute at Karnal, and the Central Institute for Research on Buffaloes at Hisar are instrumental in development of new breeds of cattle and propagation of these breeds through embryo transfer technology. The Murrah breed of water buffalo from Haryana is world-famous for its milk production.

The high-altitude states of Himachal Pradesh and Jammu and Kashmir are ideal for production of apples. Arunachal Pradesh also has a large number of fruit orchards. Tea is the other produce of the high altitude regions of Assam, West Bengal (Darjeeling), Tripura, Tamil Nadu (Ooty), Himachal Pradesh and Kerala. Assam produces some of the finest and most expensive teas in the world. However Assam tea is grown at elevations near sea level, giving it a malty sweetness and an earthy flavor, as opposed to the more floral aroma of highland (e.g., Darjeeling, Taiwanese) teas.

In the northeastern states like Arunachal Pradesh and Nagaland, shifting cultivation known locally as jhum, was practised by the tribal groups, but that has come to be less practised. In mountainous states like Sikkim, farming is done on terraced slopes. The state has the highest production and largest cultivated area of cardamom in India.

Karnataka is the largest producer of coffee in India and accounts for 59% of the country's coffee production. It is grown moslty in the lower slopes of the Western Ghats in Kodagu district. Karnataka is also the largest producer of sandalwood based products like perfumes. Sandalwood comes from the dense forested areas of southern Karnataka. The state is also the largest producer of raw silk and Mysore silk saris are famous. The other state manufacturing silk is Tamil Nadu.

Rajasthan is among the largest producers of edible oils in India and the second largest producer of oilseeds. The state is also the biggest wool-producing state in India.

Kerala produces 96% of national output of pepper. It is also the largest producer of spices which include cardamom, vanilla, cinnamon, and nutmeg. Kerala is also the largest producer of natural rubber in India (91%). The other state producing rubber is Tripura.

30 percent of Mizoram is covered with wild bamboo forests, and accounts for 40 percent of India's 80-million-ton annual bamboo crop. There has been an economic shift towards agriculture for some states like Bihar after the mineral rich areas were carved out to form the new state of Jharkhand.

Research

The Indian Agricultural Research Institute (IARI) established in 1905, was responsible for the research leading to the "Green revolution" of the 1970s. The Indian Council of Agricultural Research (ICAR) is the apex body in agriculture and related allied fields, including research and education. The Union Minister of Agriculture is the President of the ICAR. The Indian Agricultural Statistics Research Institute develops new techniques for the design of agricultural experiments, analyses data in agriculture, and specializes in statistical techniques for animal and plant breeding.

In 1983, the Nobel Prize in Physiology or Medicine was given to Barbara McClintock for her work with the complex color patterns and genetics of Indian corn.

Prof. M.S. Swaminathan is known as "Father of the Green Revolution" and heads the MS Swaminathan Research Foundation. He is known for his advocacy of environmentally sustainable agriculture and sustainable food security.

INDUSTRIALISATION

Industrialisation (also spelt Industrialization) or an Industrial Revolution is a process of social and economic change whereby a human society is transformed from a pre-industrial (an economy where the amount of capital accumulated per capita is low) to an industrial state. This social and economic change is closely intertwined with technological innovation, particularly the development of large-scale energy production and metallurgy. Industrialisation is also related to some form of philosophical change, or to a different attitude in the perception of nature, though whether these philosophical changes are caused by industrialisation or vice-versa is subject to debate. The world's first industrialised city was Manchester in northwest England.

Industrialisation has spawned its own health problems. Modern stressors include noise, air, water pollution, poor nutrition, dangerous machinery, impersonal work, isolation, poverty, homelessness, and substance abuse. Health problems in industrial nations are as much caused by economic, social, political, and cultural factors as by pathogens. Industrialisation has become a major medical issue world wide, and hopefully will become less of a problem over the upcoming years.

When capitalised, Industrial Revolution refers to the first industrial revolution, which took place in Britain during the 18th and 19th centuries. The Second Industrial Revolution describes later, somewhat less dramatic changes which came about with the widespread availability of electric power, the internal-combustion engine and assembly lines.

Most pre-industrial economies had standards of living not much above subsistence, meaning that the majority of the population were focused on producing their means of survival. For example, in medieval Europe, 80% of the labour force was employed in subsistence agriculture.

Some pre-industrial economies, such as Ancient Athens, have had trade and commerce as significant factors, enjoying wealth far beyond a sustenance standard of living. Famines were frequent in most pre-industrial societies, although some, such as the Netherlands and England of the 17th and 18th centuries, the Italian city states of the 15th century and the ancient Greek and Roman civilizations were able to escape the famine cycle through increasing trade and commercialisation of the agricultural sector. It is estimated that 17th century Netherlands imported nearly 70% of its grain supply and 5th century BC Athens imported 75% of its total food supply.

Many third world countries began industrialisation under the influence of either the United States or the USSR during the Cold War. This effort has been successful in many East Asian countries and less successful in other areas (excluding some late industrialisers in Europe that were already progressing fast before the second world war).

The currently prevailing "development paradigm" in the international development community (which means the World Bank, OECD, many United Nations departments and some other such organisations) is poverty reduction, which pays attention to economic growth as such, but does not recognise traditional industrialisation policies as being beneficial in the longer term (with the perception that it simply creates inefficient local industry that is useless in a free-trade dominated world).

INFORMATION TECHNOLOGY

Information technology (IT), also known as Information and Communication(s) Technology (ICT) and Infocomm in Asia, is concerned with the use of technology in managing and processing information, especially in large organizations.

In particular, IT deals with the use of electronic computers and computer software to convert, store, protect, process, transmit, and retrieve information. For that reason, computer professionals are often called IT specialists/ consultants or Business Process Consultants, and the division of a company or university that deals with software technology is often called the IT department. Other names for the latter are information services (IS) or management information services (MIS), managed service providers (MSP).

History

The first commercial business computer was developed in the United Kingdom in 1951, by the Joe Lyons catering organization. This was known as the 'Lyons Electronic Office'- or LEO for short. It was developed further and used widely during the 1960s and early 1970s. (Joe Lyons formed a separate company to develop the LEO computers and this subsequently merged to form English Electric Leo Marconi and then International Computers Ltd.)

Early commercial systems were installed exclusively by large organizations. These could afford to invest the time and capital necessary to purchase hardware, hire specialist staff to develop custom software and work-through the consequent (and often unexpected) organizational and cultural changes.

At first, individual organizations developed their own software, including data management utilities, themselves. Different products might also have 'one-off' custom software. This fragmented approach led to duplicated effort and the production of management information needed manual effort.

High hardware costs and relatively slow processing speeds forced developers to use resources 'efficiently'. Data storage formats were heavily compacted, for example. A common example is the removal of the century from dates, which eventually lead to the 'millennium bug'.

Data input required intermediate processing via punched paper tape or card and separate input to computers, usually for overnight processing. Data required validation in batches. All of this was a repetitive, labour intensive task, removed from user control and error-prone. Invalid or incorrect data needed correction and resubmission with consequences for data and account reconciliation. Data storage was strictly serial on paper tape, and then later to magnetic tape: the use of data storage within readily accessible memory was not cost-effective. Results would be presented to users on paper. Enquiries were delayed by whatever turnaround was available.

Present Status

As with other industrial processes, commercial IT has moved in all respects from a custom, craft-based industry where the product was tailored to fit the customer; to multi-use components taken off the shelf to find the best-fit in any situation. Mass-production has greatly reduced costs and IT is available to the smallest company or one-man band-or school-kid.

LEO was hardware tailored for a single client. Today, Intel Pentium and compatible chips are standard and become parts of other components which are combined as needed. One individual change of note was the freeing of computers and removable storage from protected, air-filtered environments. Microsoft and IBM at various times have been influential enough to impose order on IT and the resultant standardisations allowed specialist software to flourish.

Software is available off the shelf: apart from Microsoft Office or IBM Lotus Notes, there are also specialist packages for payroll and personnel management, account maintenance and customer management, to name a few. These are highly specialised and intricate components of larger environments, but they rely upon common conventions and interfaces.

Data storage has also standardised. Relational databases are developed by different suppliers to common formats and conventions. Common file formats can be shared by large main-frames and desk-top personal computers, allowing online, real-time input and validation. In parallel, software development has fragmented. There are still specialist technicians, but these increasingly use standardised methodologies where outcomes are predictable and accessible. At the other end of the scale, any office manager can dabble in spreadsheets or databases and obtain acceptable results (but there are risks).

India

India has several engineering colleges. These produce qualified engineers. Some of them get IT trained through their employer and others through independent IT training institutes. These skilled engineers can easily compete with IT professional produced by western institutes. India has become a pioneer in IT related industry, particularly in the IT service as well as software development area. It is also a leader in BPO or ITES. Indian Software and Indian BPO has been among the major growth industries of India in the recent past.-India has recently set up Indian Institute of Information Technology, or the IIIT, which are looking to impart IT related knowledge to tech graduates.

GENERAL AGREEMENT ON TARIFFS AND TRADE

The General Agreement on Tariffs and Trade (typically abbreviated GATT) was originally created by the Bretton Woods Conference as part of a larger plan for economic recovery after

World War II. The GATT's main purpose was to reduce barriers to international trade. This was achieved through the reduction of tariff barriers, quantitative restrictions and subsidies on trade through a series of different agreements. The GATT was an agreement, not an organization. Originally, the GATT was supposed to become a full international organization like the World Bank or IMF called the International Trade Organization. However, the agreement was not ratified, so the GATT remained simply an agreement. The functions of the .GATT have been replaced by the World Trade Organization which was established through the final round of negotiations on January 1, 1995.

The history of the GATT can be divided into three phases: the first, from 1947 until the Torquay round, largely concerned which commodities would be covered by the agreement and freezing existing tariff levels. A second phase, encompassing three rounds, from 1959 to 1979, focused on reducing tariffs. The third phase, consisting only of the Uruguay Round from 1986 to 1994, extended the agreement fully to new areas such as intellectual property, services, capital, and agriculture. Out of this round the WTO was born.

GATT 1947

The first version of GATT, developed in 1947 during the United Nations Conference on Trade and Employment in Havana, Cuba, is referred to as "GATT 1947". On January 1, 1948 the agreement was signed by 23 countries: Australia, Belgium, Brazil, Burma, Canada, Ceylon, Chile, the Republic of China, Cuba, the Czechoslovak Republic, France, India, Lebanon, Luxembourg, Netherlands, New Zealand, Norway, Pakistan, Southern Rhodesia, Syria, South Africa, the United Kingdom, and the United States. 45,000 tariff concessions were made influencing over $10 billion in trade which comprised 20% of the total global market at the time.

GATT 1947 in the US

The GATT, as an international agreement, is similar to a treaty. Under United States law it is classified as a congressional-executive agreement. Based on the Reciprocal Trade Agreements Act it allowed the executive branch negotiating power over trade agreements with temporary authority from Congress. At the time it functioned as a provisional, but promising trade system. The agreement is based on the "unconditional most favored nation principle." This means that the conditions applied to the most favored trading nation (i.e. the one with the least restrictions) apply to all trading nations. In the US, there was large opposition against the International Trade Organization (which had been ratified in several countries, including Australia), and thus President Truman never even submitted it to Congress. This caused other countries to lose interest and left the orphaned GATT as the world's only multilateral trade agreement, coming into force on January 1st, 1948.

GATT 1949

The second round took place in 1949 in Annecy, France. The main focus of the talks was more tariff reductions, around 5000 total.

GATT 1951

The third round occurred in Torquay, England in 1951. 8,700 tariff concessions were made totaling the remaining amount of tariffs to three-fourths of the tariffs which were in effect in 1948.

GATT 1955-1956

The fourth round returned to Geneva in 1955 and lasted until May 1956. $2.5 billion in tariffs were eliminated or reduced.

GATT "Dillon" 1960-1962

The fifth round occurred once more in Geneva and lasted from 1960 to 1962. The talks were named after Under Secretary of State General of the US, Douglas Dillon, who first proposed the talks. Along with reducing over $4.9 billion in tariffs, it also yielded discussion relating to the creation of the European Economic Community (EEC).

GATT "Kennedy" 1964-1967

The sixth round was the last to take place in Geneva from 1964 until 1967 and was named after the late US President

Kennedy in his memory. Concessions were made on $40 billion worth of tariffs. Some of the GATT negotiation rules were also more clearly defined.

GATT 1973-1979

The seventh round of GATT took place in Tokyo from 1973 until 1979. The talks managed to reduce several trade barriers in addition to $300 billion in tariffs. Negotiations covered a range of topics including government procurement, customs valuation, subsidies, countervailing measures, antidumping, standards and import licensing.

Uruguay Round 1986-1993

The Uruguay Round began in 1986. It was the most ambitious round to date, hoping to expand the competence of the GATT to important new areas such as services, capital, intellectual property, and agriculture. Agriculture was essentially exempted from previous agreements as it was given special status in the areas of import quotas and export subsidies, with only mild caveats. However, by the time of the Uruguay round, many countries considered the exception of agriculture to be sufficiently glaring that they refused to sign a new deal without some movement on agricultural products. These fourteen countries came to be known as the "Cairns Group", and included mostly small and medium sized agricultural exporters such as Australia, Brazil, Canada, Indonesia, and New Zealand.

GATT and the World Trade Organization

In 1994 the GATT was updated (GATT 1994) to include new obligations upon its signatories. One of the most significant changes was the creation of the World Trade Organization (WTO). The 75 existing GATT members and the European Communities became the founding members of the WTO on January 1, 1995. The other 52 GATT members rejoined the WTO in the following two years (the last being Congo in 1997). Since the founding of the WTO, 21 new non-GATT members have joined and 28 are currently negotiating membership. Of the original GATT members, only the SFR Yugoslavia has not rejoined the WTO. Since FR Yugoslavia, (renamed to Serbia and Montenegro and with membership negotiations later split in two), is not recognised as a direct SFRY successor state; therefore, its application is considered a new (non-GATT) one. The contracting parties who founded the WTO ended official agreement of the "GATT 1947" terms on December 31, 1995.

Whereas GATT was a set of rules agreed upon by nations, the WTO is an institutional body. The WTO expanded its scope from traded goods to trade within the service sector and intellectual property rights. Although it was designed to serve multilateral agreements, during several rounds of GATT negotiations (particularly the Tokyo Round) plurilateral agreements created selective trading and caused fragmentation among members. WTO arrangements are generally a multilateral agreement settlement mechanism of GATT.

DEVELOPING COUNTRY

A developing country has a relatively low standard of living, an undeveloped industrial base, and a moderate to low Human Development Index (HDI) score. In developing countries, there is low per capita income, widespread poverty, and low capital formation. The term has tended to edge out earlier ones, including the Cold War-defined "Third World", which has come to have unintentional negative connotations associated with it, but new terms such as Less developed country (LDC) or Less economically developed country (LEDC) have not caught on yet. LEDC is a term used by modern geographers to portray the countries classified as "developing countries" more accurately, specifying that they are less economically developed, which usually correlates best with other factors such as low human development.

Development entails a modern infrastructure (both physical and institutional), and a move away from low value added sectors such as agriculture and natural resource extraction. Developed countries, in comparison, usually have economic systems based on continuous, self-sustaining economic growth in the tertiary and quaternary sectors and high standards of living.

The application of the term developing country to some of the world's less developed countries could be considered inappropriate: a number of poor countries are not improving their economic situation (as the term implies), but have experienced prolonged periods of economic decline.

Countries that have the more advanced economies among the developing nations but have not yet fully demonstrated the signs of a developed country, are grouped under the term Newly Industrialised Country.

Measure and Concept of Development

The development of a country is measured with statistical indexes such as income per capita (GDP), life expectancy, the rate of literacy, et cetera. The UN has developed the HDI, a compound indicator of the above statistics, to gauge the level of human development for countries where data is available.

Developing countries are in general countries which have not achieved a significant degree of industrialization relative to their populations, and which have a low standard of living. There is a strong correlation between low income and high population growth, both within and between countries.

The terms utilized when discussing developing countries refer to the intent and to the constructs of those who utilize these terms. Other terms sometimes used are less developed countries (LDCs), least economically developed countries (LEDCs), "underdeveloped nations" or "undeveloped nations", Third World nations, the South, grandpa's house and "non-industrialized nations". Conversely, the opposite end of the spectrum is termed developed countries, most economically developed countries (MEDCs), First World nations and "industrialized nations".

The United Nations allows each nation to decide for itself whether it will be designated as "undeveloped" or "developing" (though many economists and other observers ignore the UN rule about self-designation).

To moderate the euphemistic aspect of the word developing, international organisations have started to use the term least developed countries (LLDCs) for the poorest nations which can in no sense be regarded as developing. That is, LLDCs are the poorest subset of LDCs. This also moderates the wrong tendency to believe that the standard of living in all of the developing world is the same.

The concept of the developing nation is found, under one term or another, in numerous theoretical systems having diverse orientations-for example, theories of decolonization, liberation theology, marxism, anti-imperialism, and political economy.

INTERNATIONAL INVESTMENT POSITION

A country's international investment position (IIP) is a financial statement setting out the value and composition of that country's external financial assets and liabilities. The IIP is one component of the capital account of a country's balance of payments, containing for example stock of companies, real estate, financial instruments, and so on. By comparison, imports and exports of goods and services are part of the current account.

BILATERAL INVESTMENT TREATY

A Bilateral Investment Treaty (BIT) is an agreement establishing the terms and conditions for private investment by nationals and companies of one state in the state of the other. This type of investment is called Foreign direct investment (FDI). BITs are established through trade pacts.

Most BITs grant investments made by an investor of one Contracting State in the territory of the other a number of guarantees, which typically include fair and equitable treatment, protection from expropriation, free transfer of means and full protection and security. The distinctive feature of many BITs is that they allow for an alternative dispute resolution mechanism, whereby an investor whose rights under the BIT have been violated could have recourse to international arbitration, often under the auspices of the ICSID (International Center for the Resolution of Investment Disputes), rather than suing the host State in its own courts.

16

Economic Policy

Economic policy refers to the actions that governments take in the economic field. It covers the systems for setting interest rates and government deficit as well as the labour market, national ownership, and many other areas of government. Such policies are often influenced by international institutions like the International Monetary Fund or World Bank as well as political beliefs and the consequent policies of parties.

TYPES OF ECONOMIC POLICY

Economic policy is a complicated area and can be broken down into three principal areas:

- Fiscal policy is the size of the government deficit and the methods it uses to finance it.
    - o *Fiscal Stance:* The size of the deficit
    - o *Tax Policy:* The taxes used to collect government income.
    - o Government spending on just about any area of government
- Monetary policy is concerned with the amount of money in circulation and, consequently, interest rates and inflation.
    - o Interest rates, if set by the Government
    - o Incomes policies which aim at imposing non-monetary controls on inflation
    - o Bank regulations which affect the money multiplier

- Trade policy refers to tariffs, trade agreements and the international institutions that govern them.

Almost any aspect of government has an economic aspect and so many terms are used. However, they can usually be seen to apply to one of these areas. For instance, agricultural policy is generally a matter of the burden of taxation and of trade in agricultural goods.

TOOLS AND GOALS

Policy is generally directed to achieve particular objectives, like targets for inflation, unemployment, or economic growth. Sometimes other objectives, like military spending or nationalization are important. These are referred to as the policy goals: the outcomes which the economic policy aims to achieve.

To achieve these goals, governments use policy tools which are under the control of the government. These generally include the interest rate and money supply, tax and government spending, tariffs, exchange rates, labour market regulations, and many other aspects of government.

The government's economic policy determines the tools and hopes that they will achieve its goals.

SELECTING TOOLS AND GOALS

Governments and central banks are limited in the number of goals they can achieve in the short term. For instance, there may be pressure on the government to reduce inflation, reduce unemployment, and reduce interest rates while maintaining currency stability. If all of these are selected as goals for the short term, then policy is likely to be incoherent, because a normal consequence of reducing inflation and maintaining currency stability is increasing unemployment and increasing interest rates.

Demand-side vs. Supply-side Tools

This dilemma can in part be resolved by using microeconomic, supply-side policy to help adjust markets. For instance, unemployment could potentially be reduced by altering laws relating to trade unions or unemployment insurance, as well as by macroeconomic (demand-side) factors like interest rates.

Discretionary Policy vs Policy Rules

For much of the 20th century, governments adopted discretionary policies like demand management designed to correct the business cycle. These typically used fiscal and monetary policy to adjust inflation, output and unemployment. However, following the stagflation of the 1970s, policymakers began to be attracted to policy rules.

A discretionary policy is supported because it allows policymakers to respond quickly to events. However, discretionary policy can be subject to dynamic inconsistency: a government may say it intends to raise interest rates indefinitely to bring inflation under control, but then relax its stance later. This makes policy non-credible and ultimately ineffective.

A rule-based policy can be more credible, because it is more transparent and easier to anticipate. Examples of rule-based policies are fixed exchange rates, interest rate rules, the stability and growth pact and the Golden Rule. Some policy rules can be imposed by external bodies, for instance the Exchange Rate Mechanism for currency.

A compromise between strict discretionary and strict rule-based policy is to grant discretionary power to an independent body. For instance, the Federal Reserve Bank, European Central Bank and Bank of England all set interest rates without government interference, but do not adopt rules.

Another type of non-discretionary policy is a set of policies which are imposed by an international body. This can occur (for example) as a result of intervention by the International Monetary Fund.

ECONOMIC POLICY THROUGH HISTORY

The first economic problem was how to gain the resources it needed to be able to perform the functions of an early government: the military, roads and other projects like building the Pyramids. Early governments generally relied on tax in kind and forced labour for their economic resources. However, with the development of money came the first policy choice. A government could raise money through taxing its citizens. However, it could now also debase the coinage and so increase the money supply.

Early civilizations also made decisions about whether to permit and how to tax trade. Some early civilizations, such as Ptolemaic Egypt adopted a closed currency policy whereby foreign merchants had to exchange their coin for local money. This effectively levied a very high tariff on foreign trade.

By the early modern age, more policy choices had been developed. There was considerable debate about mercantilism and other restrictive trade practices like the Navigation Acts, as trade policy became associated with both national wealth and with foreign and colonial policy.

Throughout the 19th Century, monetary standards became an important issue. Gold and silver were in supply in different proportions which metal was adopted influenced the wealth of different groups in society.

The First Fiscal Policy

With the accumulation of private capital in the Renaissance, states developed methods of financing deficits without debasing their coin. The development of capital markets meant that a government could borrow money to finance war or expansion while causing less economic hardship.

This was the beginning of modern fiscal policy.

The same markets made it easy for private entities to raise bonds or sell shares to fund private initiatives.

Business Cycles

The business cycle became a predominant issue in the 19th century, as it became clear that industrial output, employment, and profit behaved in a cyclical manner. The first real policy solution to the problem came with the work of Keynes, who proposed that fiscal policy could be used actively to ward off depressions, recessions and slumps.

ECONOMY OF SOUTH INDIA

The Economy of South India is largely agrarian, dependent on monsoons, as are most people in India. Some of the main crops cultivated in South India include paddy, sorghum, millet, pulses, cotton, chilli, and ragi. South India was and still is the "promised land" as far as spice cultivation is concerned. Areca, coffee, pepper, tapioca, and cardamom are widely cultivated on the Nilgiri Hills and Kodagu. But frequent droughts in Northern Karnataka, Rayalaseema and Telangana regions are leaving farmers debt-ridden, forcing them to sell their livestock and sometimes even to suicides. Scarcity of water has been a major problem for past few years in these regions along with cities like Chennai and Hyderabad.

Education is highly valued in the south Indian community, and is seen as a gateway to a better livelihood. Many of the nation's most prominent physicists and mathematicians have been South Indians. Kerala, while possessing a literacy rate above 98% also has the highest unemployment rates in India. The population growth rate of these states is also beginning to decline rapidly relative to North India.

Information Technology is a growing field in South India. Bangalore is India's Information Technology hub, and is home to over 200 software companies. It is often referred to as the "Silicon Valley of India".

Chennai, Tamil Nadu ranks next only to Bangalore in the software exports in India and grossed over Rs 100,000,000,000 in 2005.

Chennai houses the automobile manufacturing giants in the country. More than 35% of heavy vehicles produced in the country, such as cars, buses, lorries, trains and bicycles, are produced in Chennai, and it is referred to as the Detroit of South Asia. The manufacturing units of BMW, Flextronics, Motorola, Dell, TVS, Mitsubishi, Ford, Hyundai, Nokia and Saint Gobain are some of the international players in Chennai.

Hyderabad is a currently the most happening place in India. Hyderabad is the first destination for Microsoft Development Center in India. Hyderabad is known as Pearl City.

Hyderabad is also known as GeNome Valley of India (Number of Biotech and Pharma Industries) like Avra Laboratories, Bharat Biotech International, Bijam Biosciences, Biological E. Ltd, Bioserve Biotechnologies, Dr. Reddy's Laboratories, Genotex International, GVK Bio, Indian Immunologicals Ltd, Indigene Pharmaceuticals, Jupiter Biosciences, Krebs Biochemicals, Microbiomed Products, Nuziveedu Seeds, Prabhat Agri Biotech, Satyam Computer Services, Shantha Biotechnics, Tata Consultancy Services and Vimta Labs are the Top Players.

Hyderabad convention center is the south Asia's largest convention center. Guntur is the Cotton source for nearly 50% production in India. Andhra Pradesh Government is planning to establish Cotton Mills around Guntur to Make the city Cotton city surpassing the Current Cotton City Coimbatore. Currently Guntur district Port/NizamPatnam is built up to make the plan implemented. Czek Repablic is Investing 10,000 crores for this Project.

Kerala lags behind many of the Indian states in terms of production and per capita income, but in terms of Human Development Index and life standard of the people, Kerala is ahead of most other states in India. This peculiar paradox is often termed as the "Kerala Phenomenon" or Kerala model of development by experts.

There is also a large amount of disparity within Southern India. As IT companies have entered the economic arena, their high level of pay has raised the economic standing of young and educated professionals, while the poor has become less and less able to afford basic necessities. It is not uncommon to see the shacks of homeless people propped up against the buildings of large multinationals. The poor, unable to afford sending their children to school, remain in a cycle of life completed separated from that of this more affluent upper class.

Andhra Pradesh

Agriculture has been the chief source of income for the state's economy. Two important rivers of India, the Godavari and Krishna, flow through the state. Rice, tobacco, cotton, mirchi, and sugarcane are the local crops. The state has also started to focus on the fields of information technology and biotechnology.

Hyderabad, the capital of Andhra Pradesh, is the fifth largest cosmopolitan city in India, rich in culture, enduring history and industrial growth.

Hyderabad beat IT heavyweight Bangalore to bag the Fab City project, which will host India's first major silicon chip manufacturing facility. Its Due to the Governments Unique FDI Policies and the City Infrastructure.

The advent of Information Technology growth in India, the so called "Blue Chip Revolution", has fostered the growth of Hyderabad's economy. The city is sometimes referred to as "Cyberabad" because of the large number of IT firms in the city. Andhra Pradesh has witnessed a major jump in software exports. Hyderabad's IT export revenue was Rs. 81,450,000,000, an increaes of 62% from fiscal 2004. For Andhra, fiscal 2004 is particularly significant as the 62% growth in exports in fiscal 2005, was almost double the 37% it grew in 2003-2004. Other cities such as Vizag and Vijayawada have shown growths in IT exports on an annual basis. Vizag's contribution was Rs 700,000,000, while it was Rs 240,000,000 from Vijayawada.

State Owned APSRTC Bus Service-entered Guinness World Record for owning the largest fleet of buses IN 1999.

AP is the largest producer of rice in India

Raj IV-(Internet Village) Initiative by AP Government. Government's plan is to establish Broadband Network across the State by connecting Districts with 10 GB/s and Up to Mandals with 1 GB/s and up to Villages with 100 MB/s Bandwidth with in Jun 2007.

Infosys signs MoU Andhra for expansion in Hyderabad Plans to ramp up headcount to 25,000 with an added investment of Rs. 1250 crore.

Karnataka

Karnataka's net state domestic product of $47 billion is the fifth largest in India. Between 1992-2002, Karnataka attracted the fourth highest total Foreign Direct Investment approvals in India, to the tune of Rs. 21,566 million. Karnataka accounts for one third of India's Information technology exports. For the year 2006, the state is expected to bring in 37% of all IT revenues amounting to 37,000 crores ($8.2 billion). Nearly 50% of IT companies and 40% of Bio-Tecnology companies are based here. Agriculture in Karnataka, like most of India, employs 80% of the population. Agriculture and its allied activities account for 49% of the state's income. The coastal plains of Karnataka, which include Uttara Kanara and Dakshina Kanara are cultivated with rice and sugarcane. Coffee and Tea are also grown on the slopes of the Western Ghats in the district of Kodagu Chikmagalur and Hassan. Karnataka produces 70% of India's coffee, of which about 50% is exported.. The black soil in the northwest of the state, is hospitable for the growth of cotton, onion, course cereal, sunflower and peanuts.

The forests of the Malnad region produce timber, bamboo and sandalwood. Karnataka is the only exporter of sandalwood in the country. Most of the world's sandalwood oil is produced in Karnataka.

All of India's gold comes from the Kolar district of Karnataka. Karnataka is also rich in minerals which form the bulk of the raw materials for iron and steel industries in the state such as the one at Bhadravati. All of India's Iron ore comes from the Malnad region.

The first power station in Asia was set up in Karnataka at Shivanasamudra in 1902 to produce hydroelectric power. Karnataka has 18 power stations which generate annually 16,513 million units. The state, however generates insufficient power and is forced to buy electricity from neighboring states.

Bangalore, the capital of Karnataka, is home to several public sector undertaking aircraft companies, such as Hindustan Aeronautics Limited (HAL), HMT Hindustan Machine Tools, Bharat Heavy Electronics Limited (BHEL), National Aeronautics Limited and also Indian Space Research Organization (ISRO). Bangalore, often referred to as the Silicon Valley of India has the largest number of international and local Information Technology and business process outsourcing (BPO) companies in the country. A number of "IT Parks" have been set up by the Karnataka State Electronics Development

Corporation Limited (KEONICS) including Bangalore's "Electronics City" and IT parks in Mysore, Mangalore and Hubli. Bangalore is also home to prestigious higher institutes of learning such as the Indian Institute of Science (IISc) and the Indian Institute of Management (IIM Bangalore). One of the largest SEZ's in India,the ONGC SEZ is coming up at Mangalore, which is currently the fastest growing non metro in the south. The total investment in the ONGC SEZ is expected to cross 100,000 crores. At least three IT SEZ'S are coming up in Mangalore with companies like TCS, Wipro, Lotus and others investing upto more than 3000 crores and creating 67,000 jobs in Mangalore over the next three years. Mangalore is also attracting investment in the Hospitality sectors with companies like the Maurya and Leela Group investing in the region.

Kerala

Kerala's economy is predominantly agrarian. In terms of industrialisation, Kerala lags behind many of the Indian states, but in terms of Human Development Index and life standard of the people, Kerala is ahead of most other states in India. In fact, in certain development indices it is on a par with some of the developed countries. This peculiar paradox is often termed as the "Kerala Phenomenon" or Kerala model of development by experts.

Kerala follows a socialist welfare economy. Kerala's emphasis on social welfare also resulted in slow economic progress. There are few major industries in Kerala, and the per capita GDP is lower than the national average. Remittances from Keralites working abroad, mainly in the Middle East, make up over 60% of the state's gross domestic product.

However, today, the state is emerging as a future IT center of India, owing to its high internet connectivity (undersea cable landing points), along with skilled labour. The government has established two IT Parks in the state at Trivandrum and Kochi. The Technopark at Trivandrum is the second largest IT park in Asia. Kochi is a safe natural harbour, and hence on the most important ports of India. A container transhipment terminal has been proposed in Kochi. The construction of the proposed mega Deep Water Container Transshipment Port at Vizhinjam near Trivandrum is expected to boost up the economy of the state. Vizhinjam is having a natural depth of 24m, which requires no annual dredging, thus making it the deepest port in Asia. Situated close to Trivandrum city, Vizhinjam is very close to international shipping route and East-West shipping axis.

Agriculture is still the most predominant economic activity in the state. Coconut, tea and coffee are grown extensively, along with rubber, cashew and spices. Spices commonly cultivated in Kerala include pepper, cardamom, vanilla, cinnamon and nutmeg. Much of Kerala's agriculture is in the form of home gardens.

Unemployment is typically high in Kerala. Traditional low-wage cottage industries such as the processing of coconut fiber and cashew or weaving employ most workers. More than a fourth of Kerala's workers provide services.

Kerala boasts an Indian Institute of Management at Kozhikode. One of the two ship building yards of India is in Kerala at Kochi. The Southern Naval Command of India has its headquarters in Kochi, and the Southern Air Command Head Quarters is in Thiruvananthapuram (Trivandrum). There are three international airports in Kerala, Trivandrum, Cochin and Calicut. Cochin International Airport is the first International Airport in India that has been built without the Federal Government's stake.

Kerala is also one of the tourist hot-spots of India. It was proclaimed as one of the ten paradises on earth by the National Geographic traveller. The state has also won a large number of awards for its tourism initiatives. Its tourism logo and slogan have global superbrand status.

Tamil Nadu

Tamil Nadu's net state domestic product is the largest in South India and third largest in India. It is one of the most industrialised states in India. It ranks third in the country in total foreign direct investment (FDI) (Rs. 220,582,640,000). The State's investment constitutes 9.12% of the total FDI in the country. According to the 2001 Census, Tamil Nadu has the highest level of urbanization (43.86%) in India, which accounts for 6% of India's total population and 9.6% of the urban population. Chennai is referred as the Gate way of South India. Chennai is the Second leading Software exporter in India. Companies such as Cognizant, Covansys, Xansa, Verizon, iSoft and many others are Chennai based companies in India. Infosys has set up India's largest software development centre to house 25,000 software professionals at an estimated investment of Rs 1,250 crore (Rs 12.5 billion) in Chennai.

India's largest IT park is housed at Chennai. Unlike other States in India the state has many software tier II cities such as Coimbatore, Trichy, Madurai and Hosur. Chennai has become the most preferred BPO hub in India and South Asia. Chennai is sometimes referred to as the "Health Capital of India" or the "Banking Capital of India", having attracted investments from International corporations and the World Bank. Tamil Nadu has a network of about 110 industrial parks/estates that offer developed plots with supporting infrastructure. Also, the Government is promoting other industrial parks like Rubber Park, Apparel Parks, Floriculture Park, TICEL Park for Biotechnology, Siruseri IT Park, Agro Export Zones among others. 56% of India's total knitwear exports come from Tirupur, Tamilnadu.

The heavy engineering manufacturing companies are centered around the suburbs of Chennai. Chennai boasts presence of global car manufacturing giants like Ford, Hyundai, BMW and Mitsubishi as well as home grown companies like MRF, TI Cycles of India, Ashok Leyland and TVS. Chennai is also home to one of the Indian Institutes of Technology, IIT Madras. Kalpakkam nuclear power plant, Neyveli Lignite Corporation, and the Narimanam natural gas plants provide sources of fuel and energy for the nation. 55% of electricity from wind power produced in India from wind mills comes from Tamil Nadu. The town of Sivakasi is the leader for Printing, Fireworks, Safety matches Production in India. It contributes to 80% of India's total Safety Matches Production,90% of India's Total Fireworks Production and 60% of India's Total Offset Printing Solutions and ranks as one of the highest Tax payer towns in India. Sivakasi and Tirupur in Tamil Nadu are 100% employed towns, among a few towns in India.

Tamilnadu is leading producer of kambu, cholam, ground nut, oil seeds and sugarcane in India. At present Tamil Nadu is Third biggest producer of Rice in India, next to Andhra Pradesh and Punjab where there is perennial source of irrigation.

Biovalleys in Tamil Nadu include Biotechnology Incubator Park Near Chennai, Women's Biotechnology Park Kelambakkam, Medicinal Plants Biotechnology Park, Madurai, Marine Biotechnology Park, Madapam and Bioinformatics and Genomics Centre (BGC), Chennai.

Bibliography

Acharya, K.C.S.: *Food Security System of India: Evolution of the Buffer Stocking Policy and Its Evaluation*, New Delhi, Concept, 1983.

Ahmad, Imtiaz: *State and Foreign Policy: India's Role in South Asia*, New Delhi, Vikas, 1993.

Ajit, K: *A History of Indian Economic Thought. Routledge History of Economic Thought Series*, London, Routledge, 1993.

Ansari, Nasim: *Agrarian Structure, Land Reform, and Agricultural Growth in India*, Delhi, Tata McGraw-Hill, 1991.

Ashok, Vasant: *Indian Economy in the World Setting*, Bombay, Himalaya, 1988.

Bardhan, K.: *Land, Labor, and Rural Poverty: Essays in Development Economics*, New Delhi, Oxford University Press, 1984.

Baxi, Upendra: *The Crisis of the Indian Legal System*, New Delhi, Vikas, 1982.

Behari, Madhuri: *Indian Economy since Independence: Chronology of Events*, Delhi, D.K. Publications, 1983.

Bhagwati, Jagdish: *India in Transition: Freeing the Economy*, Oxford, Clarendon Press, 1993.

Bhatia, B.M.: *Indian Agriculture: A Policy Perspective*, New Delhi, Sage, 1988.

Bhatta, Sitesh: *Agricultural Price Policy and Production in India*, Delhi, Konark, 1991.

Bhuleshkar, Vasant: *Indian Economy in the World Setting*, Bombay, Himalaya, 1988.

Bookman, Zarkovic: *The Political Economy of Discontinuous Development: Regional Disparities and Inter-regional Conflict*, New York, Praeger, 1991.

Bose, Sugata: *Peasant Labour and Colonial Capital: Rural Bengal since 1770*, Cambridge, Cambridge University Press, 1993.

Byres, J.: *The State and Development Planning in India*, Delhi, Oxford University Press, 1994.

Calman, J.: *Toward Empowerment: Women and Politics in India*, Colorado, Westview Press, 1992.

Chandhok, H.L.: *The Economy: Annual Time Series Data*, New Delhi, Living Media India, 1990.

Chaudhuri, Pramit: *The Indian Economy: Poverty and Development*, New York, St. Martin's Press, 1979.

Dahiya, L.N.: *Dynamics of Economic Life in Rural India*, Delhi, Gian, 1991.

Das, Kishore: *Economic History of Mughal India: An Annotated Bibliography, 1526-1875*, Calcutta, Santiniketan, 1991.

Dasgupta, K: *A History of Indian Economic Thought. Routledge History of Economic Thought Series*, London, Routledge, 1993.

Desai, Vasant: *A Study of Rural Economics: A Systems Approach*, Bombay, Himalaya, 1983.

Dhingra, C.: *The Indian Economy: Resources, Planning, Development, and Problems*, Delhi, Sultan Chand, 1983.

Diwakar, D.M.: *Agriculture and Industry: Dynamics of Imbalances in India*, New Delhi, Manak, 1991.

Goldsmith, W.: *The Financial Development of India, 1860-1977*, New Haven, Yale University Press, 1983.

Goyal, S.K.: *Agricultural Prices and Its Impact on the Indian Economy: A Case Study of Haryana*, New Delhi, Classical, 1992.

Guhan, S.: *The World Bank's Lending in South Asia*, Washington, Brookings Institution, 1995.

Gupta, B.: *Black Income in India*, New Delhi, Sage, 1992.

Ishwar, C.: *The Indian Economy: Resources, Planning, Development, and Problems*, Delhi, Sultan Chand, 1983.

Jalan, Bimal: *The Indian Economy: Problems and Prospects*, New Delhi, Viking, 1992.